The Peace Keeper

Rev. Cheril Goodrich

PublishAmerica
Baltimore

© 2006 by Rev. Cheril Goodrich.
All rights reserved. No part of this book may be reproduced, stored in a retrieval system or transmitted in any form or by any means without the prior written permission of the publishers, except by a reviewer who may quote brief passages in a review to be printed in a newspaper, magazine or journal.

First printing

At the specific preference of the author, PublishAmerica allowed this work to remain exactly as the author intended, verbatim, without editorial input.

ISBN: 1-4241-0803-9
PUBLISHED BY PUBLISHAMERICA, LLLP
www.publishamerica.com
Baltimore

Printed in the United States of America

The Peace Keeper is dedicated to my Grandchildren, MacKenzie and Courtney King. It is also dedicated to Morgan and all of the innocence that has brought their gift of wisdom into the world to share and heal it.

I would like to acknowledge the Inner Voice of Wisdom that has continued to Guide me even when I was at the point of throwing in the towel. Because Gratitude is a Law of Heaven that is shared with the world, it is my sincere wish that my conscious gratitude provides an open door for others to learn of their own plan that Heaven is providing for their healing.

The Call Is Going out for Peace Keepers.
Are You a Peace Keeper?

The Peace Keeper

The world is in a radical state of change. When this change is complete, the changes will be such that the world will be unrecognizable as it is now. This radical state is an evolutionary shift that is occurring, and will continue to occur until the message of peace has been well established in this world. There is not one person who will not be affected by this evolutionary shift as time unveils the next spurt of growth as these world changing events unfold. The evolutionary shift amounts to the end of days. The end of days need not be a fearful time, for it does not mean the end of the world. Instead it is the end of the 7th day, for no where in the Bible does it refer to the last day being completed. Because God does not lie, the end of the 7th day must end with; and He saw all that He created, and it was good. We live in a world that is not good. The world was created to be a spiritual playground, not a physical stomping ground. The world must be restored to its original purpose before the end of days arrive.

Everyone who walks this earth will be given the opportunity to help with this process. It is not necessary to understand or know what must be done, for this information is being held for the individual who makes this choice to join, learn, and then help. Each individual that agrees to help has been given an assignment. The assignment is not a physical job, nor does it entail anything that must be done from a physical standpoint. Instead, the assignment comes out of the heart. The assignment was written on the heart before one enters this world, and at the exact moment that the call goes out to the heart, the heart hears and must respond.

The call is going out now for Peace Keepers. Peace Keepers have a Divine mission in that they are the conductors of peace. Just as electricity must have a conductor to keep it focused so the energy is not distorted and thus destructive, Peace Keepers know how to maintain peace and thus be a conduit for peace to enter the world and keep it safe until peace is evident. Without Peace Keepers, peace cannot be focused and must enter time very sporadically because it is at the mercy of individual's whose intention is not always peaceful.

The Peace Keepers have been placed throughout the world by a Divine Plan. These individuals were chosen before their birth to be strategically placed in the world, by their birth, or it was known where their lives would lead them. Eventually, the call to peace would become intense, and it would be time to answer the call for which they were placed in the world. This is their Heavenly calling, or their spiritual duty that they agreed to for before they entered the physical realm. Each of their lives has led them in a direction that has taught them everything they need to know to be a Keeper of the Peace. Events have occurred and they may have wondered why they felt drawn to remember a particular event. People have been placed in their lives that taught them specific lessons that would directly link them to their function of being a Peace Keeper. The physical personality traits of the Peace Keeper does not reveal what was written on the heart before the physical personality developed. The heart requirement is already known at the Being level, and when it is time, the world is ready for the Peace Keeper to take his/her position. This position is not necessarily a lofty position in the world. The job does not necessarily include perks the way the world thinks of perks. However, the job is an intricate part of the Plan for the salvation of the world, and without the Peace Keepers, the world and all of its occupants will perish.

If you have been called, or believe that it is your calling to be a Peace Keeper, it may be time to take your place among the saviors of the world. It is necessary to understand peace from a spiritual standpoint, for peace in the Higher Realm is much different than it is in the world. The assumptions that are held in the world now about the state of peace are incorrect, and in order to be a conduit for such a blessed position of being a conductor of peace, a new way of learning must occur. This new way of learning strips away the old ideas about what must occur for the conditions of peace to enter the world. Peace Keepers allow a very creative process to move through them to establish and maintain peace but first they must first learn about this process or what is going to occur so they are not frightened by the process. The beginning of the learning process begins as a commitment is made by the individual to fulfill the mission they agreed to before they entered the physical realm. The agreement is thus a symbolic signing of a Sacred Agreement that has already been agreed to on the heart and states that the individual will live up to the agreement of learning how to be a Peace Keeper. The signing of this agreement is not to be taken lightly, for we are kept at our word in the Higher Realms. Therefore, before signing a Sacred Agreement, it is important to seek out conformation before the Agreement is signed. The conformation comes in the way of dreams, off handed remarks by others, or something that confirms this is your path. If you do not receive conformation, this is probably not your path. Being a Peace Keeper requires deep inner self understanding. It is difficult to maintain a State of Peace if one is in turmoil. For this reason a period of healing and adjustment is usually necessary before the Title of Peace Keeper is given. Relinquishing feelings of unrest and internal turmoil is necessary to bring up into conscious awareness the unnatural conditions that are out of alignment with being a Peace Keeper. The healing will most likely occur more quickly than what is expected for other world inhabitants because the lack of peace in this world right now is without question its greatest threat.

The Peace Keeper is in direct contact with Higher Realms, as this is necessary to mobilize a peace keeping spiritual force around the world at key times to prevent conflicted areas from exploding into war. The spiritual force must move through the mind of the Peace Keeper to stabilize unstable conditions. This includes unnatural weather patterns that the conditions of peace has the ability to restore to harmlessness. Therefore, the Language of Heaven will be introduced into the inner communication as an ongoing learning process so the Peace Keeper will understand what is occurring without becoming fearful. The learning of this new Language will be paramount and it will be necessary to begin to distinguish the difference between personal dialog and communication that is being shared by the Guides and Advisors that are helping the world through this transitional period.

Do not be deceived by the voice that speaks of self praise and how you will profit individually from being a Peace Keeper. Higher Guides and Advisors are not deceived by this voice, but we are when this voice is listened to. The Peace Keeper is written in the Book of Life and his/her specific mission is to keep the peace by upholding the Laws of God that are written on the heart. This is a very lofty position in Heaven, but is not necessarily considered as such in this physical world. Trying to use the peace keeping anointing to enhance a personal position in this world will result in failure. Because the physical learning experience has given values that are not accepted in the spiritual realm, the need to learn true value that emanates from Heaven will be taught. Being a Peace Keeper is an anointing and also a privilege, the honor, prestige and reward emanates out of Heaven with blessings that far outweigh any physical reward.

If you believe being a Peace Keeper is your calling, then by all means beckon to the call and find out the requirements. Without your gift, the world will not survive, for all those who have been called must answer and fulfill the purpose that they have been assigned. It is fulfilling the call whereby the world is brought to the Promised Land, where peace and joy will never end.

Note

I have elected to use 30 days of peace as a method of inner learning and healing. It is evident that I am not consistently peaceful, and therefore out of my true element, which is Love, for it is only in Love that I can find my own reality.

Being peaceful does not mean I will look for ways to practice peace, it means that I will recognize when I am not at peace and make a correction, for it is in the correction that I learn that I already am that which I desire.

The moments in time that interfere with my ability to be peaceful means that I am seeking for something beyond truth, and in reality there is nothing beyond truth. Therefore I will begin to look at the moments that my internal conversations with myself turn to attack, defense, or when I try to look beyond my own awareness to perceive something outside of myself. I know that there is nothing outside of my own awareness that has any ability to provide me anything and when I look externally I see something that has no reality outside of the one I have already given it. Events do not give me meaning; I give meaning to events, so anything that occurs in the world is a product of my own perception, therefore my own imagination and many times nightmare. Terror is the state of mind that has led me out of my true element. As I learn that terror is not real, it will disappear from the face of the earth and the world will be restored to peace. I am responsible for what I see. When I am at peace, I see another world that offers hope and happiness for me and future generations.

My 30 days of peace is my gift to the world, for what I give I also receive. Peace to you and to yours. It is my hope that you will decide to create your own 30 days of peace and see what happens as you venture into the New World that echo's into time as inner terror gives way to inner peace. Perhaps you are a Peacekeeper and your decision to dedicate 30 days of peace will lead you to this purpose.

Blessings,
Cheril

Day One

It makes sense to me that if I can decide to give 30 days to peace, then I should be able to change my life.

These are the things I know about peace.
Peace is the state where Love abides and seeks to share Itself. This means that it is entirely possible to reach Love or God by just being peaceful, but in order to be peaceful; I must give what I desire. Giving peace is alien to me. What I believe is I must get what I desire, so this is my first correction then. I will learn how to give peace when I am feeling that I have been deprived of something or I want to engage in some internal verbal attacking. I have learned that when I have an internal conversation that is full of attack, then I am not in the element of peace and have opened myself up to attack. This is also true of defense. When I find that I am defending my position, then I am out of my true element and have opened myself up to what I believe I am defending myself against. The truth is that nothing outside of myself has any ability at all, so when I believe this I am entertaining false beliefs that are leading me away from peace. The intense internal desire to attack is very strong, but I also know that this intense desire must be within my own jurisdiction of control. The fact is that either I am in control of my own thinking process, or it controls me. For the most part, my attacking and defending is not something that is heard by others. I know how to smile sweetly when I believe I have been offended in some way, while all the while my internal process is waging war. These are the moments that I choose to heal and bring to peace. I am sure that the internal desire to attack and defend will be addressed over and over

again as I move through the 30 days that I have promised myself. My peace diversely affects the peace of the world, and as I am concerned about world peace, it must be that I can change the world by changing my mind. My personal physical experience will also change as I change my mind.

Peace is not a physical experience, it is a Spiritual Expression. Expression is how the Laws of Life move through my evaluations of my physical experience, but these Expressions can only occur when I am peaceful. Therefore, when I am expressing true peace, I am giving the physical experience the Expression of Heaven and this Expression has the ability to heal and thus change anything that I am thinking about. Heaven's reality is one of peace, so I realize that my peace carries with it the gifts of Heaven that will change the world. By remembering my obligation to myself and thus the world, I will begin to remember how to give that which I desire, for it is in the giving that I receive. Heaven's Patience is the peace I hope to attain so I can see what is really here without the violence I have chosen to believe is real. Eternal Patience creates immediate results, but this must first occur at a level that I am not particularly used to dealing with, which is my thought process. I am a Thought in the Mind of God. His Laws are surrounded in peace. The purpose of a thought is to extend the mind of the thinker. Therefore, my only purpose here is to extend His Mind into the world and heal it. When my thoughts are out of accord with His Mind, then I am attempting to do the impossible, for without His Love only impossible conditions exist and I see these conditions as they are reflected off of my own insane thinking into an insane world that I have made up.

Peace is the conductor of Love. Just as electricity flows through metal, Love flows through peace. When I have reached beyond my own physical belief that I understand peace, something else emerges that transcends the physical as my reality, for peace does not carry a physical interpretation. The true interpretation of Peace lies in the definition that transcends the physical experience, but is entirely within my ability to comprehend. I am not responsible for reaching peace, but I am responsible for relinquishing the perceived attacks on others that my ego has falsely accused. By choosing to search beyond the attack, my mind automatically joins with "Something Else." Sometimes it seems to take an ability that is beyond me to reach, but if it is possible to reach it just once, then it is possible to reach it again. The more I practice, the better peace keeper I will become.

Electricity seeks a conductor. Love also seeks a conductor. But just as I do not understand the laws of electricity, I also do not understand the Laws of Love. What I do understand are the conflicts that rage in my mind when I am not at peace. Because of this understanding, I seek for conflicted understanding. Understanding is a Law of Mind, but I have been using it to destroy rather than promote peace. The Law of Understanding states that; what I understand I love. What I love, I want more of, so I will find a way to create it. Thus, because I understand conflict, I must love it and will therefore find ways to incorporate it into my physical experience as a testimony to my understanding. Then I will boast about it also, because it has taken on the ego flair for conceit.

There is another way of understanding. If I can achieve, for just an instant, and give my mind over to peace, Love emerges in Its purest sense and fills my very Being with true understanding that is not physical, but instead Spiritual. This is a moment I cannot explain, for revelation cannot be explained, but only understood. This is True Understanding and speaks to me out of the Laws of Life that are contained in the Book of Life.

I am a Co-Creator with God. I have come here, into this physical realm, to help heal the world. The world is my inheritance that God has given to me jointly with all of the other inhabitants who have, for the most part, forgotten their mission. Therefore, in order to establish the New World order of peace a joint effort must be recognized. It is this that will bring about world peace and make the world a place that properly reflects the Laws of Heaven. This means that I am here to give something of value. This value is not anything I have physically; it is a spiritual value, which is my ability to attach to my true expression and give to the world what is needed to heal it. Let there be peace on earth and let it begin with me. I cannot teach peace as long as I am pointing a finger at someone else for violating peace. Correction is of God, and His correction is the only one that will last. God Loved the world enough to give it to His Son as His Inheritance. It is therefore my responsibility to learn how to give it to peace to keep it safe. For I Am His Son, and without my help, the world will perish.

My first decision on the first day is to decide to choose to be peaceful no matter what happens. This does not mean that I consciously know how to attain a peaceful state, it simply means that I am consciously agreeing to learn how to be something I do not know how to be. To be something means that it is a part of Who I Am and I know how to turn to Who I Am when conditions arise that intrude on my peaceful being. Therefore, I must learn how to tune into a state of mind that I have forgotten how to tune into.
Consciously, I do not know or understand peace. I know that it exists, but not in the consciousness that I understand peace. Therefore, there must be another consciousness that exists that is beyond what I now know. How I will reach this is not yet known to me.
Now my first dilemma arises., which is; how do I do what I do not know how to do? Let me see, it is not in my doing; so it must be in my Being. What I am learning is how to be instead of do. My ability to be peaceful lies in another Consciousness that is beyond my belief or physical consciousness. Beliefs I have contrived about doing have formed my perceptions about peace, so my beliefs must change so my perceptions change, which ultimately affects my physical experience and my ideas about peace. This is my other Consciousness that lies beyond my ability to physically manipulate. In order to learn peace I must also learn to trust a Higher Consciousness that does not come from what I think I know. It is kind of like flying a plane by the instruments instead of using the innate feeling that I am right and the instruments are wrong. I know there is a being level of Consciousness that can lead me to peace, where my peaceful being is safe and waiting for me to discover it. This is the Christ Consciousness that I hear so

much about. As much as I would like to believe it, I realize that the consciousness that I have been living from is not the Christ Consciousness, and it is comforting to know that I don't know. I think that this must be the journey.

My decision to find peace is a way to build a link to the Christ Consciousness. This link is also known as the Inner Guide that speaks to me and shows me how to re-attach to my being level. The reason I know that the Inner Guide and the new Link are one in the same, is because God only creates life because His Expression is life. What has been written in the Book of Life is alive and has the ability to communicate with me in the Language of Heaven. By making another choice that does not entertain the incorrect choices of the past; I am moving towards a new way of living my life and achieving my goal of peace.

Today I will be content with my decision to achieve peace and not try to push the link I have established by forcing this link to do something to make me peaceful. If this link is real, then the decision I have made will put my Internal Guide into operation. I think this link, or Guide, has merely been waiting for me to make a new decision that will teach me about peace.

Sanctuary

In the days of old, sanctuary was a church. It was a building that provided a place of refuge where one could go to get away from being persecuted by others that were not of the same moral or religious opinion. The church's sanctuary was such that even the political institutions, or town government of the day, did not violate the idea of sanctuary. To violate the sanctuary of the church was to invoke the wrath of God. Because of the superstitious beliefs regarding the idea of God, and not knowing for sure what they were dealing with, most people observed the sanctuary that was provided by the church.

Depending on the kindness of the priest or priests that occupied the church, the fate of the individual seeking sanctuary would either have a good experience or a terrible one. Today we are much more educated and sophisticated to believe that a church can protect us from our crimes against the state and society. We also have a Constitution that separates the church from the state, and we realize that to mix the two is a violation of not only the physical laws that we live under in time, but also a violation of the Laws of God. In the physical realm, when we violate a physical law the penalty we pay is having a jury of our peers decide our guilt. When we violate a Spiritual Law, there is another penalty that we will pay, but it does not seem to be as evident as the physical penalty that we pay when we break a physical law. This penalty is not because of our bad behavior. When we are ignorant of Higher Laws, we violate our being level. When sanctuary is needed for a violation of a Spiritual Law, it is impossible to find sanctuary in a church. Instead it is found within a spiritual state of awareness that is held within a part of our mind that seemingly we have lost the ability to access. The fear that arises from violating a Spiritual Law seems to be something else, but at a deep psychological level we are afraid of God and His wrath that will be brought upon us for breaking one of His Laws.

Within the physical realm there is a misunderstanding concerning the brain and the mind. Physical science teaches that the mind is held within the brain. This is a physical interpretation that goes by the premise that only what can be seen is real. If approached from a spiritual understanding, it is in fact the brain that is a part of the mind. Because we cannot physically see the mind, credit is given to the brain for vast amounts of wisdom which it does not hold. Spiritually, the brain is a tool for the mind and the mind uses it to re-interpret spiritual understanding into physical symbols or experiences. As we enter the threshold and move past the boundaries of eternity into time; in the beginning the mind does not understand how to be physical, so it uses the brain to re-interpret the spiritual identity into a physical identity. This identity learns to attach to experiences that are of a physical origin.

As long as science maintains that the brain has the correct interpretation of life, we will not understand the purpose of the spiritual sanctuary that has been provided for us and why it is a necessity.

Spiritual sanctuary is not a condition that occurs or exists anywhere within the physical realm. Spiritual sanctuary offers refuge from the inner turmoil that we experience when problems arise in our lives. Without realizing there is such a place, we will not learn how to take advantage of it. Because there is nowhere physical that offers protection from inner turmoil, except perhaps drugs, it is time to learn that there is such a sanctuary that has been provided for us when this occurs. It takes perseverance to learn how to access this sanctuary, but the effort is worth it.

It is said that we use only about 10% of our brain. This is because there is only so much that can be revealed or seen physically. On the other hand, the mind is limitless, and it is this that we use less than 10% of. The brain only has memories of this life. The mind, on the other hand can access vast amounts of wisdom that abounds in the universe and beyond. When we do not understand the difference, we bind ourselves to physical law and do not avail ourselves of the spiritual wisdom that is beyond the brain.

The brain is physical, and so it can be seen. The mind is pure energy, and because energy is unlimited, it is not bound by the physical laws that hold time and space together. Everyone has access to mind energy. The energy that governs nature are the same Laws that govern the mind. When it is not being used properly tension and anxiety are the conditions that occurs within the body. Imagine trying to hold the wind back with your hand. Physical experiences that have violated the Natural Laws of mind indicate this kind of insanity. We feel this impossible dilemma as stress, tension and anxiety within the body and these conditions are seldom recognized and understood as trying to hold back Natural Law.

Just outside of the brain is unlimited potential. It is also where sanctuary lies. When brain information, or physical experience is looked to for help, it is easy to get trapped in the belief that there is no alternate solution to physical problems. Being trapped in the brain or intellectual solution means sacrifice is in order, if not by us, then someone else who will have to perform this useless task. Sacrifice is a learned experience, not a spiritual one. Learning to move beyond the information that is in the brain gives an alternate solution by tuning us into Laws that govern the Spirit, which removes us from the influence of our problems that seem unsolvable. Spiritual Law, or Natural Law does not abide by the laws of time, or any government that is in the world. When Jesus walked the earth, He proclaimed that His Kingdom was no part of this world. He knew it was not because He was able to live by Laws that did not conform to the laws of Rome, which was in power at the time. He understood his physical body conformed to certain physical laws, but He also understood that if He wanted to, He could command a whole army of Angels that could and would protect Him. He fed the multitudes with the fish and loaves by using Natural Laws that did not conform to any physical experience that was known then or now. Just before He fed the multitude, He looked up. He was not focusing on the information that was in His brain, He was instead focused on a level of unlimited awareness that was just above His brain. This higher awareness is where the Laws of God abide. We also have access to those Laws that He used and He proclaimed this when He told the apostles that they would do "greater things than these."

Learning conflict and turmoil has inadvertently converted Natural Laws into physical law. Natural Laws and physical laws are at odds. As they are now, the two cannot live in harmony. Upside down thinking must be corrected. What is seen physically must learn how to live and abide by Natural Laws. Humanity has violated the Laws of Nature. Nature is not here to be commanded by what is physically seen. What is physically seen represents less than 10% of creation. The process of aligning physical law with Natural Law has not been left up to the occupants of the world. Instead each person has been assigned an Internal Guide that can help unravel the seeming need for sanctuary. Once the unraveling has occurred, the need for sanctuary is complete.

Each one who comes here has been assigned a task, and when the time is right, each person will gravitate towards the sanctuary that will eventually lead them to the task they have been assigned. A peaceful mind is the sanctuary that has been provided for everyone and it is within the grasp of anyone who wishes to move beyond the physical experience to something greater. The more this escape plan is used, the greater influence peace has on the world. Taking advantage of the escape hatch, or sanctuary, it the introduction into the Law of Nature and the Law of Life.

Day Two

As is customary, as soon as I make a decision, everything that is unlike the decision I have made comes up. I want to be peaceful, but something happens and it seems like my peace goes out the window. Making an agreement to be peaceful is great, but following through is not always as easy as I would like it to be.

I know why this happens. I used to wonder why, but now I know. Because peace is not a physical experience, I have to be willing to examine the moments in time when I had a physical experience that taught me that it was not safe to be peaceful. All of the things that taught me that I am not as God created me must be examined and found to be lacking in the truth. Otherwise I am harboring an insane belief that wants me to go on in my assumption that the belief is right, and God is wrong about me and peace. Now I will have to follow the process that can lead me back to peace.

I know I have found moments of peace even in my physical experience. These were the times that my mind was quiet. These moments of peace came to me as I watched the waters of a lake lap upon the shore or I was mesmerized by the beauty of nature. For a moment time stood still as I did not realize how much time had passed until the peace was broken by a sound of something physical. Sometimes it was just a moment. Other times it was longer. When I reached this state, the birds, squirrels and other small animals did not even notice I was there. Then, instantly I became aware of my surroundings and everything changed. As my physical presence returned, the small animals were also aware of my physical presence and scattered. I am sure that if it is possible to reach this state without consciously trying, then it is possible to reach this state with a clear goal of reaching it.

This is what I will have to work towards if I hope to find the peace that I am attempting to re-establish in my life.

First I have to recognize that my peace has been violated. Without this recognition, I cannot move forward. I will also have to recognize that the problem is coming from me; otherwise I will try to correct someone else for my own violation. This places me in the position of being able to move out of conflict and back towards peace.

Once I recognize that the problem is mine, I have to follow a procedure that will lead me to the truth. It is very difficult to explain the internal procedure; for everyone's internal communication is a little different than mine. It is also important to understand that the Guide that each person has internally speaks to them in the language that they understand. This includes their personal beliefs, their own understanding of the way life works, and also what must be taken into consideration as how to address the problem without introducing more fear, for fear produces a state in which peace cannot exist in. This keeps me from trying to correct someone else and helps me understand that each person has an Internal Guide, Who's responsible for leading them to peace. Therefore, I will withhold correction of another, and realize that it is my responsibility for my peace and refuse to blame another for my own lack of peace.

Being responsible for my own peace brings in a certain amount of fear, for now I know I cannot blame another for my lack of peace. This begins a journey to discover why I have abandoned peace so I can have a traumatic or dramatic experience. I now know that the lack of peace I am experiencing is not coming from the external situation that is at hand. The truth is that the fear of this situation that I am in, that has seemingly violated my peace, is merely a symbol of a past learning experience that has taught me that it is not safe to be a peaceful being. I also know that I am responsible for my own fear.

The protective devices in the mind that were instilled at the moment of creation will not allow me to attack fear. (As I well know as I try to tell myself how stupid I am for feeling this way and as I try to push away my fear and move forward, I only intensify the feeling.) Since I cannot attack it, or explain it away, and because my mind believes in its reality, I will have to find a way around it so as not to intensify the effects of the terror that I am not in control of.

I discover that my mind does not object to my questions, so I can question my mind as to why there is fear. This is one way to move around fear without setting up barriers to my goal of peace. One of the Laws, under which I was created, is that everything belongs to me. This means that everything is a part of me, and I am a part of everything. If I try to get rid of fear, my mind will follow the Laws under which it was created, and prove that fear is a possession and not to be gotten rid of, so I am defeated before I start. In order to move around this condition, I will use the Law of Understanding so as to show my mind that if fear is not present it will not be a loss. Mind was created to seek for understanding and if I use understanding, fear cannot exist in the presence of truthful understanding. So I want my mind to understand that fear is not a part of the conditions under which I was created, so it is not understandable and therefore not real. The way I will do this is to question, not the fear, but the issue that the fear is hiding, for behind the fear is the real block to peace, in fact wanting to return to the state of peace.

Before the separation, there was only Love. Love does not hide what It holds, for what Love holds are happiness, goodness, joy, life, health, and everything I want. Fear hides an experience of a physical origin that shows me that I am not real and the mistaken experience is. This seems to make fear real. In truth I do not want to look at the concept that it is possible that the experience I am having is real, and I am not; so I set up a condition of fear so I don't have to understand this false reality. In truth, it is me that is real, but until I reach the issue that is hiding behind fear, it will not understand and my mind will try to keep the false protection. Truth does not need to hide, but it does need to be uncovered so I can see there is nothing to be afraid of, and then it can be released so I can return to my peaceful state. This is what I want my mind to understand.

Sometimes I cannot find the issue that fear is hiding so I will have to find another way to restore peace to my mind. For the fear will return over and over again until I realize at a deep psychological level of mind that fear is nothing. If my mind is using fear as a protective device instead of Love the way it was intended, then I am depending on a protective devise that finds protection in hiding, as fear does. So as much as I want to hide from the external torment that seems to be occurring, I will choose to ask for Inner Guidance to help me with what I cannot do for myself. This is one of the special provisions that have been given to the world to help with the process of healing that is occurring right now.

I am learning how to access Laws that include Love. Love governs my Being. This means that I do not have to "do anything, for doing is governed by physical law. If I use physical law, I will have to force or manipulate my way through the use of behavior. At a behavior level, I am acting out, and acting out of fear. So in order to move past my intense desire to "do" something, I will choose to just be peaceful.

By choosing peace, something has occurred. The intensity of the problem seems to have diminished and the inner turmoil of having to "do" something to make a correction is not a factor. I am not sure what this means, but at least I have found that there is something else besides my intense feelings of having to do something to correct the fearful feelings. I have reached something else and have learned that there is an alternative to the fear and having to force or manipulate circumstances to make things work out for me. I am trying to match this feeling up to different times that I have attained a peaceful state without actually trying. I am looking for what is the same. For peace to be real, it must contain the same content every time. I am not sure what the same content is as yet, but there is something familiar about peace every time I have attained it, but I can't quite put my finger on it.

Memories

What is a memory?

Memories are how we keep track of past events. They help us recognize a friend or a foe. They remind us of the laughter in our lives, and they remind us of our pain. Memories are written on the mirror in our mind and we reflect on our memories often. These are the pictures that we take with our mind's eye throughout our life experience and then use these pictures to determine how we will respond when situations arise that remind us of the past memory.

Our beliefs are deeply rooted in our memories. In fact all personal beliefs spring from our memories. We are hardly aware of how our mind uses the memory process because we are not aware of how our mind works. If we want to understand why we believe and behave a certain way, or why someone else does, then the memory system will have to be examined as a source of personal belief and behavior.

How the mind stores memory

The mind works much the same as a camera does when it is recording history in that it has the ability to freeze a frame and save it. Try to remember the first physical recording that you have. Most people have a hard time remembering things before a certain age, then, all of a sudden, a memory springs to life. This is a memory of our first physical experience. It is not the first physical experience, but is the first time we became self aware. There are many more self aware experiences to come, and each self aware picture that is taken becomes a part of the warehouse of the past that the mind uses as a reference as to how to have and learn from a physical experience.

The Being level of mind

At the Being level of mind, the mind is not self aware, it is aware of wholeness. Up until the first self aware moment captured in the memory of the person who is now having a physical experience, the mind is still reliant on whole awareness for its reality, so it could be said that the person is Being whole. At a closer look, we can see that before the mind becomes totally self aware, it is not dependent on time. In other words the memory of the awareness of the a baby does not look at a clock to determine if he/she is hungry, wants to play, wants to be comforted, or etc. The memory of time is non-existent in the mind of the child, so when it is hungry, it is Being hungry. When it wants to play, it is Being playful, and etc. Here, it is seen that doing is the outcome of the Being. The child has not learned yet that to be, one must do first. This state is called innocence. Innocent memory deals with the Being level, and also whole awareness.

The shift to time

Shifting to self awareness can only be experienced in time because whole awareness or eternity is not time based. So time awareness is physical awareness and physical awareness comes from experiences that have been learned in time so they are linked and perform a dance that is not in harmony with Being or whole awareness, and what is known in eternity as innocence. The dance that is out of harmony with wholeness makes unhappiness and disease a physical reality that we try to correct physically. This is called using physical law to try to correct what can only be corrected by Spiritual Law.

Once we begin shifting into self awareness our belief system shifts into fragmented beliefs that are based on the memories learned in time. These memories are written on the walls of the body because the body is part of the physical reality and physical reality is as much a part of time as spirit is tied to eternity. The memories of time based experiences begin to lead us slowly but surely away from our spiritual nature, until at last we are totally dependent on fragmented, time based physical memories learned from experiences that have nothing to do with our spirit or Being nature, but instead regulate behavior or doing.

Behavior

Behavior is not who we are, it is what we do. Who we are is spiritual, and what we do is physical. When we judge behavior it is because our physical experience has taught us that someone else's behavior, or our own, is out of sorts with individual self awareness and is therefore bad. This judgment makes behavior real in our own mind, and does not even consider the Being except that behavior has possibly labeled us or another as "being" bad. At a spiritual level, it is impossible to "be" bad, so this is sin. Trying to do something impossible, like violating Spiritual Law is what is known as sin. In the first place, we are spiritual Beings, in the second place what we do with the physical body has no effect on eternity whatsoever so therefore is unreal. Being sinful merely reflects the unreal self aware memories that have been stored in the body that are attached to time, which began in the past and we are still carrying as if they were still applicable today. Is it any wonder why much of the world is depressed, sick, in pain, unhappy, conflicted, stressed, etc?

Body learning

Once the body has been filled with memories of time based experiences, it stops learning and depends upon the past to determine the present and the future. Because these memories are not in alignment with Spiritual Law, and because the mind is creative in nature, it incorrectly uses beliefs based on false memory to create with. If our memories or beliefs are way out of harmony, then our life becomes very destructive, either internally, externally, or both. Even if they are not way out of harmony, we cannot escape the "sin" of making memories without the constructive creative process. In the end we all pay the ultimate price because our memories are distorted and the wages of sin is death so we all eventually experience the seeming finality of death. But this too is a belief that is stored in false memory, so even death, in the realm of spirit, is not a viable threat.

Our real memory

We have become so accustomed to using false memory to help us get through life; we have forgotten that there is another way of remembering. This way of remembering reconnects us to our Being level of mind where our spiritual nature awaits us. These memories remind us of our real Home where there are other Laws that teach the truth. These memories are the ones we share with God.

The miracle

The miracle is misunderstood when placed under the fragmented memories learned in time. Using false memory learned in time, we try to make the miracle something it was never intended to be. The miracle is to be used to help lead the mind back to its reality. It cannot lead the body because it is not a part of spirit. The body performs tasks, while the spirit just is, so it is part of the Being. The miracle has the ability to restore us to wholeness by showing us the exact moment when we departed from whole awareness into self awareness and fragmented our Being with a false memory. The miracle has the ability to restore our memory to the wholeness of God, but we must be willing participants in the process. If we are trying to get the miracle to heal the body, we are trying to misuse its purpose. In order to use the provision of the miracle, it must be used properly. Distortion is not acceptable in eternity.

It is up to us to embrace the idea that there is something that we do not know. Our willingness to accept this is all that is necessary to begin the process of moving us beyond our false learning that we hold so dear in our memory. God placed another Voice in our mind to direct and help us find our false associations that we have unwittingly tried to make real. Reality does not dwell in what is false; it dwells in what is real. No matter how hard we try to make what is perishable real, it will never be real. The body dies, while the spirit is pure energy. Energy can transform, but the body only deteriorates until nothing is left. The opportunity for us to use miracles is now open to mankind. Learn how to use this provision that has been made for us during this trying time. The outcome of miracles is cumulative in effect, and will change the world.

Changing your mind means exchanging your memory. Take the Hand of Heaven and allow this Hand to lead you to your salvation. Everything is in place waiting for your return. Another memory of Heaven awaits those that are willing to let go of what they think they know. Within this new memory is life and the ability to heal the world.

Day Three

    I still seem to be having experiences that are in conflict with the peace I wish to attain. Things will be going along just fine, and then "boom," something happens externally that invades what I am trying to accomplish. The inner struggle, which is I am going to be peaceful today, seems to produce an inner feeling that is blasting my decision and telling me that it is impossible to keep peace because there is going to be an outcome to this situation that I am not going to like. I wonder where this feeling comes from that has the ability to override my desire for peace. I know I want peace, but I also feel that I cannot have it. The terror of not being in control is almost overwhelming. I can feel the inner need to have to "do" something. I want to run and do something to make this better so I don't have to continue feeling this way. But I also know that to do will not be in line with just being peaceful. I have learned that if I do something then I am using physical law, and these are the laws that govern my physical experience. This misunderstanding means that in order to "be" I have to "do." Somehow I know this is wrong, but I do not know how to correct this. There is a tremendous amount of anxiety that makes me believe that if I do something I will feel better because this will alleviate the anxiety. But then anxiety is the motivating factor for peace instead of peace being the motivating factor. Anxiety should not be a prerequisite to peace. Something is wrong, but I do not know how to make the correction.

    I think today I should look at the Internal Guide so I can realize that there is Help that has the ability to override the sabotage or mutiny that seems to be going on within. I know that without this Help I will never be able to stabilize peace within myself and keep what I know is rightfully mine. Somewhere within I know that peace is my birthright and I will strive to attain it no matter what. I am greater than the problem, and this includes any problem that is intruding on my peace. Even though I do not believe this, at a deep level I know this to be true. Carl Jung said that to know is greater than to believe; so even though I don't understand, I do know. This is going to take a great amount of faith. I never really realized how much.

I will examine what I understand about the Internal Guide so I can better understand how this Guide can help me. The Internal Guide has a specific purpose because everything was created with a purpose. Just as the purpose of peace is to be the conductor of Love or God, the purpose of the Internal Guide is to help me restore peace back to my mind. He helps me accomplish this when I make a decision to follow the Law of Peace. It is His purpose to show me my Being by helping me stabilize the incorrect decisions I have made in the past that have led me to believe I am the experience I am having instead of the Love that God created.

He lives in my mind and communicates with me, but He speaks to me on a different level than I am used to communicating at. Although His Voice is not alien to me, and I know that He has the truth, sometimes it is difficult for me to believe what He is saying and I revert to what I know, which is doing something to alleviate the feelings that seem to be emerging from a problem. How can feelings emerge from an external problem? The feelings are not in the problem, they are in me but I feel they are in the problem. It is not what I think, it is what I feel. The anxiety that arises from my perception of the problem is causing the problem, not the problem itself. I wonder just how much I am actually contributing to the problem with my own anxiety. I wonder what would happen if I had no anxiety about the problem.

It is the job of the Guide to help me straighten all of this out. It is His Job to change my perception, so my understanding shifts from a doing level to a Being level. At a Being level, I am governed by Spiritual Law, and I am no longer constricted by the laws of time, governments, institutions, or the anxiety of a problem. Spiritual Law has the ability to dismiss these laws and false perceptions by overlooking them and declaring them to be at my disposal instead of my being at their disposal. The reality of Being has the ability to change my old concept, and thus change the purpose of what seems to be external to me. Purpose is of God, but it is up to me to see this. If I believe the purpose of the government is to conduct war, collect taxes, red tape, and etc and cause me anxiety., then the purpose that I have learned in my physical experience is incorrect and must be exchanged for the purpose or function that God has given it. With the new interpretation firmly in place that my mind carries as I give up the old, a New World emerges that is upheld by the Laws of Peace that begin in my mind with my decision to learn peace as a way of life.

Perception is not reality, but true perception leads to reality. False perception says; this is the way I believe truth is because that is the way it was explained to me or; I encountered it to be this way through experience. A new perception, which the Inner Guide is responsible for, gives me a new meaning that has a direct impact on the fear, anxiety and problems I seem to be experiencing now. The new perception shows me that what I am encountering is actually the past that taught me how to follow the laws of doing amd experience instead of the Laws of Being and expression. If I want to learn how to be peaceful, then I will have to learn the new perception that will teach me how to express a new experience.

The past the old perception made with false memory keeps showing up in my life over and over again. The only thing that is different is the physical symbol. It constantly changes. But the problem is the same though not recognizable because of the physical symbol that constantly changes. This is why many people seemingly marry their parents. The new marriage relationship has become an old symbol of their relationship with their parents, so what has happened is an exchange of physical symbols; same problem just a different person or symbol. If the relationship with the parents was a way to force and manipulate to "get" our own way, the marriage will be the same. This is worked in many ways, and too many to recount here. In fact, the marriage is neither good nor bad. It simply does not reflect the Laws of Heaven because the Laws of Heaven are not symbolic, they are real. A symbolic relationship is not necessarily healthy and usually ends up, but not always, in divorce. There is another perception that leads out of the symbolism that has been given the relationship or the experience. This is the real perception that can lead to the truth, or place me under New Laws that govern my Being, thus the new experience is not reminiscent of the past. This shows me that there is a part of me that places what I have learned erroneously in the proper perspective and sees it as a symbol of the past. But there is something within that has a great investment in the past. Because the body is a part of the past, it also must receive another interpretation or I will keep it as a constant reminder of my errors in the past. It is the reminder of the past that keeps me doing out of fear, for there is no fear in spirit, but there is a tremendous amount of fear where my body is concerned. The body must be reinterpreted so I can see what it really means, for the interpretation I have given it is not something I like at all.

Physical History/Spiritual History

Spiritual information must make sense so that it can be accepted. The old cliche that everything should be accepted on faith is moving out to make way for the new. This does not mean that there is no longer any need for faith, it just means that the old way of viewing faith must change in order to make way for the new. People are much too sophisticated and informed to accept that there is spiritual information that is not in the physical interpretation of what life means. Therefore, spiritual information must make enough sense for humankind to make use of it at a physical level. As spiritual beings we are having a physical experience and are rational thinking beings because we were created that way. When anything occurs we must find some kind of rational explanation for what is happening or it eats at us. For example, we explain the reason why we do things to ourselves and others, if they care to listen. We also explain to ourselves and sometimes others why someone else is doing something. This is in fact is justification of behavior, either ours or someone else's. Justification of behavior is not necessarily a good thing. For instance, I could say that someone else treated me mean because they were a jerk. In a way I am justifying their behavior through my judgment of how a jerk behaves. Behaving like a jerk is not spiritual behavior because in order to behave like a jerk one would have to be a jerk constantly and consistently, and no one is always a jerk, so personal judgment comes from the one observing behavior, and not necessarily from the so called jerk.

Behavior is not a part of our being until we begin a physical experience. The reason for this is that in order to have behavior, we must have a body. Without a body, we could not judge behavior because we wouldn't have any. We also would not be able to rationally explain why someone else is doing something or why something is being done. If behavior does not fit in with my interpretation of correct behavior, is it wrong? In order to bring some meaning to this it must be looked at from a different perspective, which would lead to why judgment of behavior is so cherished. On closer examination the physical history of the world stems from judgment of behavior and behavior stems from experience. Because God does not have behavior, it is impossible for Him to judge or be judged, as far a physical judging occurs. It is also impossible for Him to have experiences, because everything reacts to Him and His Laws, so the physical experience is a reaction to behavior and because God does not have behavior or reaction, His reaction to the physical realm has been greatly overstated. As physical doers, we relate to experience and behavior, and because we do, we expect that God does also, but what if this is not true? Physical experience arises from our physical encounters, which is then stored in our mind as a fact, which is then stored in the physical body where the mind has access to it so it can "behave" with a body. The reaction to experience causes humankind to believe that God must be the problem, but this is impossible for God is the solution. The physical history of the world is therefore based on our decision about some else's behavior or our own learned through judgment, ours or somebody else's. In order to have behavior, we must do something. The judgment that arises from behavior, or what is being done, establishes us as having a physical experience, or as physical beings. The spiritual history of the world arose to correct an error. The Bible tells us that the mistake occurred after the creation of Adam and Eve. In order to understand what went wrong in the Garden and why two different kinds of histories had to emerge, we will take a look at what happened in the Garden. First of all, the time has come for us to understand rationally what the real error was that occurred there. Without this explanation we will continue trying to make sense out of events that we are trying to understand from a physical point of view. In other words, the *behavior* of Adam and Eve will be evaluated instead of the real so called "sin." The behavior is in the eating of the so called fruit of good and bad, or the symbolic apple. If the event is not rationally explored then we will be back to the idea that we must accept that we are sinful on faith, and the purpose of faith will be lost in sin.

In the beginning when God created Adam and Eve, they were Spiritual Beings. There essence or expression of Being was established by God. They did not have to establish their worth by trying to do something. In fact any act of doing came out of their sense of Being happy. So in the beginning, Being established everything. Something happened that turned all of this around. We look to the Bible to find out what switched Adam and Eve to a level of having to do in order to Be, because this was the issue that was raised in the Garden. Either God's creation is a Spiritual Being, or a physical creature that has do something to force and manipulate life so the being can be proven. If being must be proved through doing, then God is wrong and the serpent must be right. It seems so trivial to look at the issue this way, but this was the question that arose in the Garden, and it was this question that had the ability to turn the very Heavens upside down. It was this that God could not allow, so he devised a Plan that would restore the true spiritual nature back to all of creation, including the world. A span of time would be allowed to prove the impossible task that it was possible that a creation of God could be something other than what God had created. In order to prove that is was possible for God to be wrong about the Being Nature, a new way of experiencing life would have to emerge. This experience was based on a fearful existence, and was separate from the Love that Being was created with. At the moment the error was made, and it was discovered it was possible to do without being with God or Love, a hole opened up and a part of the Heaven's creation fell out into a place of non-existence. It is called a place of non-existence because in truth there is no where that God does not exist. The evidence of God is always in His Peace. Obviously, since the beginning of time, the world has not been a peaceful place. The world has been full of fear, and the outcome of fear is conflict. This was the lesson that was expelled from Heaven. It was the error that is was possible to be able to do something and make God second next to the doing or physical nature, thus leaving the Being or the God Nature without a Home. This new doing nature began to learn new laws that were made to force and manipulate. Not only by making an existence out of what was physically seen, but also by forcing and manipulating others to conform to a way by forcing and manipulating the spirit of individuals. The spirit went into hiding until an appointed time and all of this mess would be straightened out. The doing nature left because of the fear of God and so the Laws of God remained intact in the Hgher Realm, and the question would be worked out at a lower level that began to make new laws that would conform to behavior, or force and manipulation.

Before this happened, fear was not known. The most profound evidence of this split occurred when Adam and Eve began to experience fear. Love is an expression, not an experience, so the fear experience took Adam and Eve out of the moment and into a past learning experience based on fear. This event is most dramatically told because God cannot hear Adam anymore. The communication level of God and His Creation had been breeched. This caused Adam's level of communication to shift from the heart, where wisdom lies, to the intellect, where fear abides. In the Bible we are told over and over again that God dwells in the heart, so communication shifted, not in the mind of God, but in the mind of Adam and Eve. This shift brought about the doing level, or the physical experience. This new world of doing had to emerge because of the power that God had given Adam at the moment he was created. So powerful were the thoughts of Adam, a new world emerged that tried to overtake the Power of God and tried to prove it was possible to live in a world of fear instead of Love. God dwells in peace and peace is the conductor of Love. What was exchanged for peace was time. God is the protector of all of His Creation. The exchange was the new protection of fear. Fear became the protector as Adam tried to hide from God behind the fear he had made.

All of God's creation lives in innocent. What was exchanged for innocence was guilt. Guilt now became the backbone of time. God created everything in wholeness. The exchange for wholeness or everything being joined in love was fragmentation. This made physical love special because it did not include the Love of God, so not everyone was included on the list when people made their love lists.

God's creation was created in the "Being" of everything. The exchange was having to do something so one could be. God created spirit. The exchange was a body where information regarding a physical experience could be stored. God created willingness. The exchange was resistance. God's creation acts together as a whole. The exchange was reacting to an experience individually. God created freedom of will . The exchange was to imprison the will and make it serve a physical experience. God created His creation as expressions of Love. The exchange was for a physical experience of fear and belief that something that was not done correctly was punishable through force and manipulation. God created eternal life. The exchange was death of the physical body. The list could go on and on. The idea is that physical law and Spiritual Law are in direct contrast. In truth it is impossible to place a Spiritual Law under the rule of physical law that forces and manipulates. This violates the Law of Freedom that is upheld by the Heavenly Court. This is why God chose to give His Own Version to the world, which explains the spiritual history of the world. This Book is commonly known as the Bible. The spiritual history of the world explains our Being and the righteous heart. It tells u over and over again that the righteous heart is recognized by God and that the Laws of God abide within this heart. It explains the inner turmoil that occurs between the intellect and the heart, or the being and doing level, and how this was overcome. The physical history of the world, which is told in history books, explains what mankind has done with his conflicts and wars. It explains the conquests and and all that man has done in the world since the beginning of time.

The spiritual history of the world began right around 6000 years ago. What this means is that God did not introduce His Plan or His Seed into the world until that time. Before then, the physical history of the world was being firmly established. We commonly believe that God established the beginning of time, but the Bible does not point to this in any way. The Bible establishes the beginning of creation, not the beginning of time. Time is relative and therefore not established by truth. Up until the point that the spiritual history of the world was introduced, fear was the motivating factor behind the physical meaning for life. After the spiritual history was introduced, a shift occurred. The motivating factor for life began to move back to the heart level and Love level where The Home of God is. This did not mean that the motivating factor behind the physical experience instantly shifted and man was ruled by love. At the beginning of the spiritual history of the world the motivation factor was fear, which is clearly seen by man's interpretation of God. At this point in the spiritual history of the world, man was trying to understand God through a physical interpretation, and because his main motivation was fear, he gave to God what he understood. This is why the Old Testament refers to God as being a God of fear. Spiritual Love for the entire world was not introduced until the Christ. With the introduction of the Christ, the prophecy that God would crush the serpent with His Seed became implemented. The doing nature of man could not prevent the Love of God from entering the physical world through a man known as Jesus Christ.

The spiritual history of the world points to a Man that will be born into the world that will bring righteousness to the world by showing a new way that was founded on a Love principle, not a doing one. This man is a King, not because He will come and kill the wicked, that prophecy was fear misinterpreting Love. Instead this King is the Light of the World. The Bible says that when time was full, God sent His Son, so full of what? Time was full of every thought that could possibly be thought of that could bring about the fear factor. Everything that could be done had been done to try to prove that man could live without his Creator. This is why the Ecclesiastes says that there is nothing new under the sun. Nothing else could be done that would serve to show mankind that it was possible to live without God. God set a time when the heart of man would turn back towards His Love. The end of fear was in the works, but fear does not go without a fight. So enter the Light of the World. Just think, instead of believing that there was a love that mankind did not understand, the Son of God actually established real Spiritual Love and it was He that fulfilled the scripture of God's Seed by introducing this Spiritual Love into a place that had never know it. Fear no longer was ruler over man's innocence. He now had a choice to live from his intellect or his heart. The impact of this event from a physical standpoint is beyond our scope of understanding.

After God's Son entered the world, from now on only His Son would come. All of the fear that lived in the world would be exchanged for Love, and communication with God would be restored. The intellect would go by the way side for the choice of heart felt communication. Heartfelt communication would establish a link between Heaven and Earth to make way for a new Heavens and a new Earth. The scriptures say; "and look, I saw a new Heavens and a new Earth, and the former things had passed away."

After the resurrection of Jesus and the revelation in the Bible, the spiritual history of the world goes silent. In fact it seems to almost die. But because we are dealing with the element of time, we have to understand that what seems to have taken 2000 years, in eternity took no time at all. From a physical standpoint, God's Son continued to bring pieces of the Plan into time and leave it here for the past 2000 years. At last all of the pieces are here, and it is time to put the pieces together.

The pieces are put together through the journey of self discovery. As the intellectual communication is recognized as being based on a purely physical experience is put aside for the communication that is within the heart a New World emerges. The heart is where the Plan lies. As each individual learns how to heal their life, their piece of the puzzle to restore the world to righteousness is revealed and they settle into Laws that do not conform to time. The shift, of fear moves to the Love of God, as the world and Heaven become as one.

How 9/11 Changed the World Spiritually

No event in the history of the world changed the course of history, physical and spiritual, like the event that occurred in New York and Washington DC on September 11, 2001. The event began a new era. The new era would begin the process of joining together both the physical and spiritual identity of man into one.

Never before in the history of the world has an event occurred where it was so evident that a tragedy had world wide implications. This tragedy caused world wide grief and grief such as this has never occurred in the history of the world. Other events have occurred in this world and there have been many more innocent people killed, murdered and tortured than the lives that were taken on that fateful 911 day, but something stood out on that day and made it like no other day ever before experienced.

The events that occurred on that day had been in the making for many thousands of years, but the physical perception of the event did not begin to touch the symbolic magnitude of it. The question of who has the right to govern creation was answered on the day, but this was not something that was seen, but instead felt because of the massive overwhelming feelings of grief and sadness that were experienced as waves of compassion touched the feelings of loss. At a deep level of awareness and as a world we knew that this event would change the face of complacency and the world as a whole would be forced to change direction, for without this change the world was headed in a downward spiral motion that would end in its ultimate destruction. The forces of evil had forced the symbolic Hand of the spiritual realm to begin the process of the healing of the world and bringing into existence a New Movement of Thought that would heal the world through a process of joining both the physical mind with the spiritual mind, thereby uniting the two realms into one.

We were all in shock that day, but the terror of the event did not stop the support and love that occurred throughout the world; thus terror was not the victor, Love was. Never before had the whole world taken a stand against evil at the same instant, and this was the shift the world needed to bring it into alignment with a higher truth that will bring about the eventual peace that this world so desperately needs. The world need only give Heaven an instant of perfect Love for it to enter and give it a new interpretation. Although many believe that the feelings of love and support have gone by the wayside since 911, it is impossible for Heaven to forget. The cry that arose out of the devastation was answered immediately by Love, and we all felt it. Once this was released into the world, the world would never be the same. This would not have noticeable effects immediately, but the eventual outcome would remain until the end of time.

The old must make way for the new. The old physical interpretation of the world must make way for a spiritual one. This other interpretation was hard to hear on that fateful day because the sound of grief was beyond comprehension. For every event that occurs in this physical world that brings sadness and grief, there is another interpretation that has the ability to bring another meaning that brings new hope for something better. Without this interpretation, we are forced to accept an evil interpretation that brings loss and despair. We have a choice, but sometimes when tragedy occurs it is easy to forget that there is another way of looking that has the ability to bring about circumstances that will bring ultimate healing to the world. Most of the time we feel our choices are caught between the best of two evils, but this is no longer the case. Evil does not offer choices, it offers destruction. This day was different and the choice that was made was Love.

Every 2000 years a major spiritual event occurs. The last major spiritual event was the life of Christ. 2000 years before that, Moses led the Israelites out of Egypt. 2000 years before that, the spiritual history of the world began. Before that, the physical history of the world was considered the greater of the two. The physical and spiritual history of the world are different from the perspective that the physical history deals with mans ability to be logical and use the intellect as a source of survival in this world. Physical history deals with how force and manipulation have brought us to this day. On the other hand, spiritual history has always dealt with a righteous heart and wisdom. The intellectual understanding of a matter has never been the heart of the matter. That is, until the events of September 11, 2001. On that day, the heart and the intellect crossed paths, and nothing would ever be the same again. The shift that occurred on that day would bring about a new interpretation to this world that could only heal the world by bringing a new meaning to it that would include the heart, which is the Home of God. That fateful day, the physical history and the spiritual history at last met and stared one another in the symbolic face, and the world would never be the same again.

At a conscious level, we did not see the meeting; all we could see was the destruction. For the forces of the intellect and the spirit to meet would indeed bring about a dramatic climax that would be symbolized by an event that would shock and shake the world at its very core. The meeting of these two forces were foretold millions of years before. The outcome of this meeting would bring about a New World where peace would rule because the heart would be recognized as being greater than the intellect. But the intellect did not readily understand what was occurring, and so the clash symbolized the beginning of an unseen shift that when completed would make room for both the intellect and the spirit to reside in peace. A new life force was in the making, and the Twin Towers destruction symbolized the bringing down of both the physical and spiritual interpretation as separate so they could eventually live in harmony as one.

My first objection is about the people who died as a result of the destruction. The answer comes that they did not see death. Angels were there looking to take those who wished to go before death could be seen. Those who jumped, they fell into the arms of angels and never hit the ground. Everyone who was supposed to be there, was there. Those who were not, were delayed. The ones on the planes that hit the towers, at a deep level, understood the significance of the eventful day, and agreed to be a part of it. The plane that crashed over Pennsylvania, that particular group of people were there because of their ability to work together and stop what was not supposed to occur. Their reward in Heaven is great.

A year and a half before 911 occurred, I had 3 dreams that foretold of a "storm coming." I was told that the storm would be greater than any storm that the world had ever experienced. The second time I took heed of the dream. The third time, the dream explained that the storm would be 300 miles long. That is how many miles between New York and Washington DC.

After the attacks, and the dust settled, I was explained the spiritual interpretation of the actual event. I now understand that the event had to be reinterpreted so hope could come to the world. Evil does not want the world to hope, it wants it to be destroyed. I share this with you so you too can begin to learn that is is possible to turn all unpleasant conditions in your personal life into hope for this is the how the world will change.

The New Interpretation of 9/11

The Twin Towers represents the dual identity of man. One is physical and the other is spiritual. Both had to be destroyed so that a new idea of humanity could arise from the ashes. This is the symbolic rising of the Phoenix. The new interpretation that would emerge would join the physical experience with the spiritual expression, and they would ultimately live side by side in peace. The lion, or the physical nature of man, along side the sheep, or the spiritual idea in the heart, and a child will lead them all. The child is the innocent nature of the spirit guiding the intellect to peace.

After the destruction of the towers a time of healing would occur. This is the evolutionary shift that is occurring right now. The innocent heart must take precedence over the bestial or physical nature, so peace can occur. This is the end of the guilt of sin, which is the symbolic lower nature that governs behavior. The end of the judgment of behavior also signifies the end of the evil rule that is commonly referred to as the inner demons that bring men to do evil deeds. The outcome is the joining of Heaven and Earth as One. No longer is man at odds with God, for His Home has been restored. It is no longer observed as just a physical organ that pumps blood to the body. God has returned Home, and the world rejoices for peace as at last come to the world. Evil has lost its home, for the heart has been returned to Love. The new building in New York is the symbol of the new man that will walk in Love instead of fear.

It is interesting to note that after the Towers were destroyed, a light was placed and remained for a while where the Towers once were. Light is symbolic of spiritual wisdom. Because it is physically impossible to destroy light, the light stood as a reminder to the evil forces that there is a Force that is beyond the comprehension of evil but not beyond the comprehension of man.

If you look at where the Pentagon is located, it looks like the heart of America. Evil forces tried to destroy all of the heart, where the Home of God abides. The destruction of the Home of God is impossible, but the part that evil did claim was destroyed. The heart is symbolically now free to choose to allow God to return to His Home and so is the world.

Heaven has moved into the world, but most of the occupants have not noticed. To everything there is a season. The season has arrived that earth's occupants take note of the symbolic language that is occurring in the world and begin to learn how to use the information that has become available to work with the evolutionary shift instead of fighting it. Heaven has It's Own Plan to heal the world and bring about peace. We have the choice to learn of our own individual plan that will add to Heaven's Plan or continue on without recognizing that this world altering event has occurred. The choice is ours, but whether or not this Plan will be carried out is not our choice. There are many opportunities that are emerging to help others find and use methods to help ourselves, others, and world situations by learning what is expected and how to use what is being offered. The Miracle Response is dedicated to help with this process.

Day Four

I am constantly looking for a way to solve the problems that I am encountering throughout the day. I am beginning to learn that the resolution to my problems is not in how I have gone about solving them in the past. Instead the resolution lies in maintaining a state of peace. I am learning that there are levels within the mind that are just like states in the United States. In other words, there is a State of Florida and a State of California, and just like there are different states in the Union, there are States of Being. For instance, I can be in a Happy State, or I can be in an unhappy state. I have not recognized these as States before, but now am beginning to understand the connection and how we use States of Mind to represent things in time. Just as when I am in Florida, I cannot experience California; when I am in a State of Peace, I cannot experience a state of war. This does not necessarily mean that the war going on in the world is not in my awareness, but now I recognize war as a state that lies in my physical awareness and not my Spiritual Awareness and I can shift my awareness any time I please.

My physical awareness is what makes my physical experience. The "state" of my mind where awareness lies needs direction. It is where my belief system lies; whereas my consciousness is how I direct this awareness. My physical awareness is a result of learning how I became self aware. Without self awareness there is only whole awareness and this is where reality or God dwells. The reason I have put this together is this: It is known that God is Omnipresent, Omniscient, and Omnipotent. This means that He is everywhere and everything all at once and only exists now. This being the case, then if I am not "aware" of this then I have removed my self from the State of His Grace, which lies in His Peace. Time is not a "now state" and if I can only have peace now, then to have it I will have to let something else go that conflicts with it.

My self awareness began the first time I recognized myself through a physical experience I was having. Before that, I did not see myself as being separate from whole awareness. Usually separation from the whole aware state is brought about by a traumatic experience, or a physical event so diametrically opposed to wholeness, I was immediately shocked into a realization that there was something that did not originate with wholeness. This is where my physical consciousness began and when I began to separate from knowing how to be and instead trying to do.

In my Spiritual State, it is not necessary to have consciousness. The true purpose of awareness is whole and complete and within Itself in the Spiritual Realm. When the separation began, a new way of learning was introduced. This new way of learning involved consciousness, as revealed in the story of the Garden of Eden. The onset of the separation brought on self awareness through the decision that it was possible to live without the Wholeness of Love. This self aware state of learning how to do was the introduction of fear into awareness, and out of this emerged consciousness. Consciousness was the way that a self aware person could make decisions, not based on Love, but instead based on fear. The fearful state was how the physical state of doing emerged, which is force and manipulation, as is clearly seen in the story of the Garden of Eden. As soon as the self aware state began, the couple began to try to manipulate their way out of the situation through blame. Now, instead of the extension of Love that was evident in the world, the need for projection because of denial, which leads to blame, began. This would force the state of self awareness, or doing state of mind, to be governed by something else other than Wholeness or God, because in the State of Peace there is no projection of blame. There is only extension of Love.

It is only possible to find Love, or God in the State of Peace, so awareness that did not include wholeness "stepped out" of the Whole Aware State into a self aware fear based state. The only place where self awareness could call home was the body. So self awareness that is held in the body is based on a self absorption of ideas that have nothing to do with truth. What emerged from this state were beliefs that now defined the physical belief of fear. Self awareness needed a way to make decisions to try to avoid fear, so consciousness was born out of a need to make decisions without God. Instead of looking for reasons to Love, self awareness looked for reasons to hide, if fear was a clear and present danger. Also, because it is impossible to create constructively without God, a new way of creating emerged that was destructive in intent. Intention is not always a good thing. Without spiritual Love, the best of intentions are not supported by Spiritual Laws and are therefore not necessarily approved by Heaven.

Intellect, which explains the reasons for fear, was made to replace wisdom, which explains the reasons for Love. Because fear is always seen as something "out there," the external world was a result. The external world always had shadows that were holding something that brought danger, and because fear is outside, the attack always seemed to be coming from someone or something else. I never realized that the fear the shadow produced was really being made by me, so I was really afraid of my own shadow. But my intellect told me the shadow was real, so I believed it. Intellect also told me to judge what is occurring externally and to see how someone else's behavior measures up to mine. Mine was always so much better, because my intellect told me it was. My intellect became my insane method of judgment, and wisdom of wholeness or God took a backseat to the stored intelligence that I had self righteously collected. Self consciousness came as a result of self awareness, and self righteousness was a result of my self awareness. Now, instead of God completing the creative process, my consciousness could do it for the fear based beliefs that I had self righteously collected, but I was always afraid. I had forgotten how to be peaceful, and when the idea of peace intruded on my conflicts, I just knew that peace couldn't be the right road. After all, I must have to do something to make all of this fear and inner turmoil go away. Peace doesn't do anything, it just is, so that couldn't be right, could it? Self awareness could not connect to my Peace State, so only a partial truth emerged. This partial truth began to be looked at as my truth, and because each person holds their own self awareness, no one totally agreed with me about anything. This was especially true of the fear state, because a self aware person holds their own fear based thoughts, and what is true for one is not necessarily true for another.

Well, in order to undo all of this mess, I had to look to another Plan that would bring everything back into wholeness. The Plan included another kind of Consciousness that was not self directed and would instead have the ability to direct the State of Whole Awareness. From a world perspective the Plan would not be introduced until the Spiritual History of the World began, which was 6000 years ago. For millions of years, up until the Spiritual History of the World began, the intellect was busy learning how to force and manipulate its way out of fearful experiences. After the Spiritual History of the world began, the new Plan was set into motion that would invalidate fear as directing influence of the intellect. The Plan would re-introduce Love as being the real State, and fear as being a product of a self aware intellect, which learned how to make a life filled with fear. Self consciousness would become whole consciousness as one chose to unite with the Plan. The Plan would take 6000 years to unfold. This seems like a long time, but in Eternity, time does not have any significance. So in Eternity, the Plan took place immediately and was over the instant it began. In time, the Plan seemed to prod along, and it would take thousands of years for the question of the right to Authorship of awareness to be answered. Either it was Love or fear, the home of the intellect or the Home of Love, because both claimed authorship, but one was eternal, and the other was earth bound.

It has seemed like my own personal Plan has taken this long, after all it seems like I have been at this forever, but as I look at how my life symbolizes the problem and the solution that the Plan has taken, I can see the parallel. From an individual standpoint, this was difficult to see, but from another perspective, it is all the same thing. The split is symbolized by Adam and Eve leaving the Garden. My split is symbolized by me looking to my physical experience to give me meaning. The Garden really represented the idea of wholeness. My wholeness was represented by a connection to my heart that was also connected to the eternal State of Peace. Outside of the Garden was where self aware beliefs of the intellect could grow and flourish. My physical beliefs began to flourish when I looked outside of my "own garden" or heart for reality. Thoughts and feelings, when joined are the creative process. Thoughts, when joined with feelings of fear, produce the self aware or intellectual state. From here comes the belief that it is necessary to force and manipulate circumstances to avoid what is not wanted, or what is wanted. It is impossible to think alone, so when I quit thinking with God I invented a new voice that sounded real. That voice was my intellect, but my intellect does not know God. Thoughts that do not know God are known as beliefs, and it is the belief system that keeps the world from joining with the Wholeness of God.

So this is where I find myself now. I have believed my purpose has been to work and avoid fearful outward circumstances, or force and manipulate to get what I want, but now I know that my True Purpose is to attain Consciousness that leads Whole Awareness. There is a part of me that does not want to accept the New Consciousness, and this is what I am up against every time I attempt to reach the State of Peace. My self awareness that wants me to believe that the only states there are, are the ones that exist in the United States, but I know this is not true. The intellect and self aware state is very powerful and contains false beliefs that will lead me to the destructive purpose of fear. But I am learning that I have another choice, although I am not totally sure of how I am going to make this choice, I know that peace has the ability to lead me to this State and bring new alternatives that I have not thought of.

Can Time Heal?

There is a belief that time heals all wounds. The premise of this belief is that the further you get away from a painful event in time, the less the pain is felt that is associated with the event. A real question must be asked; is it possible to heal with time? To examine this concept, we must first address the nature of time. For something to be healed it must promote healing by offering an idea that has the ability to heal. Does time offer this? Is it possible for a non-feeling, non-caring idea that only has the ability to move forward really have the ability to heal? Is time able to sooth the soul when something happens that seems so catastrophic we do not have any idea how we can move beyond our pain? If all we have to look forward to is relief from a non-feeling source such as time, this calls into question our relationship to our Creator because, from this premise, time offers us a better way of healing and we can forget the Nature of God to heal us, because time can do a better job. By relying on what we think will end our pain, sometimes we are apt to just make it through anyway we can. This does not necessarily heal the pain and some people go on for years not understanding how to move on. Thus, time did not offer healing, because if it did then there would be no more pain associated with any event.

Perhaps this is not true at all. Perhaps we do not understand the provisions of healing that God has provided for us. There is an alternative when we believe we must rely on a source such as time to heal us, for it is possible to find real Help when we are in such pain. Sometimes it is a miracle that helps us to move on, and miracles have nothing to do with time. Miracles help us find a strength that does not come from what is known in time. Looking beyond what we think we know helps us to handle the misery that is too painful to speak of. This involves finding a place within where time does not rule. Finding this place means finding a place of peace that we all have the ability to reach. We all have access to this state because we were created with this fail-safe sanctuary, but we have forgotten how to access and use it. The state of peace is our solution, but until we remember that it is there, and appreciate it, we will turn to what we believe is our answer, and time will not hear us when we call.

Learning that there are different states of mind that we have access to, places us in a position of control. We learn we do not have to wallow in pain or depression., but this takes practice and a focus we are not accustomed to using. Our mind is like a horse that continually goes home to what it knows. In this case it believes its shelter is in time. Finding another state of mind where peace is prevalent shows us that we can move beyond any perceived problem and join with something Higher that can lead us to something we have never thought about. All ideas that can heal our pain be it psychological or physical come out of peace. All solutions that can heal the world come out of this place that is found within, but we do not access it because we do not believe that it works because of the false assumption that time holds what we need. We are living in perilous times. We are not being asked to heal the world, just ourselves of the internal pain and conflict that seems to be endless. How can peace come to the world if we cannot even find peace within ourselves? If we are not responsible for ourselves, then who is? If I blame another or blame circumstances that seem to be beyond my control, then I am a victim, and someone else controls my life. This is not the role God would have us play.

Look for the solution that lies within in any circumstance that seems to be beyond your control. For every problem there is a solution. By concentrating only on the problem, the solution is removed by the onslaught of the problem. By looking for and reaching for the solution, you will remember how to access the part of the mind where God still abides. No one can do this for us, it is an individual choice that remains open to us, but is not evident unless we search for it. There is another way. The answer does not lie in time or in a belief that has been born in time. It comes from me and it comes from you. By learning to access and use another state of mind, we can heal not only ourselves, but also the world because accessing this part of our mind joins us with something Greater than ourselves. Learn to be a part of the Healing Force that will move the world beyond any perceived conflict. It all begins by learning how to access peace.

Day Five

It only seems appropriate that if I am going to choose peace for the next 30 days then I will have to choose to give one purpose to everything and that one purpose will be peace. Doing this means that I will have to at least begin to attempt to understand everything from a peaceful state. In Heaven everything has one purpose, and that one purpose is the one that God gave to everything. This is the Living Law that does not conflict with anything because there is nothing that can conflict with a Living Law.

I think I must be crazy. In fact it seems that this is being proven every time I try to prove to myself that peace is real and conflict is not. I am constantly being shown the reasons why peace is not real and conflict is. The inner struggle is immense and it proves very difficult to focus on peace as the solutions to all of my problems. There is obviously something within myself that does not want peace, otherwise peace would be evident. I thought that all I would have to do was choose peace and it would be given to me, but obviously I have been delusional to think this. I don't think that it has not been given to me, I think instead I have placed blocks up myself that are standing in the way to the peace I desire.

There is something within that knows that it is entirely possible to live within a peaceful context. I can feel it. What is it within that knows, for it seems that this is what I must get in contact with if I am to learn how to be a peace giver? It seems to me that there must be remnants of peace in everything if God is in everything. So to find peace I must uncover the false premise that conflict is real and peace is not. The conflict is hiding the peace. My questioning is a sincere request for an answer that I have no idea of how to find. If I answered myself, I know my answer would be in error, for how can understanding peace come from a premise of understanding conflict? I know that I must ask a question sincerely in order to hear the answer. I must also understand my question. This opens up communication at another level that I have grown unaccustomed to working with. Most of the time I rely on my intellect to answer my questions. It seems as though my intellect does not have that answer to this question. It seems to be merely skirting around the issue. As I listen to the voices within, I am not reassured. I am looking for a reassuring Voice that can speak to me of the truth that I seemed to have forgotten. I know this Voice is real and has the ability to teach me of my reality. I really want this Voice, or Inner Guide to take away all of this mess that I have accumulated, but I know this isn't how it works. It seems as though if I could simply get what I need, then everything would be alright. But I have had all of the physical comforts and money that seemingly ended the inner turmoil before, but it was only a temporary fix. I seem to constantly move in and out of turmoil. A lasting peace cannot be brought about by physical comforts, can it? This is probably a trick and my intellect is making sure that I know what it is I think I need to bring about peace. I wish these voices would just shut up. The more I try to deal with them, the louder they become. The more I try to reason with them, the more that seem to enter and give me more input about what I need to bring about peace. These are the voices that demand of me solutions that I have no idea how to perform. I do not have the resources to do what these voices are dictating to me. The lack of resources brings on constant worry. It seems as though if I run off and do something that these voices are demanding, I will only delay the peace that I am seeking. I want a lasting peace, not one that is temporary. If I try to run away from the problem, then the problem will remain.

    I remember having a dream once. It was like a movie I once saw. It was a dinosaur movie, and a child was being accosted by a t-rex. The man told the child to stay perfectly still and the monster would not be able to see her and would leave. I wondered why this dream presented itself to me. As I re-examine the dream now, I realize that being quiet in the midst of turmoil is necessary to maintain peace. I also realize that being peaceful is a way to keep the voices quiet. If I am quiet, they cannot hear my thinking process, for these conflicted thoughts are attracted to turmoil and if I refuse to negotiate with them, they loose their ability to see or understand my mental process. The intellect cannot understand peace so it shuts up. This leads me to understand that I have two thought processes. One I have learned through my physical experience and governs how I do; and one holds my Being and governs Who I Am. The one that governs my doing insists that I do something to bring about peace, and the other explains that I am the peace that I am seeking. What I learn from this is that I have a choice as to which one I am going to listen to. Even at this, the voices that demand me to do something are never silent unless I make a conscious effort to move beyond the mental chatter. Moving beyond the mental chatter is sometimes seemingly impossible.

Within every problem, the truth is evident waiting to be revealed. The problem is merely hiding the truth by dictating a false reality or identity that has nothing to do with wisdom. The problem constantly tells me how to do, so I can be. If I can just live up to the expectations of the problem, then somehow I think I can solve the problem, but problems cannot be solved as a result of making a temporary solution and I cannot solve a problem with a problem. If it is a temporary solution, the problem will evolve again and one only knows how it will show up. What I need is stability introduced into my mind that will allow me to see something else. The stability introduces the seeds of truth that lie within the problem. Before, I was trying to make the truth "do" something to ease my conflict, now I see that the truth will lead me down a different road that can change my perception so I can see what is really going on. Truth does not do anything, it merely is. It can only "be" what it is. If I desire peace, then I must learn that to do anything means that I am trying to move outside of Being, and this will introduce fear. Fear is a state of not being, so fear removes me from life and towards death. The state of not being means that I am trying to make the Laws of God not real, and violating the Laws of God places me in a fearful state. Not because God is going to punish me, but I fear that He will at some level because I am not being what He created, but trying to be something else. What I learn from this is that moving into a state where there is no peace, seems to separate me from the peace of God.

When the separation first introduced the idea that it was possible to live without Love, or God, a new state of awareness arose. In order to "house" this state of awareness, a new receptacle was made. This receptacle was the body and so the mind/body illusion began. Self aware body thoughts also could not extend the Peace of God, so the realm of time began and projection took the place of extension and fear took the place of Love. Because the Thoughts of God were created in innocence they would have to be restored to the innocent state before they were allowed to extend Peace. Otherwise, God's Peace would be contaminated with the projection of fear instead of the extension of Love. Fear makes me want to prove my reality by forcing or manipulating someone or something so I don't have to look at what I am trying to avoid. Love does not do anything because within the purpose of Love there is nothing to prove. The opposite of innocence is guilt, so instead of extending innocence, self aware thoughts that evolved in time used guilt from behavior to prove reality. So it is the guilt of learning a state of mind without the Presence of God that makes the flesh weak. This is because all of the self awareness learned and stored in the intellect, without the Presence of Love brings about a state that does not exist, but seems to in the mind of the one that holds thoughts that are in opposition to truth. The spirit is strong, because it extends the Laws of God, and these Laws carry within them the truth of Life. On the other hand, self aware thoughts that project guilt do not have the Laws of Life within them and look to time to get. This is where the intense feelings come from. I really want to follow my innocent state, but because I have forgotten what that is, I feel irrepressibly drawn to the guilt of trying to do something. Now that's intense.

Learning how to crack the shell of the illusion of the false notion that I have the ability to live without the Love of God seems to be easy on the surface, but I know the truth is that the shell *seems* to be impenetrable. I know that I am dealing with the most creative force in the universe, and must respect the fact that my knowledge of this creative force is beyond my ability to understand, as of yet. In order to crack the shell, I will have to learn how to work within the boundaries of the Laws under which the mind was created. If I do not learn how to work within the boundaries of the Laws, the violation that has occurred to the Law will work against me, as I have well learned in regards to trying to obtain peace.

Innocence

There is a wisdom that is so ancient it bubbles up inside my mind and has the ability to be transported past time. This ancient wisdom is innocence and it contains everything that is needed to heal the world. There are scatterings of this wisdom that is seemingly found in time. It is seen in the turns of the seasons, the wisdom of nature and the innocence of a child. These scatterings alone do not hold enough power to bring the healing of the world because they must be understood. Something else is needed. This something else is the link that unites all of these scattered pieces of wisdom together. This link is the idea of Love and is found in the mind of every person who walks this earth. It is to the idea of Love that we must turn to allow innocence to flourish and heal the world for without innocence all life will perish.

When a person re-connects to Love and begins to disconnect from the boundaries and barriers that time and space sets on the mind, it begins to connect to another Source that is powerful enough to move the forces of nature and gentle enough to cradle a child's innocence. As one searches for this ancient source of wisdom, a pattern begins to emerge. This pattern is revealed each time the mind is freed from a past perceived hurt. Each step taken becomes a golden thread that binds together the fallen innocence that is scattered in the world. It is this connection that will save the world. There is nothing else. If there were then Love would be a lie and all of the betrayal and pain found in the world would be the truth. Connecting to innocence unites us to the ancient Wisdom found in Heaven. Heaven cannot unite with what it does not know, but we can align our mind with innocence by perceiving a new way of thinking. We cannot pursue a new way of thinking until the old way is given up as something not wanted.

We think we know, but do we understand how the seasons change? Why the innocence of a child is so precious? The wisdom of these things is what is worth pursuing, yet we get caught up in the "wisdom of the world" which teaches us we are something we are not. No wonder there is so much treachery and pain in the world. The constant demand that we become something we were never supposed to be overwhelms every mind that makes such a demand. The intensity that this strain causes is seen and played out on the faces of those that walk this world and on the face of those that makes such a request. Our next challenge is not world peace, conquering outer space, feeding the world or global warming. It is not protecting the environment or the world economy.

The next challenge that we face today is preserving something that we all are born with and is re-introduced into the world each time a child passes the threshold from eternity into time. The trait that is so cherished in our children is called innocence. This is the challenge for this millennium; how do we maintain and keep the quality of innocence in our children while bringing them up and teaching them to become physical beings? Spirit, by nature, is innocent. If we can keep our children innocent, they will heal the world. They can teach the world how to Love again without being threatened, for what they carry into the threshold of time is unconditional Love. What they learn in the physical realm is that it is not safe to love unconditionally and so the programming begins. This is fear and can only be learned in time. It is fear that threatens the existence of the world, nothing else.

In the physical realm there is a strong tendency to believe that being physical is the greatest expression of Spirit. Being physical is not an end, or the final way Spirit can be interpreted, but instead just an avenue of expression of the Spirit. Being physical should be a blend of the Spirit, which is soft and yielding and also innocent, to the physical, which is a way to express the Spirit through the manipulation of physical matter or molding it to the Glory of God. God's Glory isn't found in the body. It is found in our Being. A true holy encounter reveals the innocence that each one of us still holds and it is beheld by one looking through innocent eyes. Innocence is a gift from God and God never takes back what He has given freely. The miracle restores our innocence and it is the gift that is being extended unto mankind by God so we can remember what the rest of creation already knows. Take my hand and help me gather the wisdom that is tossed about in the world. Let us join together in a new understanding that brings us back to the simplicity of life. All of the harsh undertakings found in the world is simply a futile attempt to make a statement that screams; "I am not the innocence that lies scattered about in time. I am greater than this." But there is nothing greater because there is nothing else. The wisdom of the world is merely nothing because it does not contain a drop of innocence that a child offers to the world every time one is born.

Day Six

Today I have been thinking about beliefs. The song says, "if only you believe." Well, I thought I believed in my dreams, but I found out that beliefs aren't enough. Perhaps it isn't that it isn't enough, it's just that when I try to proclaim something new that is in opposition to a belief that I hold as reality, then I just can't move beyond the old belief. The new reality I wish to express is seemingly caught up on a feeling that this just isn't going to work, and eventually I end up giving up. Perhaps I have been working with the wrong process, for I have tried to change my beliefs so they would align me with my desires and it seems to have had the reverse effect.

Boy, I have read a lot of self help books that target the belief system. I tried that for quite awhile, and I now realize it takes too long to change a belief by using affirmations, denial or visualization. I think I was trying to oppose a belief I already held with another false belief. This brings us another question; what if I change the belief to something that will lead me to another problem. Trying to change a belief means that I will have to work very hard to overcome what I have learned in the past, which I have already accepted as my reality. If my own mind is relying on the old belief for its reality, then the old belief will be protected from my affirmations, denial or visualization through resistance. I have felt this many times when I have entertained a new idea, and then felt the inner resistance begin. I have tried to move past this resistance through my own will power, but to no avail. Oh, my mind hears what I am saying, but once a belief has been established as real, my mind will not easily give over to my persistent bombardment of what I want it now to believe. The belief I hold just moves around the new belief I am trying to instill, leaving me frustrated and wondering why what I am doing is not working. Finally I learn it is the mind I must engage where the belief is stored, not the belief itself for it is the mind that *holds* the belief system and also the Law that can change my mind.

I have done all of the things that self help books have suggested. I wondered if there was something wrong with me, because after all, I followed them and did as they suggested, but with little or no results that were supposed to change my life. It took me awhile, but I finally understood. When a self help book is written, the writer is already coming from an aware point of view, which means that they probably came into the physical plane with the information they are sharing. Everything is easy if you already know how to do it. For quite some time, I became angry at these writers. I also became angry at those who would offer a class and tell me to just go ahead and spend the money and move beyond the restrictions I had placed on myself and explaining to myself that I was worth it. (The belief that I held already knew that I was not worth it.) Well, that didn't work either. I read one book once that explained how the girl in the story tricked her mind into believing that she already had a job, and she got it. I tried that too, and my mind wasn't so easily tricked. Still, I "believed" that I had to work with my belief system to change my mind. Now I know that my belief system is in total error, and my beliefs do not want to give up the authority that they have in my mind. So, now I know that I must learn how to move around my beliefs so that they are not a factor in my decision to complete my mission of peace. Once again, the creative process of the mind is beyond my own ability to "will" a new belief, or talk myself into one. The belief has been established as already *being* real by me, and because mind works at the "being level," I will have to show my mind that what I have been trying to be from past learning is in error. But I cannot show myself how I have been in error. That task is left to the Internal Guide, for He can see the problem and I cannot.

Never underestimate the power of a belief. But also never underestimate the power of the mind; for the belief is held within the mind and the mind answers to an Authority that is Greater than the beliefs that hold the mind spell bound. When truth enters, the mind is silent and knows that truth is present. All belief chatter cannot out shout the silence of truth. Because for the present I do not know what truth is or what truth means, I am sure that I must remain in the silence of peace, for peace is the conductor of Love, and where there is Love there is truth.

So much of the world is based on our beliefs, in fact I am told for anything to happen, I must believe it first. But belief does not know, and belief does not come out of the silence, it comes from what has been explained to me by another, or something that I have chosen as my own truth. It seems to me, for something to be real; it must come from knowing, not believing. But I live in the world of beliefs, so I will have to work at changing my beliefs so they can reflect something real. That is how the world will change. If I change my belief, I can change my life, and thus my perception of the world will change and if my perception changes, then the world will also. The first thing that must occur for this to happen is that I will have to go under the assumption that everything I have learned is false and be willing to place it up for the healing process. The reason I will assume this, first of all, time was not created by God; it was made to establish a reality not created by God, so therefore an unreality because it is impossible to create without God or Love. Chaotic creation without Love makes a reality that was started in chaos, so I will have to assume that my beliefs are chaotic. Introducing another belief and not understanding exactly how Love works in the creative process will only make another belief without Love. So in order for a chaotic belief, which exists in my mind, to reflect the Laws of God it will have to be looked at by me in a new way. This means that my beliefs will have to be given a new perception that originates with Love that does not come from my own personal belief system or from what I think I know. Because I do not know what this new perception is, stability that does not come from me will have to be introduced, so I will have to reach out of time or my beliefs that tell me time is real and touch the process that has been designed especially for this purpose. Touching this is beyond belief, but not beyond my ability. Learning how to accomplish this will be the introduction of Spiritual Law into time through my own mind. It will begin with my beliefs and allow me to work within my own belief system by showing me another way of using my beliefs. Otherwise the process will be too frightening, and the process is designed to eliminate fear, not establish it as real.

My beliefs do not want to change on their own. They are like misbehaving children and I can feel the resistance to change when I make a decision to change a belief. The harder I try to hold myself away from the belief I have established as real, the closer it gets. Resistance is futile. A Law of Mind states that the mind cannot move away from anything, it can only move towards something. So, if I am experiencing what I don't want and try to move away from it, I am in fact moving towards it. This is insane, for I really do believe I can move away from a belief I do not want. But that is not how the mind was created. Because what I don't want seems to be real to my mind, I have to find a way around it so I can stop moving towards it. My Inner Guide can introduce a new perception into my belief and help me to see my belief in another way. This will show me how the belief I have held has been a hindrance and then stop the continual chatter from the misaligned belief. The instant my mind understands this, it will not oppose the help that is being offered. The correction is automatic as I do not have to do anything to change except be willing to see my belief another way.

In order to establish peace today, when a belief arises that is in opposition to my peace, I will begin to notice the belief and how I am being expected to try to correct the problem that is in fact arising from the belief.

The Apple Core

When I was ordained, in 2000, as I lie in bed one night, I saw a vision of an apple core. I thought perhaps the vision was for another person who was going through the same process of Ordination that I was. Her personal vision was to feed the hungry in Detroit, and she did not know what she was going to call her organization or how she was going to accomplish this task. I had listened to her discuss it with others, and it was the next morning in the twilight of sleep that I saw the vision of the apple core. My belief was that she was to call her organization The Apple Corp.

Sometimes the best intentions, or intentions of the heart, get lost in the scattered drudgery of every day life and her vision did not come to pass. So it was the vision of the apple core stayed with me. I have received this kind of vision before, although not necessarily an apple core, but the kind of vision that speaks volumes about something. Sometimes I can tell what the vision means. Other times the vision takes years for me to understand. I put the vision in the back of my mind. At times I would pull out the vision and examine it and wonder what it meant. Other times I would try to make a circumstance resonate with the idea of an apple core, but nothing seemed to fit. That is until the last week of March, 2003. I was thinking about the apple core and how to create a class of a spiritual nature around this idea when all of a sudden I was flooded with the information concerning what this vision meant. The following article describes the meaning of the apple core. Because a vision speaks volumes about one subject, it may take some time before the vision is appreciated.

The Meaning of the Vision

In the physical realm we communicate by means of the spoken word. In the spirit realm, the spoken word is considered primitive. Whole ideas are conveyed in pictures because they can convey so much more than words. For instance dreams; one picture in a dream can explain a whole problem and also the solution at the same time. Before the language of spirit can be understood, which is also the language of the heart, the symbolic language of pictures has to take on a personal meaning. But this is getting me off the subject. Let me share with you the story of the apple core.

In the beginning there was Adam and Eve and the Garden of Eden. Everyone knows the story of the temptation and how the of the eating of the apple sent Adam and Eve out of the Garden and into the world where they would have to fend for themselves. In order to understand the significance of the apple core, the apple peel and the meat of the apple and what their symbolic representation was when the apple was eaten, must be understood. The Bible explains the Spiritual History of the world. It begins by showing us that Adam and Eve were in direct contact with God. The story takes us through creation and begins to get really interesting just before the eating of the apple. But before the eating of the apple is examined, what must first be examined is the motive. This is done because to understand life as it is now, we must be motivated through our understanding before we anything will happen..

The Bible says that Eve was tempted, so what will first be examined is the idea of temptation; what is it? In the beginning there was nothing else besides what God created. Nothing was known outside of His Creation and because there was nothing else, what could possibly tempt Eve? Something had to enter her mind that was unlike God or His Creation; so the temptation was to make something real that was not real. It is impossible for unreality to spring from unreality, so the temptation was not a real viable situation, but instead a question that entered.

This is where the symbolism of the eating of the apple comes in. The symbolic breaking of the skin of the apple was the symbolic breaking of the protection of God's Laws and venturing into what was unknown to God. This was the question that entered that was not founded on truth. Because in truth there is nothing that He did not create or does not know, the unreality of another dimension began that did not reflect the Light of His Love. God could not place His recognition in the unreality of the temptation. To do so would in effect be saying that the temptation was real and violating the Law of Peace meant nothing. Even at this, He still recognized Adam and Eve because they were a part of His Creation. But the place in which they entered was unknown to Him because He does not create a place where it is possible to be tempted. Therefore, the temptation that entered was to make something real that was impossible to make real because it did not carry the backing of God's Laws.

Temptation is not known in the eternal realm, so it was a new way of thinking that was meant to alter with the old way, or the way that God held His Thought. In the Mind of God, where eternity lies, only Love is known. Also, because Love is a thought of the highest vibration that is held by God, a lower vibrational thought had to be introduced into the mind that was unlike Love. This lower vibrational thought was fear. Love, unlike fear, is an internal idea that is held in place by God. In order to use the new vibration of fear, a new arena would have to emerge outside of the protection of Love, or God. This new realm would only be real to those who used fear as a protective measure.

In the eternal realm everything is surrounded by peace. It is difficult for us to understand that peace is the atmosphere of Heaven and it is the atmosphere of peace surrounds the idea of Love and keeps the Laws of Heaven from the intrusion of conflict. The new idea of fear had to be cast out of the peaceful condition of Heaven into an atmosphere that was dense and could hold it. This atmosphere would have to be one that was unfeeling and uncaring, and devoid of higher vibration. Thus began the physical reality (unreality) known as time and space.

This new home made from fear could be used for other purposes that did not reflect the Laws of Heaven. It could be a place where it could be proven that fear could be used as master instead of Love to protect and defend the occupants. This new idea of fear, or beliefs that respond to fear, is represented by the meat of the apple. Eating the apple was symbolic of ingesting a new thought form, or fear, that had nothing to do with Love. Whenever we ingest something we take it into the physical body. The physical body thus became the recipient of how the mind could hold fearful ideas that did not reflect Heaven's Laws of peace. These ingested ideas could be cast into the new atmosphere known as time and space. And because time and space holds the physical reality of man, what was being held in the physical body was played out on the screen of time. The external world became a place where the internal conflicts held within the mind/body awareness could be played out.

As the story unfolds, Eve blames the snake for her temptation, but the temptation that she tried to cast outside of herself came from her mind and it is impossible for a thought to leave the mind that it originated in. Adam did the same thing. As a world of people, we have been "eating" the apple since the beginning of time and trying to blame others for the ideas we hold. We have cast guilt into the world by looking for ways to cast blame upon others for fear that originated with us. This is why fear is the original sin. We do this in many ways and this is called being deceived. Eve said: "It wasn't me, it was the snake." By blaming others we hope to escape the Laws of God that have been written on the heart that state; everything that is happening is coming from me. Unfortunately, breaking the Laws of Life is being shown to us by getting what we do not want while being physical because blame does not atone for our mistakes, but the fear we have used for a false sense of security since the beginning of time would have us believe this. After Adam and Eve were cast out of the Garden, they learned to live by physical law, or by the sweat of their brow. This symbolism shows that their mind was no longer looking at the idea of Love for understanding. In other words they chose to learn a new way of understanding creation. It is this that led them to using physical law or trying to force and manipulate their outside circumstances. This also led them to believe that through domination with fear tactics they could rule the earth. The new laws of force and manipulation helped them compensate for their own inadequate feelings of fear. This would mean that the original purpose of Love would have to be twisted in order to use the idea of fear because it is impossible to create anything without Love. So it was, the purpose of Love became distorted to make way for the purpose of fear, but this was so only in the mind of the one doing the twisting for it is impossible to distort the purpose of Love.

Since time began we have been eating the meat of the apple. We have tried every way that is possible to get our outer life to fit what we want internally, but we can't do that because getting violates the Laws written on the heart. Before we are physical, we are spirit so we must abide by the Law even though we do not know how it works. Being physical means we manipulate or force physical matter to bend to our way of thinking. But trying to physically force or manipulate someone else is actually a way we try to manipulate their spirit by trying to get them to do what we want. We also try to manipulate outside circumstances (or events in time and space that are not real) so we can have or get what we want, but generally our wants stem from a sense of fear or guilt. When we do not believe that Spiritual Law is true it is because Higher Laws seem to violate the laws that we have been associated with while inhabiting a body. The belief that it is possible to violate Spiritual Law and use physical laws to manipulate another is a bite of the apple.

Sooner or later the meat of the apple is totally ingested, and because there is nothing left to eat, something else is introduced. So now the question becomes whether we will cry over the loss of what is gone or look at what is left. Everything that can be accomplished without Spiritual Love has occurred, except possible extinction of the human race. Every inhumanity that has ever been done has already occurred. There is poverty, starvation, lack, war, hate, conflict, muggings, sexual offense, and the list goes on. Is this what we yearn for? It seems so, for we would rather choose to continue on in the state of affairs that we have learned from our past fear then learn the Lessons of Love. Change will not come easy.

Because fear was introduced into the mind, a new plan was formulated by God to bring mankind back into the fold of creation. Because God could not violate His own Law of Peace, or the condition where Love presides, the Plan would allow for mankind to use the physical laws that he had chosen over Spiritual Law for an appointed time. For a time it would look like fear had dominated over Love. Also, because God was not physical, He could not use force and manipulation to formulate His Plan. Seems like an impossible situation at best, especially sense at a physical level we cannot even comprehend accomplishing any task without forcing or manipulating something or someone. After the physical history of the world had been well established, the Spiritual History of the world began. This is included in the story of the Garden of Eden, but the physical history actually took millions of years to accomplish, while the spiritual history took about 6000 years.

Slowly but surely the plan began to take shape through means of prophecy, vision and also the "seed". The seed of the spirit was buried deep within the apple. It could not be violated by anything that was going on in the external or fear state of the physical realm represented by the meat of the apple. While the apple was being ingested by mankind, the seeds of the apple remained safely inside the apple, so the Seed of God could not be diminished or taken from its core.

God looked for a pure heart in the offspring of those appointed to carry His Seed to carry out His Plan. Even though these men were physical, the seed would be activated to carry out the Spiritual History when it was time to move mankind in the direction of the Plan. Each story of the Bible is indicative of how God used His Seed to impregnate or keep alive the spirit that lives deep within the heart, for the heart is the Home of God. The story of the Israelites is how Spiritual Law was re-interpreted to compensate for being physical. By using this re-interpreted law of spirit the Jews were protected because God responds to what He recognizes, and His Laws are clearly recognizable by Him when the heart is read. The Bible tells us that the Law was written on the heart of Israel.

At last we see the prophecy of the seed coming into the physical realm when Jesus is born. He said Himself that he did not come to add to the Law but instead fulfill it. What does this mean? Mary was impregnated by the "Seed" of God. The birth of Jesus was the symbolic end of the eating of the meat of the apple. The physical history of the world was passing away to make way for Spiritual History of the world by introducing a New Idea that emanated from Heaven. This New Idea or Seed was Innocence and is known as a Child of God. The birth of Jesus ushered in a new way of responding to the Seed of God. Jesus was the example of what was to eventually evolve from the Spiritual History that was introduced into the world and how mankind was eventually going to respond to His own spirit which entered time on the Wings of Love. The seed of Innocence was introduced and the end of fear would soon arrive.

Fear produces guilt, and innocence is the opposite of guilt, so in order to be innocent one must be Loving, but this Love is Heaven sent, not physically learned. Physical love demands sacrifice and it is used to force and manipulate others. Beginning with the Birth of the Christ, Innocence would eventually take the lead, as Innocence was buried deep within the core of every individual that entered time. The activation of Innocence is upon us, but the world must make way for It. The apple has been eaten to the core. There is nothing left for fear to make. All ways of learning how to force and manipulate have been used to the max. The next step that humankind will make will be the one towards Innocence that is backed by Love. With the lifting of the veil of fear everything will change and the way humankind relates to the world will be taking a dramatic turn.

Value must shift to take a spiritual flavor. This means that what we value externally or physically will begin to loose its appeal. It will do this through revolutionary means. The fear that we learned as a motivating factor will be forced to become non-existent. The internal value will shift from what we have to who we are. Fear will not go without a fight and we will see this being played out in the arena of time. Fearful events will precede the coming of truth. This is not truth that is bringing this fear, for truth does not rely on fear for reality, it relies on Love. This effect will be the fear that is exiting while trying to maintain its position, but the fight is pitiful and cannot prove a worthy opponent to Love as it become stronger as we learn of our Innocence. We, as a Spiritual Beings first, agreed to come into time at exactly this moment to help with this process.

So, what exactly is the core? The core is the essence of man's spiritual nature. This is the turning point in the Spiritual History of the world when man begins to look inward for his truth. He stops looking for ways to manipulate with fear and turns instead to his true nature, which is spiritual. He looks at the true seeds of creation that are held within the apple core and begins to understand that he can live life another way, and this other way is how Love is introduced into time and the New World is created where only peace abides.

We feel incomplete because of the separation and the rest of creation is incomplete without us. Slowly but steadily we will make the change, but it is up to us to recognize the sign of the times. If this resonates with you it is because this message is already in your heart and has been waiting for someone to put it into words. The ones hearing this message now are the ones that will lay the foundation of the New

World that will be ushered in. The only way that this can be done is to learn how fear is ruling your life. Each person has been assigned a mission and a Plan has been drawn out to specifically help that individual reach their purpose. Heaven is holding out a Hand and all we have to do is reach upward out of time and hold what is eternal. It is our eternal nature that we are seeking for, not the physical things that are only temporary. We have the opportunity to use our essence to usher in the seeds of true creation, or we can be like Lot's wife and continue to look at the past and mourn for it.

This is a time of extreme turbulence in the world. It is essential that we begin our journey back to the core and allow the journey to lead us to the destination. Up until this point, we have tried to lead our destiny, but our destiny has already been decided and it was this we decided before we entered this realm. Each step that we take advances, not only ourselves, but also the world to healing. Let us not retreat into our fear and try to force the world to respect our position on how we believe things should be. We do not know how things should be, but the opportunity is now open for us to learn.

Day Seven

It occurs to me today that there is a paradigm shift going on. It is a shift that is occurring just below the immediate consciousness that is known to the world. I know that this shift is real because I can feel it, and others have confirmed that this is how they feel also. The evolutionary process of the world is shifting and this shift will be so monumental that there will be nothing left untouched by the effects that occur. With each evolutionary shift, consciousness has evolved and has become something greater. This means that the DNA of the inhabitants of the world will evolve also. The outcome of this shift will be peace. This is the New World and the Promised Land that Jesus spoke of.

This shift will not be an easy one, just as the evolutionary shift of living in the ocean to living on the land was not easy. The old ways of doing things will no longer be accepted, and because change is not easy, the shift will entail much conflict; internally as well as externally. The effect of this will happen globally and will be seen in weather patterns, war, disease and other disasters.

The beginning of the physical history of the world introduced the state of fear. The beginning of the Spiritual History of the world was to introduce Spiritual Love into the world as the alternative to fear. Spiritual Love is not represented by physical traits, or a physical interpretation of Love. As it is right now, the attraction of physical love is mostly based on fear. This is denied at many levels, but the truth is that inadequacies within the self, force us to try to find a balance with another person. Most of the time though the one we are looking at to fulfill us is also inadequate and wants the same thing from us.

Everything in time was first a spiritual expression and then arrived in time, so it still maintains at its core elements of truth. Once it was transferred to the physical realm, false expressions became external and were thought of as threatening and brought about fear because it seemed as though, and still does, that mankind has no power over them. The elements of the world are known as water, fire, air and earth. The spiritual expression of emotion took on the physical trait of water. Air, which is our interpretation of thoughts; but in truth are the physical symbol of the eternal thought system. Instead of thoughts being held within the mind, the brain began to be the interpreter of our thinking process. Re-interpreting spiritual thinking into physical thinking where the intellect dwells. Brain thinking is the intellect, and intellectually we believe that it is impossible to be in control of the weather, where most of the air resides. Before there was form, there was the creative process at the mind level of awareness. At the physical level, form took over the creative process. In other words, the only way to create anything was to force or manipulate it with a physical application. The last one to recognize is fire, which took the representation of light to keep the physical world alive, for without light everything would die. Before the separation, all of these elements were not separate, but instead moved as one entity which made them inseparable. There was no ruling force, for they all worked in harmony with one another. They emanated from the Eternal Mind where Love did not separate the elements. Peace was the state that kept all of these elements together without conflict. The separation changed all of this.

God lives in the heart. A more accurate statement is that we live in the Heart of God. If this is true, then I can only imagine the Heart of God being ripped apart when the elements shifted into a separate or physical state, which made the world separate from Him. Before this, there was only peace. So peace is my ability to unite all of the elements of water or emotion; air or thought; fire or spirit; and earth or form, together and heal the world at the elemental level.

Just this morning, I read in the headlines that there were over 13,000 killed in a tsunamis brought about by an earthquake. (The real tragedy of the tsunami was that more than 150,000 lost their lives, but at the time of this writing this fact was not known.) Last year, there were 4 hurricanes in Florida; this is the element of air that is represented by the turbulence in thought systems found in all of mankind. Hurricanes also involve the ocean, and the movement towards land is the attempt to unite the elements. It is our inability to recognize all of these elements at a form level that disrupts the earth and weather patterns. The fires in California and other parts of the world that burn out of control are the element of light unleashed because we have separated it from its source. The unrest in the ocean, which also brings about hurricanes and tsunami's are also indicative of the unrest at the emotional level of mind, which is represented by the ocean. These elemental forces must reunite, and it is up to the occupants in the world to help by first of all bringing peace at an individual level. Because peace is the ability that everyone has access to, peace is the salvation of the world for it is only here that all elements are joined. This is where the Heart of Man is in alignment with His Creator and because the Knowing of God sees everything as Being One, catastrophic world events end as everything is seen as whole and complete. Without completion, the displaced elements will continually try to reach completion by destroying form or land. Unfortunately, people live on land along with their possessions.

    The consciousness of the world must shift. My only purpose here is to help this shift occur with as much peace as possible. I have believed my purpose was to make money. For many years I have been trying to place myself on a track of learning that led me away from peace, and in fact led me towards the belief that I had to do to be. Doing is not the true state of mind, Being is. The doing level of mind is where the elements are separate because they have been cast outside. The constant struggle of doing is in truth my attempt at uniting the elements without the conductor of peace. This has made me very conflicted, especially when what I am trying to do does not work regardless of how hard I try. Doing is not the way of the new consciousness that is being introduced at the elemental level. So if it is not in the doing, it must be in the being. I learn this by first of all learning how to "be" peaceful, for it is here that I am recognized by the creative process or the Creative Mind. I am a thought in this Creative Mind, but until I recognize that my thinking process is not in alignment with the Eternal Mind, I will continually try to "do" something that will make a correction. I can't correct this, I don't know how.

For 2000 years, the world has been being bombarded with everything it needs to join these elements together. Innocence is recognized by the Creative Mind, for it is through innocence that the Creative Mind is expressed. The opposite of innocence is guilt. There is no doubt that the world is guilty, but guilty of what? I guess it is guilty of using separation to prove that the Expression of God is not something that is needed to provide a living environment. But the Laws of God are written in the Book of Life. If this is the case, then I have not been following the Book of Life. Instead I have been following the guilt of the world that proclaims me separate from the Mind that created me. So I struggle at doing something I don't know how to do.

Unity is a living Law, which means it was written in the Book of Life. In order to access the Laws in the Book of Life, I must unite under one purpose, for purpose is also a Law of Life. The one purpose that I can choose is the purpose of peace. Even though most of my thoughts do not wish to look to peace, which lies in the Being level of mind, I have the ability to lead my thoughts to a peaceful state.

Let My People Go!

Six thousand years ago, the Spiritual History of the world began. Before the Spiritual History of the world began, there was the physical history in the world. The physical history of the world denotes the physical struggles that have gone on since the beginning of time. When the Spiritual History of the world was introduced into time, something occurred that was so dramatic and was so diametrically opposed to the physical history, a new way of life had to emerge that had nothing to do with a physical interpretation of reality. The introduction of spirit in time created a major shift that was not necessarily experienced as an earth shattering event at the time, but that moment would eventually shape the World into a place of peace governed by the Laws of Heaven instead of man made laws. Just like a snowball that starts at the top of a mountain is of no consequence; by the time it gets to the bottom of the mountain, the small snowball has become a mighty avalanche and has the ability to change the face of everything it touches, so the Spiritual History of the World would change the shape of it beyond the wild imaginings of anything that man could foresee.

The snowball that began 6000 years ago has taken on the power of an avalanche and is ready to change the world from the physical face it has worn since time began to the spiritual face that reflects the Laws of Heaven. Just like the caterpillar that changes into a butterfly, the ugly worm becomes beauty and the transformation is felt throughout all of creation. This is done through a re-interpretation. In time, the physical interpretation becomes a spiritual one that reflects the will of Heaven.

Critical

We are at the most critical point in the history of mankind that has not occurred since before the days of Noah. The forces of nature are going to wipe out mankind if we do not take heed of the lessons that were given previously in the records of the spiritual history of the world. The terrorists that hold the world at large as a hostage of fear must also come under the scrutiny of Spiritual Law so that the world can know that terror is merely nothing when viewed through eyes that do not see terror. Seeing the world through eyes that do not see terror must be taught, but this teaching is not placed under physical scrutiny for physical scrutiny does not have the correct interpretation of Heaven's Laws. The Law's of Heaven are shared with the occupants of time through a process of re-interpretation.

I am not a pessimist. I am optimistic that we as a society, can rise to the occasion and use the lessons that were recorded as spiritual history to help us through this. We all believe in something, and so did the people in the days of Noah. But their beliefs did not save them, and neither will ours. False beliefs look out into the world and see terror that is not there. If our beliefs do not change, we will allow our own false belief system to dictate to us our own destruction and that of the world. False beliefs of terror must be re-interpreted to reflect the Laws of Heaven, and it is this that will heal the world.

The unseen war

There is a war going on. An unseen war that is being fought in the realm of spirit, but Heaven does not respond. Everything that we need to end the war has been extended into the physical realm for our use, but our failure to recognize what has been given is preventing the world from receiving the gift of salvation. Because we do not use the gifts and because we do not understand what they are, the gifts have no ability to stop the onslaught of the devastation and destruction that the world is and will experience until the gift is recognized.

Expression and experience

God or Love is not an experience, Love is an expression that happens now. It is the expression of Love that must be released into the world to heal it and protect it from the *experience* of terror that is occurring right now. Over and over again, the spiritual history of the world indicates for the people to just make an effort to return to God, so He can show them the way to safety. Not much is asked, just an effort. The effort that is involved is giving up beliefs so that something else can enter and take the place of the false belief. In its place is another explanation awaiting our acceptance. The problem arises from the notion that we already know what is true and what is not. The beliefs that we hold onto are the ones that are literally preventing the Holy One from entering and expressing through us the peace that has the ability to calm the terror in the world that is occurring right now. All that is asked is that we be willing to let go of what we do not want so something else can emerge. This is the exchange and the re-interpretation of what we think we see.

Let my people go

We expect that God will perform up to the standards we have given Him, but God does not respond to our standards, because He has His Own. Because God dealt with the physical body in the Old Testament, we assume He is still dealing with our physical nature. God is Spirit, and the way He dealt with mankind had to switch to the spiritual nature of man so Heaven and Earth could unite under a spiritual interpretation that was greater than the physical one that man had given to himself. Eventually God would deal with the world at a spiritual level and mankind would have to turn to his spiritual nature to help bring the world under Spiritual Law, otherwise mankind would continually have to deal with form, or physical law. Physical law is force and manipulation, and it is difficult if not impossible to deal with the natural forces of nature through force and manipulation. By the same token, terrorism can not be forced or manipulated into subjection. The Laws of God will deal with these forces, but it is up to us to use an ability that we are unaccustomed to using, and that is our spiritual ability.

Our spiritual ability has nothing to do with what we believe or what we think we know about handling the affairs that are out of control in the world. We have imprisoned our will, and with it the Will of God. To let our will go is to let God's People go. These are the spiritual thoughts that have the ability to heal the world. We do not know what these thoughts are, so we are being asked to turn towards our spiritual nature and ask. No more than this has the ability to change the outcome of the terror that is held in the mind of the occupants in the world today.

Just as in the days of Moses, God told the Pharaoh to let His People go, we are being instructed to do the same. This did not mean that the people of God did not have a certain amount of trepidation concerning their release, and it required faith that did not come from their past beliefs or anything they experienced previously. Instead it came from a prophet that said he knew. Moses came with authority and the Laws of God were *expressed* through the man known as Moses by the miracles he performed.

Releasing the Will of God

When we are born, we are all born with an innocent nature. The innocent nature becomes trapped in the physical experience and believes falsely that the physical experience is reality. Reality lies in the innocent nature that we were born with, not in the experience. Right now the experience held in the world is terror. In order to return our mind to innocence, we must retrace our steps to find where it was lost so innocence can be released into time and heal the world. Who has ever heard of an innocent child leading a terrorist attack? Innocence will introduce stability into the world that it has never known. Up until now, we have believed it is our place to change innocence so it cannot be taken advantage of. But now, we are being asked to keep it and allow it to change the world. *"And a child shall lead them all."*

Fear of being innocent

We have an innate fear of being innocent, but being innocent is our true state of being. Fear is also what is preventing innocence from expressing peace into the world and removing the terror from our own mind. Until it is removed from our mind, we will believe we are the victim, and not in charge of our own destiny. This will force us or them to try to manipulate or force others to conform to a way of thinking that is not acceptable for anyone. If you want to test your innocence against a false belief, ask if the specific belief you have is something a new born baby would believe. If not, then the belief is false and needs correction. Innocence expresses innocence, whereas beliefs are based on past experiences that do not hold our innocence as having value, but instead force our innocence to be a slave to an unwanted physical terror.

The next step

What is the next step? It is up to us. Those of us who dwell in this place called time are being called on to choose to release innocence. The other choice is to continue following the way the past road has led us down. The right choice is obvious, but not easy. But we are not asked to do it all ourselves, but our willingness to be a part of the spiritual history of the world is necessary. Things are only going to intensify until enough of us make the choice to release our own innocence that has been chained to the past road of terror. We don't have to walk that road, and what we decide will be the decision that is made for all. The choice is individually made, and Heaven holds its breath while you make yours. What you ask for will be given. Choose again and the world will change because of your decision.

Day Eight

What would happen if I could unite all of the elements within myself, and then direct them for good? For it seems that my most of my directing ability has been bent towards self destruction. I did not realize that my self destruction was also helping to destroy the world. But still, there is a Consciousness that has the ability to override my self destructive tendencies. This is the Consciousness that I have indirect contact with when I am in my "doing" mode. Even though I am not aware that it is there, it is, and this Consciousness would not allow me to totally self destruct. But I am also aware, in some way that I am not sure of, that this part of Consciousness needs to have my agreement so I can help the world through this transitional time. There is also a part of me that disavows that I have some kind of ability to help the world make this transition. But I am also aware of how powerful my beliefs are. My belief system would have me constantly doing something to reach an unattainable goal, for if I reached this goal I would be able to prove that I am not written in the Book of Life, and I would not be real and I really would self destruct. I am only real under the circumstances that I was created under, so to prove otherwise is to prove my unreality by separating all of the creative elements. It does not seem that I could possibly have at my disposal the elements of wind, water and fire, but I it has been explained to me that I do, but my ability to use these elements is limited because of my limited perception. Limited perception comes from the belief that I have to always do something. My true reality is proven in my ability to "Be" everything, not in making pitiful attempts to do something that I do not know how to do. I have been trying to "do" little by using limited beliefs that are based on a consciousness of doing or self awareness. I guess the question to ask is if it is possible to have an unlimited belief. The answer that comes back is that the question is not simple and will require a great deal of explanation, which will take time for me to understand. Time was made specifically for this; to use as a means of making something understandable to limited beliefs. Making the effort to move beyond the level of doing has brought me closer to the level of Being or whole awareness, which combines all of the elements. Beliefs do not know about the elements because they come from limited understanding. Intellectual understanding is wasted if it does not include the wisdom of the heart. The journey is one that leads from the intellect to the heart. I wasn't sure and didn't know that this was the direction that my Being Consciousness was leading me towards.

The number eight represents abundance and prosperity. I have been looking for this by trying to attain financial gain, but the Eternal Mind does not understand financial gain. This Mind only understands what has been written in the Book of Life, because this is where Life originates from. Money is a physical solution to poverty, but it also leaves out the rest of the elements that are necessary to sustain life. All of life is held in the elements of creation. My Internal Guide has the ability to interpret the spiritual aspect of abundance into the physical interpretation so my physical assets will remain until I am certain that I have the ability to make it without them. This kind of interpretation can only be realized as I learn how to live through the wisdom of the heart and not through my intellect where false beliefs lie. Belief would have me understand that it is stupid not to look for financial gain in every solution. Wisdom would tell me that I am safe and financial gain is a demonstration of a willing heart, not a way to force and manipulate to get what I want. I am learning however, that it is entirely possible to place these beliefs under Spiritual Law, but this takes time to learn. Beliefs rely on time for their reality, while wisdom relies on peace and truth. Everything must be brought into line with the truth so there is nothing in opposition to it. Even what does not understand truth opposes it in some way. Ignorance is not bliss, for the crimes that have been committed against the heart must pay the penalty. The penalty is not from God, but it is from the belief that punishment is certain for not adhering to the Greater Laws that the Universe lives by. These beliefs were not written in the Book of Life, and are therefore in opposition to Reality. Everywhere I look and everything I do seems to proclaim that money is my freedom, and I find this very hard not to pursue what I believe is my salvation. But I also know that if I follow this road, I will retreat and not find what I am looking for. I am seeking a spiritual solution to the seeming physical problems that always seem to be present.

My purpose here is to give peace to the world. The way I am to serve my purpose and give peace to the world is through healing. The place to start is with myself. I can only heal the world with forgiveness. It is a circle. If I break the circle, then I am trying to live outside of my purpose. This is when my peace seems to dissolve and I find myself at odds with the circumstances I believe I cannot control or find my way out of. So, now I will look for a way to make a correction. The problem that arises from this is that I will try to find a physical way to try to fix the problem. But the solution is not in the physical realm of fixing, it is in the mind where the elements and the creative process reside. If I do not engage the mind, where the problematic belief is, the solution will elude me. If I get trapped in the illusion that the solution is in the physical realm, I will have to "do" something to make the correction, which is in my present state, chase money. The correction does not lie in doing, it lies in being. I constantly remind myself of this, but it seems to fall on deaf ears. Doing means that I think I can resolve the problem by finding a physical source that will make me feel better. This temporarily resolves the issue, but it always comes back. False beliefs seem to be the only game in town as I begin to pursue what I believe is my salvation, which is money. This is the physical solution, and this is played out in many forms including the prevalent addictions that plague society. The physical route leads to addiction and eventual death, as the physical solution always ends in death because the Laws of Life do not emanate from the physical, they emanate from the Spirit.

"Never reject anything that is good and offered to you." My sense of value has been warped, for I have believed that the value is in the thing offered. The truth is that the value comes, not from the physical aspect of the gift, but instead in the spirit in which the gift is given. This also must be looked at from the aspect of how a gift is given. Sacrifice from a spiritual point of view is not possible. When I associate the physical attribute with a spiritual gift and believe that I have to sacrifice, then the gift is lacking in spiritual content. The physical gift means nothing without the value of my heart behind the gift. If I cannot give at the level of spirit, then my gift has not been completed. This is why, when the widow gave just a few pennies, Jesus saw past the small amount given and saw into the heart of the woman and proclaimed her gift righteous. This does not make me wrong, but instead places me in a position of first of all, recognizing the thought, and then engaging the Internal Guide to help make a correction. This is healing, for healing is not a physical thing that is done, it is a happening at a level that is higher than the mind/body experience where false beliefs are held. These beliefs are in opposition to the truth because they did not originate at the Creative Level, but instead at the mind/body experience level.

The Value of a Dollar

In our society it seems as though one of our main concerns is money. Most of the time, when we look for a job, we do not look for work on the basis of whether or not it will be something we love to do, rather it is based on how much it pays. There is a predominant belief that our own value lies in how much money we make and how many material possessions we have. The true creative process, or what we do best, is often set aside in favor of material wealth. From a spiritual standpoint value must shift and be appraised in another way. Because we have to follow Laws that conform and answer to a Higher Authority, when we do not follow those Laws, we are in violation of those Laws and will therefore pay the price for doing for material gain. This is not because we are being punished, it is because value has been placed where there is no value and a correction must occur so Laws can be used for our protection and also for our happiness.

Much of what we learn about money and material possessions comes from our parents. Just as our parents teach us what was taught to them. When we are born, we know we bring value to life without ever being told. As we become indoctrinated into the physical realm, well meaning adults teach us different laws that conflict with Higher Laws of life. Many times we are taught the "value of a dollar". By learning the value of a dollar, the value of our own being is brought into question. The focus of value begins to shift in our mind that value is outside of ourselves and so we begin to pursue a path where we believe value lies. Seeking for value is a Law of Mind, and wherever our mind believes there is value, it will seek to obtain it as a precious commodity. In our physical life, when we learn that money has more value then we do, we cease to have the value we were born with. This places us in violation of a Spiritual Law and if correction does not occur, we will find it very difficult to be successful because we will be settling, or doing what we don't want to do to "get" what we want. This also places us in a position of being in violation of Higher Laws because giving and receiving are a part of those Laws and getting is unheard of in eternity. Using this violation will teach us as we mature that we will constantly be in a "having to get" mode in order to survive. Being to get is in opposition to Spiritual Law so survival has shifted from a constant, or Spiritual Law, to an inconsistent belief. This also forces us to try to prove our being through doing something that will guarantee our survival.

Each individual that enters the physical realm has entered with a particular gift that they came to share with the world. This gift is what they love to do, and it is called the creative process. It is an internal gift that creates constructively on the physical plane with physical resources. Because it is a gift that God has shared with this particular individual, this specific gift is what he/she has agreed to share as a talent with the world. Sharing is also a Spiritual Law and when the creative process is not shared, another violation occurs. Each creative gift is a part of a Grand Plan, that when it is all put together, becomes the salvation of the world, or the Second Coming of Christ.

The gift is unique to each individual because of the energy or vibration that is attached to each individual as they enter the physical realm. To be in denial of the gift is in essence to be in denial of the Self. By going contrary to the nature or vibration that an individual possesses is to bring about problems of stress, conflict, unhappiness, disease and even the possibility of death. This could be likened to the sun deciding that it did not want to shine its light anymore. The question would be; how could it be turned off? Yet that is what we do when we deny our talent and trade it for a few dollars. Because we are God's Treasure, our own value is even greater than the value of the sun, and yet we do not see ourselves as thus and so we try to turn our gift off and pursue what is seemingly acceptable to those who occupy this world and tell us what we must do to be happy. However, happiness is Who We Are and we must vibrate at the level of happiness, or where our creative talent lies, or our vibration becomes destructive in nature, if not to ourselves then possibly others. The creative process is how we create a life, whereas money makes a living. If we use our creative potential to make a living we will make a life that is less than satisfactory that excludes us from our true potential. Our value at some point has to shift so we can understand that value lies, not in anything physical, but instead within ourselves where our creative potential lies.

God does not understand money. It is a piece of paper that does nothing because it holds no creative ability within itself. At its greatest potential, it can burn and be transformed into smoke. Only God's Creation has value to Him, and it is this that is His Treasure. When we do not value ourselves, but instead find value in a piece of paper, He does not understand. As He looks to us as His Treasure, and we look to money or a piece of paper, we devalue the gift of creativity that He has instilled in each of us as the gift we have come to bring to the world. But there is another purpose for money that has escaped our notice. Money is a tool that can be used to support the creative process. When it becomes an end instead of a means to reach an end, the tool has mistakenly taken the place of the creative process. When money becomes our goal, we are not supported by the Higher Laws of Life because these Laws cannot support paper as having creative value.

This means we are pursuing death which is supported by physical law. The new purpose of using money as a tool becomes a way of supporting us in our true creative ability. Instead of going to work to "make" money, our creative process that is shared with God becomes the strength to uphold the monetary systems of the world. The new foundation of money is built on sustenance instead of paper. When viewed from the other way around, a piece of paper cannot uphold all of the economic systems in the world. It is too fragile, and does not have the backing of the creative process or God. We have to ask, what has more value, money or an individual? We have all heard of stories of individuals being turned away because they do not have the money to pay at hospitals. This is a violation of Spiritual Law, and eventually the price will be paid. Not because we are being punished, but violations of Spiritual Law are cause and effect, so what one sows, one also reaps. As we learn to find the same value that God does, we learn that we live by Grace, not by money. The reason we find it hard to use our creative talents is because we cannot use them until we appreciate (another Spiritual Law) or understand our own self worth. If we are using our creative talent strictly to make money, or value the money over what we give to another, it is our belief that will have to be straightened out so our creative process will support us.

We all know people who seemingly do well just working for money. It is difficult to tell by appearances why another does well or why they do not. We are all on the physical plane learning different lessons. It has come to the point in the evolutionary process that it will become more and more difficult to just work just for money. The element of creativity and love will have to accompany the reason for doing anything. The stress of holding ourselves away from this purpose will become obvious by how we feel and we will suffer the consequences of our decisions. Learning a lesson such as this has not been left to our discretion because we do not know how or when we began to believe that we had less value than money. A Plan has been devised for each individual to help him/her get in touch with the value that God has placed on them. It involves healing and re-learning Laws that the rest of creation lives by. How do we get in touch with this Plan? We ask and because we want it more than what we have learned to value on the physical plane, our request is granted. With a sincere request we are introduced to people, we find others, and our dreams begin to take on a significance that we may not have been in touch with before. Learning the Plan that has been specifically devised for each individual is the journey that we hear so much about. It is the journey of self discovery. It takes trust and faith because following a path that does not seem clearly marked seems beyond our capacity to undertake but this is the journey. It is up to each person to make the choice to live as the rest of creation lives by learning to appreciate what is real.

Day Nine

Nine is the number of endings. It is putting a rest to the spiritual educational process that began in the number one cycle. The education process is different at a spiritual level than it is at a physical level. The spiritual level of education is found in the dream state when dreams occur about going to school. Many times these dreams make me feel like there is something that I have not completed, or I have to keep returning to a class only to find that I have not done my homework. This kind of dream is showing me that there is still work that needs to be done because I have not learned what I need to learn in order to make the shift from a physical reality to a spiritual one. Dreams are very symbolic, and the symbolic language of the spirit, or the Internal Guide, must speak in the language that is represented by the physical, but from a spiritual level that has a complete different meaning than the interpretation that I have place on what I see. So I must learn how to interpret the symbolic language, not on my terms, but instead a shift must occur in my mind so I can relate to these symbols so they can reveal their meaning to me instead of me giving them a physical meaning. Everything in the physical language has a spiritual interpretation, but I have it reversed. I believe that everything in the spiritual realm must means something physical. With this as a foundation, I will never find reality, for reality is not time based, it is eternally based. I cannot determine what this language is, so it must be explained to me. As I begin to learn the symbolic language of the mind, I can also learn about my physical experience or what it is I am learning here from another perspective. Otherwise events and situations that occur physically seem to make no sense at all. This confusion arises from the physical belief that nothing is related and as I try to make corrections without seeing their relationship, I try to fix an impossible situation. Nothing can be corrected unless it is wholly seen, which will reveal to me why certain events occur in my physical life. In the Spirit Realm, everything is connected and in order to see this connection I have to disconnect from my false beliefs of fragmentation. The place I can do this is in a peaceful state. Peace teaches my mind that I do not have to associate with problems that seem to overwhelm me. It seems like the solution is not here and false beliefs will drag me out of truth and into a denial of peace. This also is a problem; I also want to believe that I already know the answer. I know that I don't, but the direction of the physical dominion held by belief over the spiritual truth is very strong. I don't believe the truth because my belief does not hold the truth. Once again, I will have to learn how to engage the mind without the belief.

My false belief system teaches me that to solve a problem, I will have to go outside of my own awareness, or what I know, for a solution. This means that I will have to do something in time, because these beliefs originated in time and do not believe in the creative ability that is my inheritance. Time holds no answer because there is no meaning for time, except to move forward. True inheritance lies in the elements that seemed to have been ripped out of my awareness at the sacrifice of my innocence. Once innocence has been sacrificed, the Creative Process cannot recognize the guilt that must take the place of innocence. But the Creative Process still recognizes me and as I learn how to re-establish the connection that I have forgotten through a peaceful mind, I find that what I have forgotten to "Be" is still there.

Time, where false beliefs want me to look for reality, cannot complete my thought process. Time cannot complete thought because it does not know how. I know this, and yet my belief system still goes there trying to make something occur outside, in time, as if this will somehow permanently fix my feelings of loss. The loss in internal, not external. Finding an external solution will not solve the problem, but still the search continues as I reach for something I know isn't there, but my belief swears it is, so I keep looking. The completion of thoughts lies in a process that begins in the mind and is completed there also, so it is impossible for it to be elsewhere. It seems ridiculous to look at a thought and believe it can be completed where it did not start. A circle must end where it began; the Alpha and the Omega, the first and the last, the beginning and the end. What begins in the mind must also be completed there. Thoughts that get lost in time begin with brain or intellectual thinking, or what the world deems as logic. Brain thinking begins as our innocence is lost and replaced with logic. The brain is how I explain a physical reality, or what is happening in time to myself. As I begin to accept my physical experience as a real alternative to my spiritual expression, I begin to rely totally on the re-interpretation of the Language of Spirit into the language of the logic that the brain explains which is now physical. This is now my new reality as my intellect explains my new reality to me. The problem with this is that I have limited myself to a physical interpretation, when in reality I am unlimited. Once I have accepted my limited physical experience as real it means I have forgotten how to access the Language of the Spirit and so I will have to relearn it. This is why Jesus said that in order to enter the Kingdom, I would have to become as a child. A child realizes that he/she does not understand what is seen and waits for the proper interpretation. This is the job assigned to the Internal Guide that has been assigned to each person that has taken on the task of healing the world.

How the Ability to Communicate with Heaven was Lost

The Silent Scream

Have you ever had a dream where you were trying to scream and as hard as you could try, but could not make a sound? Silent screams occur because we believe the ability to communicate with Heaven has been lost. Our cries for help are going unnoticed, we believe, so the dream state shows us that we believe our ability to communicate with something greater than ourselves is non-existent, or that help cannot hear us. There was a time in each of our lives when we didn't make silent screams. Communication was open and we had the ability to share our inner thoughts with God. He communicated back with us and we felt safe and secure in the knowledge.

For each one, the moment when the silent scream began is different. For me the silent scream began when I was four. (I have sense found the silent scream began in infancy before the ability to physically recollect was possible) At four I was very sick with dysentery and was taken to a hospital. Up until that point, my inner communication was in tact, for the most part. I understood how to communicate with my physical cries and that produced results. I was learning how to verbally communicate, but still held on to my inner ways of communication. How I know this is that the hospital event left me with memories of being alone. It is only in time that we can experience this feeling and it becomes a self awareness that is stored in the body that explains what you are and how you should act.

Before the hospital visit, I don't have a lot of physical memory. After the hospital visit my physical memory became a bank filled with how to get what I didn't want. Children at this age do not have logic. They are filled with innocence and when a situation is not explained to them, they make their own assumptions and live by those assumptions even when they become adults. The memory is stored deep within the body and all physical associations are based on the false memory that surrounds an event that is traumatic. It is stored as a picture and although the symbol of the event changes, the memory of the event occurs over and over again. The traumatic learning event becomes a precursor for events of the future, because the mind learns from experience.

The memory of an event must be traumatic for a false memory to occur. When we are children, the mind does not distinguish the difference between the physiology and the psychology of what is occurring. If a traumatic event occurs physically, the mind tries to understand it from a psychological standpoint, because at the fundamental level it is psychological, not physical. Innocence therefore attaches emotion to a physical trauma, which has nothing to do with the body in reality, so it is this that violates innocence. The chief indicator about what is happening is how it is felt about what is occurring. If a child feels loved and cared for, they create good memories. If not then they make their own assumptions about the physical experience based on trauma. Trauma cuts off the ability to communicate with the eternal realm and leads to the silent scream because the body has now taken on a psychological tendency that it was never supposed to have. Once innocence is assaulted by a traumatic event, then it is still an event that innocence does not know how to deal with. This is why spanking children leads to trauma. A child being spanked may feel like he/she is receiving a blow to the psyche, not just the body. If this is the case, the implications of spanking sets into motion events in the future that we have not even begin to imagine. It is not true that children have no ability to understand. What children lack is logic the way adults do because it has not yet emerged. Everything in an innocent life is about psychology and trying to make sense of why their psyche is being assaulted when trauma occurs and then trying to make a decision based on an assault because no logic is present. Making a decision alone begins self awareness. Self awareness is not present until a decision is made about the external conditions that are occurring outside of the body. Self awareness is self understanding, and this is how individual consciousness begins.

Whole understanding is evident in a baby when they are born because it is written in their psychology, not their body. To them, the body is a part of their psychology. When trauma occurs psychology becomes a part of the body and the element of time begins to take carry meaning as each physical event become associated with an event in time. When we are children, we are not time dependent, we are eternal dependent. Time means nothing until we begin to associate with it. Our early years flow by and it seems like it takes forever to get from one birthday to the next, or from one Christmas to the next. As we grow older and become time dependent, time becomes a determining factor as to how we will have to live our life. We have to be on "time" for everything because time dictates that we adhere to these laws and because this has now become the answer to our questioning mind we begin to look externally for our meaning. With children, this just isn't so. This explains why time goes so much faster as we get older. We loose the ability to tune into the eternity and begin to only look to time as reality. In eternity we have forever. In time, the further we get into our physical lives, the less time we have. We begin to associate with time more and more until we are totally reliant on a non feeling force that doesn't care one way or another about us. It is consciousness that makes time valuable, but it is entirely possible to learn how to use consciousness in another way that is not out of sorts with the spiritual nature.

Possibilities

What would happen if this world and the people in it were not time dependent? What if they did not have to wait for a specific event to happen in time that would be the determining factor in their life that would lead to happiness? What if it were possible to live wholly happy right now without waiting for an event? Learning the value of time has placed us at odds with the whole state of eternity. Wholeness takes all things into consideration and brings about the best outcome for all concerned, while time is physically dependent and only looks for what is best for one on a personal level and through a fragmented memory. This does not necessarily mean that one person does not have the best interest of everyone involved, but it is difficult to determine this when an emotional outcome is expected that will bring expected happiness to one person only. Time based decisions are, first of all, decided on a past learning experience, and are only made with what is physically understood about how to bring temporary satisfaction to the one.

Possibilities occur that are not time dependent when we are not attached to the outcome. Attaching to the outcome assures that the one will be satisfied, not the whole. Therefore, the attachment comes from what is physically understood about outcome, thus leaving out the wholeness of the spirit. Memories of how something did work out, or how it did not work out, are memories. When we try to recreate the past feelings made from the past we are not using our whole mind. This brings anxiety to the body because at a deep psychological level we know something is wrong. Innocence, or the true creative level of mind, does not know how to force or manipulate, so it makes a new belief system so it can function in time. These beliefs find ways to force and manipulate circumstances, which sometimes are successful, and sometimes not so successful. The true creative potential of innocence is fearful, and out of this fear belief becomes the way to have a physical experience. This is why most of this world believes that experience is the great teacher. Once this memory has been stored, the possibility of changing this is impossible without Higher Help. The implications of storing false memory is beyond the physical comprehension because the physical comprehension relies on experience as the teacher of this world. This is a trap, but not one that cannot be undone.

Help is open to us any instant we desire it. We do this by reopening the link to whole awareness that has been closed off through the belief that we are physical instead of psychological. We are at least responsible for recognizing that the link needs to be re-established. We begin this process by learning how to establish peace within ourselves. Peace is not a physical quality, it is an eternal one. Any time we decide to find peace, we avail ourselves of all of eternity. All possibility resides here. We are multi dimensional and have the ability to reach out of time and touch other possibilities that do not exist in time. Einstein did this and walked away with relativity. Edison did this and walked away with the light bulb. I am not saying that they did it in one moment, but their persistence paid off. In that one moment the course of the world changed because a new possibility entered the realm of the one that refused to accept the past as the only possibility there is. These men were radical thinkers, and in order to move out of the pattern of experiential beliefs, it is necessary to become a radical thinker also.

Every person who walks this world has been given a task to perform. Beginning to use radical thinking is the direction to take to move in the direction of this task. Radical thinking does not mean radical behavior, it means that thoughts are introduced that shake up old memories that are relied upon as fact. The assignment or task is attached to the innocence that must be released through radical thinking. Releasing innocence restores the memory of our task or assignment. Most individuals realize there is something that they are supposed to perform. It is like there is something that needs to be done, but they just can't remember what it is. Some remember their assignment, but most don't. There are specific guidelines that must be followed to find this assignment, but until each person realizes that they really have one and then make the decision to find and use it, these guidelines will never be found because no one will look for them. Once the individual begins to realize that there is another way, innocence is released and it is only in this condition that innocence can function normally. When it is not functioning properly it is because a violation of Spiritual Law has occurred and this has forced innocence to adhere to physical laws that do not comply with Higher Laws.. It is up to us to realize the violation and begin the process of letting go of false memory. This is called healing. We would not knowingly allow an innocent child to suffer, yet this goes on all of the time within our own psyche. The tragedy of this is that it is seldom recognized until the problem becomes so acute; addiction, disease, depression and other symptoms occur. Up until now this suffering may not have recognized for what it is, and it is customary to try to push it away, but the time has come and the world must look at what has occurred and steps must be taken to heal at an individual level and set innocence free. It is in the freeing of our innocence that we are restored to health. This will not occur until the false memory is addressed which is hiding the innocent nature.

New possibilities can only occur through innocence. This is because God does not recognize the logic or the intellect of an adult who has learned logic as truth instead of wisdom. Reality is His; it does not belong to individual intellect. Our time dependent memories are keeping us from the internal communication that is shared by the rest of creation by forcing our innocent nature to tolerate the violence that was perpetrated upon it long ago. God has given a Plan to this place called time, where our logic resides. His reflection of Love can even touch the remotest places in time to give it meaning, but it must be done through the innocence that has been scattered about in time. Innocence must come under the dictates of a New Consciousness that is greater than the one that has been learned in time. Our recognition of the violations that have occurred within us is the first step to bringing the healing Power of Love into time. It is only through the inhabitants in time that this process can occur. This is why it is important to heal. Without first healing and then releasing innocence, we will never be able to hear His Call and remember our eternal Home.

Impossibilities

When we look out into the world, it is difficult not to see all of the things that we do not want. There are wars, starvation, unhappiness, lack, unfairness, addictions that affect the lives of many. I am sure you can come up with a few things in your own life that seem to be beyond your control. These situations are called impossibilities because they do not contain the Power of Love to give them meaning. If they had meaning, they would mean something that caused happiness that would be shared with the all of humankind. The Light of Love must touch the unhappy innocence so it can be healed and return Home. The Bible tells us; "and a little child will lead them all." This is because without the innocence of a child it is impossible for God to give the solution. Solution is of God, just as purpose is. We do not want a partial solution, we want a complete solution. Completion is of God, but we do not trust God because we have learned to look to false memory for our truth. This makes God unfeeling and uncaring. False memory brings a false association with the Creator, which points a finger in blame. Blame places us in the position of taking over the role of God and trying to do His Work by trying to bring some kind of meaning to the impossibilities we see in time because we don't think He is doing what He is supposed to be doing. We cannot do His Work, we don't know how. We are not even asked to. We are asked to return to Heaven its innocence that has become trapped in a time experience and in a nightmare of a false memory. This time based experience wants us to believe that truth comes from the experience, and not from God. We do not recognize that this is happening because we believe that what we behold or see in time is true. We cannot even conceive that we made it up and can change the outcome of our beliefs.

The silent scream comes from the nightmare that we see no way out of. It is the child that has lost its way and does not know how to return to Heaven. The silent scream is a prayer that we do not understand is being answered, but not in the way we think it should be so we do not "hear" that we are being invited back Home. The answer always comes from the restoration of innocence back to God. The innocent thought trapped in time needs to be returned to eternity where it will be reunited with Love and be able to operate under the Laws that it was created under. Time is not a living commodity, but eternity is. When innocence returns to eternity, we take for ourselves the equal of the psychological face that innocence has. The physical experience is cruel and our belief that it is real keeps our own innocence locked in a vault surrounded by fear that tells us over and over, "don't look in the vault at your innocence, for you are guilty and so you must be punished for what you have learned." God does not see us this way. Our innocence was created in Love, and it is our connection to the Divine. When innocence is returned, it once again is surrounded in the Love that it knew before it entered time. Because Love is real, it echoes back into our own mind, all is well and safe. It is this reconnection that allows Love to enter the world and heal it. Without this, it would be impossible.

Day Ten

Today I am reminded about the true abstract ability of the mind. I know that I am not abstract, because I constantly look for detail. Pick, pick, pick is all I seem to be able to do. It is judgment that I am dealing with. Judgment that began in my past somewhere, but where I am not sure. The symbol of what I am picking at is in fact an echo of my past learning or a memory; otherwise I would be at peace. Peace doesn't continually pick at me. For an instant the chatter in my mind stops, and then it's as if someone pulled a switch and I am flooded with emotion that disturbs me. Every fiber of my physical being seems to be screaming at me to do something, but I am remiss of what I should do. My safety does not seem to lie in the peaceful state that I have agreed to journey on for 30 days. Instead it seems to be outside of me, and in the protection of a safely laid plan that I can escape to…somewhere…but where. The problem will only return again in another symbolic form. I know that there is nothing outside of me, but I don't believe it. If there is nothing outside of me, then why do I get the consequences? This hardly seems fair especially when I am really trying.

If I can just remove the judgment from my beliefs so that my own judgment does not return to me and I suffer the consequences of the judgment I have placed on the situation that seems to be outside of me and occurring now. No one said it would be like this. No one said how hard it would be to continue in a peaceful state when all I want to do is run, but run where? I want to hide, but I can't hide from my own thoughts. Everything I am experiencing is in complete opposite of the abstract mind. The abstract mind does not pick, for it does not pick out a subject to dwell on. It looks for what is like Itself and joins with it so it becomes stronger. When I am in turmoil, I am outside of this abstract mind and am alone. No wonder I feel like running. But when I am in this unreasonable state, it is difficult for me to focus on peace, where I could join with the abstract mind and I would be helped along in my decision to maintain peace.

Judgment keeps me from joining with the abstract possibility. My judgment keeps a world full of terror real, for without my judgment, could it be true? If peace comes from me, then I will have to reach out of the condition that terror has made within my physical experience. I still don't believe it. I also realize that peace is beyond belief. I am reminded of the Bible verse that says that to reach God is the peace that passes understanding. But understanding of what? There must be a purpose of passing understanding, but as for me, I want to understand everything. Perhaps this means that to reach this kind of peace, one must reach past what one thinks they understand. Or, perhaps it means that first I understand the problem, which eradicates it, and then reach the peace that passes understanding. Obviously to pass something means that you go by it or around it. I used to believe that this statement was not to be understood, but now I am pretty sure it means that where God dwells no understanding is necessary; it just is. It is kind of like revelation. Revelation cannot be explained, it can only be understood. I have explained revelation before to others, and the response was kind of like a big yawn. To me though, this revelation was beyond my wildest imagination.

My first revelation occurred probably 25 years ago or so. I was driving down the street at night and looking up at the stars. All of a sudden I was filled with the awareness that there was no death, and that life continued on and on. It was as if I peered into eternity and saw one of its secrets there. This was the abstract mind. I only saw a speck of it, but within that speck the whole was revealed. I guess you could call this the hologram. Now, try to explain that kind of revelation to someone else. All it produces is a yawn. Peering into Heaven is extremely personal. We have all had these visions before, but as we get older and more receptive to the physical state, we forget.

I am an observer. I have known for a long time there was something about the mind that I was supposed to learn and share, so I watched, observed and asked questions that most people do not ask. I became a massage therapist in 1984, or I should say I took the classes. It wasn't until a later time that I began practicing it. It seemed as though I was drawn to it. The first time I made the connection between the mind and body was during a massage. I was working on a woman and she was complaining of a sore back. She complained that she had not had this pain in her back for 20 years, and I wondered to myself why a pain that was seemingly gone for many years would all of a sudden reoccur, so I asked her when the problem began, and the physical event that kicked off the pain. Most people do not associate physical pain with a psychological trauma. She told me that her mother died, and then the pain began. I didn't know what that meant, but I wondered to myself and stored this event because it seemed important to know.

As time went on, I began to ask for color associations. I discovered the language of the mind and how I could communicate with it. The color associations told me if the problem was guilt, sadness, fear or anger. Black is the color of guilt; blue is the color of sadness; yellow is the color of fear; and red is the color of anger. With this as bases, I probed further and began to learn the Laws of Mind and how to work within the context of the belief system that the individual had made while having a physical existence. At a very basic level, the mind is extremely simple. Complication comes from all of the physical determinations that have been made about the physical body and the experience that the body is having.

I became fascinated with the communication system that occurred in the body. I could actually begin to understand the communication process between beliefs that were occurring. I saw the effects of forgiveness as a past judgment dissolved with the realization that the past was over. I worked with one gentleman who forgave his father who had passed many years before. He asked me what the color pink meant, and I immediately realized that his father was sharing love from his spiritual state or eternity.

I know that death is not real. When my son made his transition over

3 years ago, I refused to give or offer him up to death. This did not mean that I did not grieve; it just meant that I did not give him up for dead. Since then I have received many confirmations of his continued life. Communication does not stop, it just changes. It is most easy to maintain communication while peaceful. Being in the state of constant sadness pushes me away from the reality of Heaven, life, and peace. The reality of Heaven lies in the abstract mind, and if I can remain in this peaceful state, I can see the abstract mind creates a bridge across the hole of limitation and loss.

Ok, so I guess I am feeling better. I can change my mind and decide not to look at my lack of peace and focus on what is real. I have a choice.

The Death of a Child

On October 18, 2001, my son Bruce made his transition from a physical unreality to a spiritual reality. His physical body was 33 years old. To judge the reason for his passing is to miss the purpose. Judgment of a physical experience is detrimental to the body of the one holding judgment. Placing judgment on anything that happens in the physical realm means the purpose of Heaven has changed from a spiritual purpose to a physical one. In truth, we were only supposed to find purpose in the Love that we were created to Be. So instead of trying to understand the why, which brings judgment, the new question that would not bring judgment is, "what is it for?"

Three days before his death, I awoke from a night's sleep with these words echoing in my ear, "death will be sudden and unexpected". I wasn't sure whose death it was going to be and even thought perhaps that it might be my own. When I heard this Voice speak, I was sure that the words spoken would come to pass. The Voice was not threatening, it was just informing me of an event that was about to occur. Once I received the physical message that it was Bruce that had made the transition; the first thing I had to deal with was the shock. The grief and the sadness were, and at times still are, beyond words. This, however, is not about my grief and sadness; it is about moving beyond the death experience to a place of peace where difficult situations can take on a new meaning that cannot be grasped when approached from a physical point of view. Dealing with physical death can only be grasped from a healthy standpoint when it can be accepted from a new level of understanding, and this can only be where there is no sadness or grief. It is hard to believe that there is such a level of understanding when grief seems to be all encompassing, but I can assure you that there is and it is attainable. In fact it reaches beyond the level of dealing with the death of a child.

When death occurs, especially to a loved one, we seek to understand the meaning of such an event as it is difficult to remain focused. Focusing on another way of understanding reveals other Laws that have the ability to help us move beyond the idea of death to a place of healing. One of the Laws that helped move me past grief was the Law of Appreciation. This Law states that what we understand we appreciate, and what we appreciate we love, and what we love we seek more of. In reverse, this Law looks like it is unkind. How can anyone appreciate death? Using the Law of Appreciation improperly leads to reliving the event of death over and over and trying to understand what happened and its unreality. This is revealed as the law of death becomes a real event in the mind, and it is impossible to overlook what we make real, so I decided to make his death an unreality. The seeming reality of death leads to questions of why this had to happen, which then leads to self explanation, which is understanding. The end result is love of death, which now becomes a reality and then I receive more of what I focus on. The Book of Life does not have the inclusion of death. By understanding and using death as a real experience, death could become an occurrence that would become a common element in my life. With death firmly in place in my mind, I would begin to experience this violation over and over again. By accepting the death of another, I also begin to believe that it is possible that I too will die in the end. This would force me to believe that I can defy the Law of Life and do what I was not created for, which is live eternally. We were never supposed to understand death, but now that we have we think we need an explanation, and the physical interpretation leaves us in shock and grief ridden. We are all joined at a level of our Being we do not consciously understand, so we cannot perpetrate a belief about another's death without accepting it for ourselves. This will bring about a tremendous amount of anxiety and feelings of not knowing what to do. The extreme sadness that is experienced when a loved one dies is in direct correlation to the self because of the Eternal Law under which we were created that does not recognize differences. What works for someone else must be the same for me. This is a Law of Mind and when it is used incorrectly it will bring consequences that are not happy ones. Some would say that the denial of death is not healthy, but my question would be; why is it healthy to force the idea of death on the living if death in itself is not healthy. In fact it is the end of life, and how healthy is a body with no life? The correct use of denial is the denial of death, not life.

We cannot die, but the physical body can and does end. When the body is not perceived anymore we feel that life has ended and perceive a sense of loss, but the loss is not seeing the body anymore. These are the times that I feel as if I were thrown into a deep pit because of the loss of not being able to see him anymore physically. I have to crawl out of the hole and look away from death and see that life is reality. As I look away from death, life creeps back and I remind myself, sometimes over and over, that life is real and death cannot possibly be my reality or the reality of my son. I have been through the death of a loved one before. In 1973 my sister passed over along with her husband. The car they were traveling in ended up rolled over in the median, and they both left the physical plane. I had forgotten the reaction of people. One of the things I remembered is that people are sad for you because they are tuning into their own unresolved grief and fear of loss. People who didn't even know Bruce were just sobbing. This sadness is directly connected to the feelings of being separate from our Love Source. The love and kindness shown during this kind of event is beyond comparison.

The face of compassion is kind. There is no gain from compassion, only a shared love that is not always evident in every day lives. When there is a loss of loved one, friends and acquaintances want to know what they can do. I don't know how many people told me to call them regardless of what time it was if I needed anything to call. Finally I understood that people are trying to make up somehow for what has been taken away. This comes out of a frustrating attempt to resolve something that is in fact impossible to resolve. From a physical standpoint it is impossible to give back the love that we believe that others have lost, but we can still feel the deep sense of loss and try to fill up the hole through offerings of love the only way we know how to give it…"if there is anything I can do, just call." Love is not a physical attribute; it is a spiritual one that is shared with the occupants of time. The out pouring of love that others give when a loved one makes their transition is beyond question an attribute that comes from the heart. This is truly a moment when we reach out of our physical reality beyond to an awareness that has the ability to heal and bring peace even when it appears that it is impossible to find it. We feel this from the people that offer their support at such a time. Offerings of love are truly the greatest blessing that we receive during such a traumatic time.

I found myself constantly reminding myself that Bruce was alive, and I felt better. I could climb out of the hole when I reminded myself that there was no such thing as death and not act like a blubbering idiot. I began to look for signs that spoke to me of his love and the Law of Life because what we seek, we will find. His daughter was 5 at the time of his transition. At the funeral home she was constantly coming up to me and pinching me on the behind. The day of the funeral, just before I awoke totally, I felt a gentle pinch where she was nailing me. It was a gentle nudge to let me know that he was still around. Love still communicates with us because it does not die. This was the message of the Christ and the crucifixion. His resurrection was proof that Love does not die. The physical experience does not hold Love because Love belongs to God and shares it with His Creation, and not one of His Beloved is lost in death.

The night before the funeral there was a beautiful pink sky. The clouds were light and fluffy and pink is the color of Love. I had seen this kind of sky before and was reminded in my mind that one of God's Creation had been taken Home. In the morning there was a slight rain and then the sun broke through. A beautiful rainbow appeared in the sky. A rainbow is a promise of life. Funny how that works.

The moment of the funeral arrived. I was putting the body of my first born in the ground. There were over 200 people there. I had decided I was going to speak because I couldn't let him leave the physical plane without saying something and telling others how I felt. The minister spoke, and then called me up to the podium. These are my words that I share with you now to offer hope that is beyond the grave.

The Tribute

Is it possible to measure a life by the moments spent in time? When the moment ends, what is left? Words that are left unspoken, deeds that fall short of the expectations we place on ourselves. At times I cannot bear to look. The pain of the moments I believe I have lost brings unspeakable sadness. It wells up inside my chest and is released through my eyes. But I know it will only last a moment.

Who demands that the piper be paid when it's time to go and how do we know what the payment is? Perhaps it is not this way at all. Where is the constant? What is it that always remains the same? Sometimes we forget we are not our behavior. The small victories that we perceive in life are at times paid with the price of pain that is too demanding. But pain is hiding something that has greater value then the lessons of sadness and grief. It comes to me in flashes, but seems to be buried in the pain of the moment. But then this flash moves me beyond the annals of time and brings the sweetness of peace. Buried beneath my pain is hope, but beyond hope there is Love. This is what remains the same; this is what never ends.

Love breaks the barrier that time places on our mortal lives. It moves beyond time and space to a focus within our own mind and joins us to an idea that transcends something as insignificant as time. Within the protection of Loves embrace we are all united. There is no difference because Love looks beyond what is different and focuses on what is the same.

When something like this happens, we all want to know what we can do. We feel the pain that another is experiencing and we want to fix it for them. What we feel that has been ripped away is a source of love. But Love never dies, and only Love is real. So this gift of Love is what we are left with. This is what is constant. This is what is real. Perhaps this is our lesson. Death does not claim victory over Love. It still exists. It is alive and well. We do not have to "fix" Love, Love fixes us, but it must be invited in.

When sadness does not claim its victory over me and I am quiet, I can hear Bruce's voice speak to me. Death did not claim his Love and I am comforted.

As I look out over all of you, I am deeply grateful for all of the blessings and thoughtfulness that your Love has given. Words could never say, but my heart knows, and I thank you.

As time passed over his life and I began to try to fill in the gap that had been left in my soul, I began to focus on the one thing that was very difficult for me to deal with. This was the idea that he left this plane of existence alone. Just today I was thinking about how a band of angels were there for him. That thought was interrupted with "no it was not a band of angels, it was an army", and this leaves me with an intense feeling of peace and gratitude.

Day Eleven

I was just thinking yesterday, I remember the first really vivid vision I had. I was dreaming, and all of a sudden the dream went lucid, which is I realized I was having a dream. The colors in the dream were very vibrant, and the texture of the dream was something that is missing in the element of time. Perhaps in this state of mind, all of the elements are together and peace can actually be felt. Anyway, I was standing in the ocean looking toward shore. It was extremely bright and the sun seemed to only be illuminating this particular place on the beach and then out to the ocean. There was darkness that covered everything else. As I walked to the shore, I was greeted by a person there, and because I know that if you wake within a dream, the dream characters can answer your questions, I therefore asked this person where I was. She replied, "do you see all of that which is held in the darkness?" As I peered into the darkness I could see towns and cities with the hustle and bustle of people walking and going about their business. As I was standing in the light, I was told that the world contained very little light, and by the measure that I could see, the percentage of light to darkness, the measure of light was extremely was small compared to the darkness. I was then told that most of the world is in darkness, to which I replied I was very pleased to be standing in the light. At the time I thought her response was odd as she said, "it may not be as wonderful as you think." Because it was my dream, and I figured she was my dream character, I asked her what she meant by that. All she said was, "you'll see." I tried to grab a hold of her, but she disappeared leaving me with a big question…If I was in the light, why was the premonition ominous? I always thought being in the light was a good thing and brought about blessings. At this point I was just a little cocky, and because I did not really understand the significance of my dream, and because I assumed by what I had read that I was in control of everything, I believed that the universe answered to me. Whoa!! am still working on that one. I also now realize that my old belief system is very abrasive and wants God to answer to it. This is called trying to bring truth into the illusion and this is definitely backwards. The world will not change as a result of fixing the illusion, it will only change as a result of looking beyond the illusion, and where God brings peace to the mind and shows the world that the illusion of terror and conflict is not real. This shows me that I am in control of my life, but this cannot happen under the law of force and manipulation. Instead I was to learn how to understand and use Spiritual Law, or the Laws that were written in the Book of Life, and how these Laws were to be introduced into the world.

Well, that dream marked a point in my life when all of what I had made in darkness would be revealed to me, one thing at a time and I can honestly say that what I had made was not so pretty to look at. As the story of Job goes when he proclaimed, "the thing I fear the most has come upon me," I could truly understand what he was talking about. On the other hand, on this lifetime journey I learned about peace and how to reach it,; I learned about miracles, and also how the salvation of the world would be attained. I made an agreement in my heart, and as I reached beyond my own understanding of what I was getting myself into, I said…let's go for it. I wanted to know everything. I wanted to know what the Christ knew and how He used performed the miracles spoken of in the Bible.

I learned about Spiritual Agreements and once such an Agreement has been made in the heart, the Agreement will not end until it is fulfilled. There is no turning back on this journey and I decided the quicker I could get through it the better. I did not realize how difficult the journey would be or how my life would change. Not visibly, but internally I am a different person. It appears that I do not have much from a physical viewpoint, and have felt that I was worthless because of this, but my value was changing and I was learning how to find the

Value that God had placed on me. False belief does not want me to find the Value of God. Because of a beliefs inability to access the Light, I am their source or their home and as long as I believe in them they will maintain control over me. This is a violation of freedom that is guaranteed to me by the Laws of God, so the old belief system would have to be exposed for what it is.

I always knew that when I turned 50, the world was going to go through some dramatic changes. It was like innate knowledge and even though I didn't know what this meant I just knew. I am sure that everyone who enters the physical realm enters with a certain piece of the puzzle that will heal the world. They also are expected to place into motion their piece of the puzzle by tuning into it. I notice though that there are people in my life that have very spiritual numbers, like the number 11 is a higher vibration number. I think that perhaps these people were placed in my life to support me through my journey and in my mission. This, in the end of learning, can bring about a great deal of appreciation, but while the intensity of a problem is exposed, I have felt very upset with the individual who is symbolizing the problem instead of feeling appreciation towards them. It's difficult to appreciate someone who you believe is causing your upset, so I began to look for ways to work around the upset.

The visions have continued, but visions are symbolic in nature. Sometimes there is an empathic link established to the realm of spirit. This happened to me, but it still took awhile for me to understand. Still the Language of the heart is there, and if one truly wants to learn, they will. It begins with honoring something within. I also think that, because each person has come into the physical realm with their own mission, depending on what that mission is, they receive the information that is pertinent to their mission. When a visionary says that anyone can do what they do, like Edgar Cayce, this is true, but because the physical realm is limited, if a mission is out of balance with the Sacred Agreement it is a little more difficult to obtain spiritual information that is not in line with the individual's purpose. I know because I tried. One way to investigate how to find out and then fulfill the Agreement is learning a little about astrology. Astrology is a spiritual map of the physical journey through time. What better way would God give a message, except to write the message in the Heavens?

I wouldn't go to California if I did not have a map that told me how to get there. By the same token, I did not enter the physical realm without a map. Most astrologers believe that the stars give individual meaning to each person. The truth is that the stars have received their meaning from the those who agree to enter the physical realm. Once here, most people usually forget and astrology is a way of studying energy that is unique to each individual. It also reveals at what point in their lives certain energy is working to help bring about the healing of the world that has been assigned to the one specific individual. Astrology is also a spiritual time clock. The houses move forward, like time, and the planets move backwards, like space; which is paramount to time and space. I remember the statement; "what happens when and irresistible force meets an immovable object?" The answer is nothing…they just pass one another. The same is true with time and space. Time is the irresistible force, and space contains the immovable objects, which are the planets. This is proof that nothing happens in time. But the astrology wheel, can also be shown how we continually repeat the past. Because time moves forward, and space moves backwards, and in our physical condition we are joined to these forces. When we try to move forward to try something new, the counter clock wise motion of space plucks the invisible intention and places it in the past, so an individual repeats the same mistake over and over again. Unless a decision is made to move beyond the constant shifting that occurs within the mind caused by the shifting of time and space, the past is always repeated. Most people do not believe that it is their energy that is associated with the stars because they *believe* that they are a separate entity. So much for the power of belief. Hmmm…so now I am thinking…if nothing is happening as time and space pass one another…maybe on a lesser scale, nothing is happening in this world at all. The idea that it is just an illusion is beginning to make sense.

The way out of the constant shifting of time and space is to make a decision. When the mistake of the separation was made, a new Plan had to be drawn to end the separation. Physical form cannot create because creating is a being function. Physical form performs tasks, so it learns how to force and manipulate matter. The way to use the ability of creating at the physical level is through decision making. Incorrect decisions use force and manipulation as method of psychological persuasion. Correct decisions use the true creative ability that lies within. Correct decision making can only be done through a corrected consciousness that does not use false beliefs based on false memories to make reality. Corrected consciousness realizes that in order to access whole unlimited awareness, one must move beyond the scope of physical understanding. or the belief system that has never been in contact with unlimited potential. So now, I am learning how to rely on my decision process so I can use decisions correctly instead of using them to my demise. It is also a lesson in healing. By finding the past hurts that began from an incorrect decision made in the past, I can learn how to access now and it is only in the now that the eternal is present.

These are perilous times. I am grateful that I began my healing awhile back and I am learning how to depend on the Greater Plan for the restoration of peace to the world. I know that the one that is being implemented by the physical world will not work. It is like Martin Luther King said…I have been to the Promised Land. I have been there also, but you can't get there from here, or from the world's plan to bring peace. My decision to give 30 days of peace still has its challenges, but they are not as great as they were 10 years ago. Peace comes from me…it all does. If I can't find peace within myself, how can I make the claim that I want peace? Peace is a shared lesson, and so once it is learned it is given to the world, but until it is learned within it is difficult at best to share the lessons of peace. The prospect of doing something to be peaceful always looms, and I have been a good learner of this false lesson. It has been in the undoing of the false lessons of doing that has led the way. Just like the dream foretold, it hasn't been easy.

Miracles in Motion

The world is in peril. The conditions have become such that the destruction of the world is eminent. The inability of the world's occupants to establish a condition of stability does not come from a lack of trying. Instead, it comes from a lack of understanding.

For millions of years, the world has been moving towards this particular point in time. In took millions of years to populate the world to the point where collective irrational reasoning would have the ability to make a frequency that had the ability to, not only destroy the world, but also the universe. The problem that lies at the core of irrational thinking that is making an unstable vibration that does not resonate with creation the way Love set it up. This out of sync pattern will eventually cause the world to spin off of its axis, thereby creating a domino effect that will eventually destroy the entire universe.

Humanity is not equipped to deal with the immense issues or the questions that must be answered to eradiate this extreme condition. Humanity does not know how to deal with the out of pattern vibration that is threatening the universe, so Heaven has opened its doors, and for the first time in the history of the world, humanity is being invited to join with a Plan that will bring about the ultimate healing of the world.

The Plan does not require humanity to do anything. Because of the level that the problem is occurring at, physical doing interferes, and in fact brings about conditions that increase the intensity of the problem. What is needed from humankind is physical awareness that there is a Plan and then an agreement to support the Plan that is already in motion. This plan involves miracles, for without miracles, this world would not and could not survive.

Miracles are Heavens Gift bestowed upon the world to bring stability into unstable conditions. Because humanity does not understand miracles, it is essential that they learn how not to interfere with them by learning the miracles intention and their purpose. What this means is that in order for them to work properly, belief must be withdrawn from them. Belief is a limit, and because the potential of miracles is unlimited, human belief is a hindrance. Belief is backed by good intentions, and good intentions are not enough to affect the vibrational level of error.

What is needed from the occupants of the world is to recognize that there is a Plan to heal it. Support of miracles at an individual level is a way that one can step aside and allow miracles to move ahead of the vibrational error and create another vibration that can stabilize the catastrophic conditions that are occurring in the world. Humankind does not know how to do this, but miracles can and will if they are supported. Once this happens, because miracles have the ability to move ahead of time, outcomes of disaster change and the unnatural forces of nature that are creating havoc in the world become stable. Natural disasters are being made by unseen forces that must be dealt with and because only light can shine these evil forces away, it is essential that Heaven and Earth join as one to complete this mission. This cannot occur until the Plan is accepted by humankind as the one that has the ability to establish peaceful conditions in the world. The responsibility of the occupants of the world is to accept that there is a Plan that is in effect that has been designed by Heaven to restore the world to peace. Without this recognition, nothing will happen, for the Plan must work through willing participants that agree with the Plan. It is impossible to physically see this Plan, but the results that will be played out in this world will change it dramatically.

Supporting miracles is a way to place physical symbols that are used as a way of trading and doing business, under Higher Laws that do not conform to physical laws. This would include the monetary systems of the world and other physical assets. The Plan is not designed to destroy the physical symbols of time and make them obsolete, for in so doing, panic would be exacerbated and would speed up the vibration of destruction. Instead, miracles have the ability to re-interpret the symbols before this recognition occurs in the individual mind, thus protecting the world from a global collapsed monetary system, and also natural disasters.

This Plan is designed by a Higher Consciousness that has the ability to direct unlimited awareness or potential, so the Plan is flawless.

THE PEACE KEEPER

Contrary to what may be considered popular belief, it would be impossible for God to destroy the world, for to do so would mean that God would have to violate His Own Laws, and God does change the purpose of what He has Created. The vibration of Love that is echoed through miracles is the One that will save the world. Miracles are the bridge that must be supported, but your awareness is needed so this Plan will work. Please join with me and support miracles to keep the world save for future generations.

Day Twelve

Using peace, where the Laws of Love abide, is different than using what I have learned in my physical experience and I am therefore unaccustomed to using these Laws. The most profound lesson of learning to be peaceful is that it is impossible to be dishonest. In other words, the Inner Guide knows when I am fooling myself. Honesty is not a physical trait, but a spiritual one and when physical behavior is attached to honesty, what emerges is not the truth at all. Because being honest is a psychological and not physical trait, if I am not honest within, I will hide even from myself what I am not being honest about. With this understanding, if I do not get it right then I will not move forward until I do. The Laws of Love emanate from the heart, and the One Who lives there understands the Language of His Creations. If the Language of the Heart, or the Home of God, is violated then communication is blocked. Learning how to be dishonest internally has blocked the Internal Communication process. This has led to fear, and a fearful heart cannot House the Spirit of Love. The Internal Guide, or the Interpreter, has the responsibility of aligning communication to the point where the block to the communication process is so small that it is almost indiscernible. At this point, revelation occurs and the separation ends, but this is a gradual process so revelation occurs when the heart has been unblocked enough so communication can break through.

What is used as personal or worldly interpretation of our physical life can be quite different from the Guides point of view. So before the answer from the Interpreter can be heard, I must first understand my question from the Interpreter's standpoint, otherwise I will be looking for a different answer. For instance, from a physical level, when I think about going to work I think about going to a physical job to make money. My real work, according to the Guide's interpretation, is not about going to a job and making money at all. My true work is healing so my mind can be aligned with peace. So, if I am looking for ways to enhance my physical career while working with the Internal Guide, I will not necessarily hear information about my physical career and will probably assume that my question is not being answered. This has led me to great consternation because I have believed I needed to be working successfully in order to fulfill my spiritual purpose. In other words I thought I had to get in order to give. This has led me down many paths of disappointment. To learn that my Source does not come from what I do and instead comes from just Being is a very tough lesson. I eventually knew that if I pursued my old way of trying to make a living by working for money, it would not work. At some level I knew that I was not supposed to work for money; it was supposed to work for me. But lessons of my past has shown me that my source is not God, but instead money. This of course came from beliefs that I had learned while learning how to have a successful physical life. I also learned that a Law of Mind says that I was created to only move in one direction. This brought about extreme conflict in regards to "making" or working for money. This was so especially as I learned the so called law of money that says I am supposed to save it. But in order to live and be comfortable I also had to spend. These two opposing ideas bring a lot of conflict into the mind because it does not know how to do both, so beliefs are made, one supports spending and the other supports saving. This would work ok, but when I was using one belief to do say…spend…the other belief brought about guilt because it said I should be saving. But if I saved, the other belief would point out the things I was missing out on by saving. This is what the purpose of the Interpreter is, to help sort out the conflict because guilt leaves the mind without peace, but so does fear, and the fear of not having money seems very real. In order to understand the correct perception, all of the so called learned beliefs must be stepped away from to make way for the correct perception. This explanation is just a small example of the ways the Laws of Love have been violated. To decide to use peace instead of conflict is not as easy as it sounds. If the question was evident, then the answer would be evident also, but because of the inner turmoil created by past efforts at being physical, the question is for the most part hidden behind the fear created by the conflict. The real question to ask in situations that seem to bring up conflict is…how can I heal this so my own perception is not standing in the way of a new perception entering? The new perception introduced by the Interpreter does not oppose truth, so truth reveals Itself to me and I am healed.

It seems I am always trying to work with truth, but actually I am opposing it. I want to hang onto my past beliefs about how the problem should be handled, so I cut myself off from truth. Beliefs don't know anything. If they knew, they would not be beliefs. The belief of how something should be handled always leads to fear. Fear is the basis for guilt because if there were no fear there would only be Love, and Love does not express guilt.

Fear is always fun. Yea, right…But I have learned I am responsible for my fear, and because fear is not real I have to be the one to find a way to make it unreal in my mind. When every fiber is screaming at me to run, if I want Help from the Interpreter, then I am the one that has to look away from what seems to be over powering and what I am fearful of. Fear has no power, except what I give it, for it was what I made to take the place of Love's Protection, but fear does not protect because it does not know how. The advice of fear is…run or hide. I have learned that what I am really afraid of is what I want, and if I am afraid of what I want, I cannot have it. Sounds simple on the surface, but I have been trying to find ways to look around fear for quite awhile, and there have been times when the task seems impossible. But I am told that it is indeed possible to ignore what is really not there. That's a funny one. I am afraid of what is not there because only Love is real.

I have had some pretty gruesome experiences with fear, and in the end have found that it is not real. It is impossible to conquer anything that is not real. It is also impossible to have what is known as healthy fear. How can anything that is not real be healthy? The Laws of Health were written in the Book of Life, and I am positive that healthy fear will not be found there. Love and fear are opposite, but what has no reality cannot oppose anything, so when I have opposed fear, I have recognized it as having reality. Boy, I know that I have sure made a mess, but it is getting better. There is only healthy Love and because only Love is real, when I use fear to help me solve a problem I am really relying on nothing at all.

    I do an exercise with my granddaughter. I take her into her imagination and show her that behind the doors in her mind, she is in control of everything, because after all it is her imagination that is creating her reality. I also have tried to introduce her to her own Majick. The practice of Majick in this context is actually the Laws of Love. I have told her that children have more majick than adults do, and children love this. She has explored the medicine in animals through Medicine Cards. Children are extremely majickal, but they also have a keen interest in learning about the physical realm and how to be physical. Sooner or later she will want to explore her majick, and when she does, I will be happy to help her. I don't think she realizes just how weird I really am, or that all grandmothers don't do the same things I do. That's what great about kids…they just accept.

To Spend or Save

    We live in a world of conflicting values, which creates inner turmoil. We were not created to understand conflicting values, but only to move in one direction. When we were taught that we must save our money, it created a fear of spending, and so we try to balance that which cannot be balanced. For our mind cannot do both, spend and save without making an error thus projecting fear and guilt onto the monetary system of the world.

The creative ability of mind

At our basic level we are creative beings and that creativity moves in one direction. That direction is towards the benefit for everyone. This is the Plan that was devised at the moment the separation occurred. It is this Plan that we must find and get into the "flow" of so we will not find ourselves in opposition to the direction the Universe is flowing. What this means is that we begin to find and use the latent creative ability that lies within. We do this by finding out, first of all, how we are violating the Laws under which we were created because we cannot put our creative ability to use until we find out how we are violating this ability. Our creative ability is one that is shared with God, and because He does not violate His Own Laws, He does not allow us to use the talent we share with Him until we learn how to live in harmony, or not abuse our talent. One of His Laws that has been violated is the Law that states; our mind was not created to move in two directions at once. An example of this is spending and saving.

The Instruction Manual

Everything comes with an instruction manual, except us. We have at our disposal the most creative force in the universe and are trying to use it within the context of our physical experience. What this means for us at a physical level is that we have given authority to an outside force that has no creative ability whatsoever. For instance, when we use money to try to give us meaning, we lose our meaning in our money. This does not mean that money does not have a purpose; it just means that in order to use it properly it must not take precedent over the creative process that we have been instilled with. The conflicting views that we have all learned are held within our awareness, which is the creative level of mind, and we are in constant conflict about what we should do. This conflict is being played out in the global arena in many ways. One of which is the global monetary system. If we do not learn the Laws under which we were created, we will continue to get what we do not want because we are in violation of Universal Laws that all of Creation lives by, except for mankind, who has continually tried to create his own set of rules and laws that do not work.

The greatest error

Our greatest error is in our decision to "teach" our children the laws of experience. When our children enter the physical arena, they already have or intuitively know the Laws of Life without our interference. But we go about trying to teach them something that is so alien to their understanding, that eventually they become filled with anxiety or depression. As they become an internal mess because of conflicting values, we watch helplessly and do not know what to do. One of the simplest solutions is to find the error, or the violation that has occurred that is opposing the Law. This helps the child to realign themselves with truth or the Laws written in the Book of Life. This alignment helps the child understand their Being, and gives them a sense of power over their external circumstances where the frustration appears to be occurring. Better still is to keep the child connected to the Law that they intuitively already understand.

The law of money

There is no law of money. There is only the Law of God, or the Laws of the Universe, and the Law of Mind that lives under the protection of these Laws. The ability of money to have its own energy source is ridiculous. We are the source, and without this realization we will continue to try to "get" so we can "be." The Law says that we are already it, so when we pursue something else we are trying to violate Laws that were created for our protection and then teach our children how to violate the Law and adhere to physical laws that are about doing and not Being.

Because of our own hang ups about money; we tend to teach our children what we have been taught. Our own fears concerning the conflict we feel inside now resonate with the false law of money. We teach this through example when we go to work everyday and forget our creative ability, which is protected by the Law, and instead of having money work for us, we work for it. Does this cause depression?

You bet it does, and yet the insanity continues. The vibration of doing what we dislike resonates within the creative ability of the mind and we see it being played out in the terror that is held in the world. Such is the destructive creative power of the mind that supports laws that are out of sync with creation.

What we can do

First, we can realize that we have made an error. There is a corrective process that can help us align ourselves with Laws that will support us in our endeavor to end the conflict. We are now living within a time when we are being shown our mistakes, and then we can ask for assistance in the correction process. The purpose is to get the world moving in one direction so the conflicts end. This must occur at an individual level first, for "as within, so without." Our children must be guided. Instead of being taught that the experience is real, teach them that they are having an experience. We can show them that money is not an outcome; it is a tool to use to help increase their creative ability that they share with eternity and have come to give it to the world. We can reward them for their creative ability instead of rewarding them for doing what they do not want to do; as in cleaning their room. Rewarding them for their creative ability teaches them that it is ok to be creative and they learn that money is a tool to expand their creative ability.

When we teach children to collect things, we teach them that things have more value then they do. Things do not have any creative ability, our children do. Instead of teaching children to respect our possessions, we can teach them to respect our feelings; and because our possessions fall under the protection of how we feel, what we own falls in the proper order. Our feelings come first, and so do our children's feelings. It is not the possession that ever has value. It is the feelings we have attached to the possession, so teaching children to respect feelings will teach them in a language they understand because children do understand how they feel.

Our children are our greatest resource; money is to be used as a tool to establish this fact by supporting their creative ability. Thus eternity is expanded into time through our children as we switch our value. Children are an integral part of the family and within the family dynamics everyone plays a part in holding the family together. House or room cleaning may be one of those dynamics. The value of unity is a Spiritual Law, and children are more likely to live within the context of what they know at an intuitive level. As they are included in the family value, or unity of the family, they understand their importance that contributes to the family dynamics. Thus, their personal value is appreciated as the value instead of what they "do" at a physical level.

One way to help them learn the value of themselves is to teach them to pay themselves instead of saving. Paying one self is not conflictive, as it is learned that money must move in one direction, which is continually towards the idea of sharing. Sharing, when used under the Law, or paying oneself is perfectly acceptable and not selfish or done at a level that is not considered creative.

We can also share truth with them, and when we are low on funds tell them that they have to be replenished, not that we have to go to work and do something to "get" money.

When we have money to share, give it to them, not as a reward for something they have done, but instead because everyone benefits when the Law is kept through sharing, and what you give you receive. By doing this we also teach them that the refusal of money is not a punishment, but it is like being low on groceries and we must go and replenish what we are low on.

This is uncomfortable

The undoing of what we have learned incorrectly is bound to cause uncomfortable feelings. A new way may seem like it flies in the face of everything we know, but in order to move towards a New World understanding that lives by the Laws that the rest of creation lives by we will encounter uncomfortable moments and learn to heal the source of the problem. Our efforts at learning the Law are needed now more than ever. Learning the Law is like depending on instruments to fly a plane. Sometimes it just doesn't feel right, but if we depend on our instincts instead of the instruments the plane will most likely crash.

We have depended on wrong instincts for a long while and the world is indicative of these incorrect instincts. There is another way of using instincts that brings into play our intuitive creative ability that joins us with our eternal nature. We can only learn this by stepping beyond what we think we know into Laws that are greater then what we have learned while having this physical experience. It is our decision to move beyond this experience that will lead us to a New World and under this New World, peaceful conditions will be ushered in for our children.

Day Thirteen

So much moves through my mind everyday, it seems like it never shuts up. My friend, Vivienne does palm reading, and when she looked at my palm, she said, "boy, your mind never shuts up, does it?" That is putting it mildly. The desire to understand has become an obsession. I thought it was possible to become enlightened spontaneously, but from where I have been sitting, that just hasn't happened. I have wondered if I am stupid or what. Now I realize it has nothing to do with how smart you are. It has more to do with the righteousness of the heart, although I thought I knew what that meant also. My interpretations of what all this means has been wrong. My agreement to learn in a new way has certainly led me down paths I really did not want to go down. Even the fears that I hold and have held are not even about what I thought. I have always been amazed at how the mind interprets its physical surroundings. I am learning that the mind was created to understand that everything belongs to it. What I have learned to fear is what I have learned to believe does not belong to me. These refer to my so called learning experiences that I have accumulated in time. Experience teaches me that I am separate from that which I desire, so I will have to try to find a way to get it. Getting is not a Natural Law, Giving and Receiving are. Getting is forcing or manipulating a circumstance so it turns out the way I would prefer. The Problem is that when I decided to change my mind, I also had to change how I went about making life work for me. The old ways of getting just quit working. Now I have been learning that what you give you receive. This has been the hardest lesson for me to learn. I always thought that it was better to give than to receive, so I gave just about everything I had away trying to get in return. What I didn't realize was that this Law was not about the physical ability to give, it was about how you felt about what you gave. If God reads a righteous heart, then He looks for the value of the heart. If the value I have in my heart is about what I think I should get when I give, then my sense of giving is warped. Giving is not about getting, it is about receiving. It sounds pretty easy, but because there are no mistakes in reality, I have to be sure my understanding of it is right, but this understanding does not come from my own standards, instead it comes from an internal knowing that it is right.

It is hard for me to comprehend that the universe and everything in it works at a vibration of thought. I never really gave my thought process much ability, outside of the ability to tell myself how useless and stupid I was. I also got into guilt a lot. It is really difficult in this world not to get what you want without using guilt. Using guilt is a form of force and manipulation, and this is physical law. Only experience can teach us how to be guilty, so either the experience is wrong, or Heaven is. But I have really wanted my guilt. Learning how not to see myself as guilty, and how my physical experience has taught me over and over again that I am guilty, has created a terrible conflict inside of me. The worldly experience is impossible to live without acquiring guilt. If I don't pay my bills on time, I am guilty and therefore punished by receiving a shut off notice, or a late fee, but what if I don't have the money? This circumstance only exacerbates guilt. I am expected to figure out how to give when I don't have. The only way I have found to alleviate the inner turmoil of guilt is to find a way to reinterpret the experience, for it is the learned experience that is in error, not me. Either I am real or the experience is; there is no other choice to make. I am not saying that learning how to make the right choice, or change my mind, does not give me moments of doubt. Quite the contrary is true, but once the error is exposed that is lurking in the experience, the issue is gone forever. I don't know of any physical solution that bring a resolution such as this. Physical solutions are only temporary, like getting enough money to pay a bill temporarily. Next month, the bill shows up again, and the issue of having enough money will occur again and again until the Law of Giving and Receiving is understood, not at a physical level, but at a spiritual one.

I have been wondering a lot about how the Christ fed the multitudes with one fish dinner and some bread. He never lacked for anything because He did not believe in lack. To not believe, is to not hold a certain belief. If you don't hold the belief, it is because you have not had an experience that taught you otherwise. Christ had faith, for only faith could feed that many. Faith is the assured expectations of things hoped for and the evident demonstration of a reality though not yet beheld, so faith is greater than belief. Belief cannot see beyond itself, but faith can. Faith sees evidence of a demonstration before it occurs because it is sure it will occur. Belief is a conflict. If I believe something will happen, then I must also believe that there is a possibility that it won't happen. This is conflict, and I am quite sure there is no conflict in Heaven. Faith has nothing to do with belief, for faith will work without it.

One thing I am learning for sure, and that is that the Language in Heaven is quite specific. In this world, words are thrown around without realizing the impact that communication has. I also really never knew how receptive my mind was to suggestion. The other day I was watching a cooking show. The lady who was demonstrating the cooking had a note next to her dish that said something like; older women are still hot babes, but now it just comes in flashes. I thought that was kind of cute and chuckled to myself without thinking too much about it. For two weeks after that, at night, I had these terrible hot flashes and I couldn't figure out why. Finally, I began to question myself as to why this was occurring, especially since this had not gone on in quite awhile. Immediately I realized I picked up the suggestion from the cooking show, and I released it. Learning how to become consciously aware about how my mind/body awareness learns has helped me to realize just how suggestive my mind really is.

The more I have learned, the more I can see that it is thought that is creating the worlds reality. The problem arises from the insane belief that there is something that is in this world that has any kind of ability that I do not have. Everything comes from me, but while I am still learning how to neutralize my experiences with miracles and make what seems to be occurring right now ineffective, I will still have the fear that must be dealt with. Fear learned in the past doesn't just go away, for the mind never forgets. Once it thinks it has learned that fear can somehow provide protection, the more evident it becomes that the error must be corrected and brought to place where the fear can be exchanged for Love. Love + thought & emotion = eternity, and it is peace that surrounds eternity. Fear + belief & experience = time, and time is surrounded by guilt. This equation is the vibration that is out of alignment with Heaven and only one is real. It is entirely possible to reach peace without leaving this earthly plane, so reaching out of time, or guilt, must occur so Heaven and Earth are joined as one. Until this correction is made this world will continue to be full of the guilt that is not known in Heaven.

Joining Psychology and Technology

Within the context of time, shifts are constantly occurring. These shifts are usually violent in nature and once they are over, it is only then that it is possible to look back and see the significance of what has occurred. We have traveled far along the paths of time, technologically and psychologically, and although it seems that these two abilities do not have anything to do with one another, the time has come where they must cross paths. This must occur to insure that the world will remain in tact and be safe for future generations. The avoidance of learning how to combine these two abilities must occur to avoid total annihilation. Humankind has not yet learned the impact of technology on the psyche. The physical inability to understand the ramifications of how the mind works has the ability to bring about the destruction of, not only humankind, but eventually the world and the universe at large. As a logical and informed society, we want to examine all of our options so unintentional errors do not upset the delicate balance of nature. We are moving in unexplored territory, and without a guide to inform us if an error has been made; we may unwittingly create conditions that are irreversible by setting off chain reactions that are at first unseen, but eventually deadly once manifested.

Even though there has been a tremendous amount of information that will help humanity deal with the implications of the effects of the "psychotech" society, the information is not complete. This is because no one in this world has access to, or is in a position to understand the ramifications that are occurring, that is until after the event has occurred. For instance, it was not known the impact that setting off the nuclear bomb would produce until later. Looking back, technology brought into existence a force that has the ability to destroy the world. The psychological implications of this has shifted all of humanity towards a new psychological mind set. This is evident in the fact that no one feels completely safe anymore because it is known that at any moment some nut could completely destroy the human race. When the bomb is dropped, there will be no looking back, for there will be nothing to look back on. The psychological impact of a technological invention that has the ability to destroy the world has formed a gap between technology and psychology that is impossible for humankind to bridge. There are many who contribute to the ideology of keeping the world safe for future generations by propagating a physical solution, but the problem is psychological, not physical. Thus, the physical solution has proven to make the gap greater. Using violence, or war, as a means to advocate world safety is somehow an insane notion no matter who is using it. Not doing anything also seems somehow not to be the correct way to approach the problem, so just what is the answer, for if we do not find it, and quickly, the future generations of this world will not have one to worry about.

The world was created to be a spiritual playground, not a physical stomping ground. The intention of humanity was not to make a world that was dangerous; it was just that they never had all of the facts. In order to bring all of the facts together, and because humanity really does not understand his spiritual nature, something else has been introduced to help humanity deal with the seeming incompatibility of

Natural Laws, which are governed by the spirit, and physical laws, which are governed by humanity. This new movement of thought is what is commonly known as miracles.

Miracles have many abilities that are not understood because physical laws do not have access to this information. They believe they know what the purpose of miracles are, but they are mistaken for belief has nothing to do with miracles. Miracles work in accordance with Natural Laws, not physical laws and humankind has been trying to force and manipulate nature, or Natural Laws, for thousands of years. Trying to force or manipulate Natural Laws that are not understood by humankind will result in unnatural consequences, such as hurricanes and tsunamis that have capacities that are far beyond the bomb to destroy the world. The lesson is this; butt out. Miracles have the ability to fill the gap between technology and psychology. That is their purpose. Filling the gap between the two dimensions opens up new possibilities that are not destructive, but instead helpful and harmless. Miracles are Gifts bestowed upon this generation to help humanity learn how to live within the structure of peace.

There is an evolutionary shift that is occurring. When it is complete, the world will not resemble the world as it is known now. This shift must occur so that it is understood that Natural Laws are greater than the physical laws that are being used to try to force and manipulate Natural Laws into compliance. Humanity will not stop the insane notion that Natural Laws must be manipulated to serve the lower nature until an inner shift occurs. This is because of the fear of loss that has been learned as a result of the false assumption by humankind that without exerting control over nature, nature will not provide enough, so Natural Laws have been raped to prevent a loss that in reality does not exist at all. The conditions that occur in this world as it stands right now are impossible.

Ever since the beginning of the Spiritual History of the world, God has provided an escape Plan that has proven fool proof for those who chose to believe that there was another way. Because of the radical conditions of the world, a radical Plan was formulated to bring about conditions that would keep the world safe. This Plan is found in miracles. Miracles have been introduced into the world to provide a New Movement of Thought that has the ability to bring about peaceful conditions to the world without harming anyone or destroying the structure of the world the way it has been set up by humankind. The purpose of miracles is to undo what has been unintentionally done because of fear. This undoing process works at many levels, but in order to understand the potential of the miracle, and how it works in individual lives, it must be studied so it can be understood. Miracles will only work if they are allowed to follow certain guidelines, and these guidelines do not fall under the category of physical technology or understanding. In other words, the miracle does not work according to force and manipulation, which is physical law. Instead, it works from a Natural Law perspective without undermining the technological advancements that have been made, or will be made, in the world. The purpose of the miracle is not to destroy what has already been established, but to eliminate the destructive potential of fear that has been produced because of the human inability to reconcile Natural Laws and physical laws. The miracle has the ability to move ahead of our own thinking and introduce stability with a new movement of thought whenever there are fearful circumstances that would end in disaster. This is so not only to an individual level, but also the globally. Because the miracle is not restricted by the laws of time, which physical law is, the potential of the miracle is mind boggling. However, there is a catch.

Miracles were specifically designed to help humankind deal with the inability to solve the dilemma of bringing together technology and psychology and the fear of destruction that these two together exacerbate. Therefore, miracles are for the specific purpose of dealing with this seeming gap that only exists in the physical mind. Without the error being revealed to the physical mind, worldwide destruction at a physical level will occur. Because the miracle must work by the conditions of Natural Law, which is respectful of all creation, the miracle must move through the mind of physical individual's who support miracles with their permission.

As stated before, miracles do not work according to laws the way humankind understands them, so they are not bound by physical beliefs. In fact, miracles are actually limited when they are believed in because they can only use what they are given by the physical mind. If the miracle is limited by what is believed about them, they can only work up to the potential of that particular physical belief. If the physical belief about them is incorrect, they cannot work at all. This is causing the miracle to be bound by physical laws that do not have the answer. It is therefore imperative that miracles be given free reign to move through the physical mind by giving them unlimited permission to achieve whatever is necessary for them to achieve to bridge the gap between psychology and technology, or physical law and Natural Law.

By showing physical support of miracles, we purposely join with the Natural Laws that govern all of creation, and thus join with Heaven's Plan to heal the world. Allowing miracles to move through our mind is a symbolic gesture of trust that Heaven knows what the problem is and knows how to "fix it."

Plans are currently underway to open a Spiritual College of Miracle Education that will help individuals understand the Spiritual Plan of using miracles to help heal the world. Because it is not always feasible to go to learn about miracles, an I Support Miracles Campaign is underway, which will give individuals, businesses or any other interested parties the opportunity to join the Spiritual Plan to heal the world and bring about peaceful conditions that will never end. Please see miracle-education.org for further information.

Day Fourteen

I have been called a mystic and a prophet, but I have also been called a kook. "Give it up Cheril, because this is never going to work." I've also seen the roll of eyes and how the conversation is changed when I have spoken of matters of the heart. I have also been completely ignored, when in the middle of a sentence an individual has just gotten up and left. This brings up feelings of sacrifice. In other words, if what they were saying held value and I listened; then when it was my turn to speak and I was ignored, then what I was saying did not. This will humble you a little. On closer examination I have found that the outward voice or circumstance is merely a resounding of my own internal beliefs. Funny how that works. My upset at someone else over my assessment of their assault on my journey are merely my own doubts being played out in the outer realm. I never used to look at it that way. Now I try to look at what others are saying and if there is an upset on my part, I look for my own inner turmoil that has brought about the response from them. This doesn't always work because of the feelings of being unjustly treated, but the more I practice, the better it is. The truth is neither one of us is correct and both need a re-evaluation or re-interpretation of what is happening. It lies in how the Interpreter shows me the correct way of seeing or understanding the conflict. With the introduction of stability into my mind, we both are corrected. This correction is the miracle. Mostly, others do not know that I am attempting to make a correction so the upset ends for both of us. I don't want to be upset and conflicted anymore. I also do not want to sacrifice myself for the cause of others. Supportive; yes, but sacrificial; no. I want to be peaceful without explanation.

I have learned that when I do not place value on what is happening externally, another value appears, and what I thought meant one thing; it did not mean that at all. But it is difficult at times to quiet my false associations or beliefs in what something means long enough to see another value. This is the inner battle that everyone faces, but most do not feel that they are worth the effort of correction. As long as people believe this, they will not make the effort to look beyond what is already believed to be truth. Truth, in time, is distorted because the creative ability has been distorted.

Before the separation the creative ability used spirit, thought and emotion for the creative process. These unhindered creative processes were vibrations of happiness and joy. Happiness and joy are states of Being but without emotion they are just words, so emotion is the "gas" that gets the creative process moving. At the physical level, I have had the emotion to create, but nothing has happened. This is because of the level of form. When I place form above the creative process, the process stops or is brought to a halt. This is because if I have to "do" anything to join with my creative ability then I am in error.

Once the split or separation occurred, form or the existential level, also know as physiology, began. Form is the only place that fear can reside, and the true creative ability that is shared with the Creator, form is not recognized. The Creator is Mind, and Mind only recognizes the thoughts that live within it. At a physical level, we believe we are a body and when physiological thoughts intrude at the creative level, the creative ability works defectively. This leaves in its wake frustration because the mind was created to understand completion. At a physical level mankind looks in time for reality by attaching to time based results, but time doesn't hold the creative ability. When the creative ability is brought into time by attaching to results the creative potential is denied. This is because false beliefs that began in time believe time can somehow complete them, so they are attached to a result in time, which is always in the past. This is because they arose from a past experience that could not be creatively resolved, so time became the great solver of problems. We have all heard..give it time and everything will be alright. That is garbage. I have given it enough time and still time has not given me what I want. This because time is not creative within itself and has no idea how to create anything. It just moves forward. This is an attempt at trying to place a result outside the mind instead of where its own awareness or the creative process lies. This leads to the feeling that something has to be done to make a correction, which leads to internal anxiety or depression when the problem cannot be discovered so it can be resolved.. Following this path leads to guilt because at a very basic level we understand we are in violation of The Law of Creation by trying to create without God. This is why we are anxious or depressed. This guilt is then cast into time and the world is the recipient of the destructive elements of the creative process, for the mind must create. If it is not creating constructively, then it will make something up that is destructive. This inability to attach to the creative process at the level of time is a projection of guilt. Guilt is the so called creative ability of our false belief system. Guilt is then written on the walls of time and played out in the physical experience. Over and over again what is given, which is guilt, is then returned to the one who is trying to resolve the completion issue by projecting into time the distorted creative ability of attachment. The law of giving and receiving is accomplished, but destructively instead of constructively and lovingly. Completion can only happen at a spiritual level, where the creative potential or true possibilities lie. Otherwise it is the past that occurs over and over, and impossibilities are the conditions of the physical experience. Using guilt to complete life is death in disguise. The creative process must unfold, not be given a result by beliefs that do not even understand the process.

    The creative expression must be returned to God. This can only be done by untangling form, or the physical experience, from the true creative ability of the mind. This takes "time," but the new interpretation of time is precisely for this, to untangle the mess. The question is…how can I believe this will happen if my belief system only believes in the reality of time? Jesus, when He was on earth answered this. He said, "Blessed are those who have not seen and yet believe." Before His Birth in the world, there was only belief. After His Birth a new way of interpreting life began. He said, "I did not come to add to the Law, I came to fulfill it." Fulfilling the Law meant that the *physical interpretation* of spirituality came to an end. A new interpretation would emerge that would explain the spiritual nature at a spiritual level and so an Interpreter would become a part of the physical mind that would help the beliefs that wanted to know The Law and understand how The Law works. Understanding can only occur in the mind and because Understanding is a Spiritual Law, it is part of the Inheritance. Mankind would have to learn how to access the Interpreter to move beyond the shadow that the guilt of form had left. Jesus told His disciples that He was going to send a Comforter. The Interpreter, Guide, and Comforter are the same thing, and by any other name is considered the Holy Spirit.

Without the body there is no shadow. The Light shines unobstructed if there is no form, and so it is the form that is holding innocence in bondage that must be corrected. Innocence lies in the creative ability that lies in everyone. The creative ability is invisible to form, so is therefore a part of The Law. Form must be brought into line with the creative process. Because form is not the end all, using the creative ability with only form as the outcome violates its purpose. So it is the absence of the creative ability that is bringing guilt into the world. For 2000 years, since the birth of Christ, Innocence has been being introduced into time. All of the pieces of the puzzle are here. They have been left by the visiting of the Son of God. For God Loved the world so much, He gave it to His Son so it could be healed and follow The Laws that the rest of creation lives by. That is why I am here, to help with the correction process, but first I had to learn how the Law had been screwed up. Just being an observer does not heal the world. It is like cleaning up an oil spill. All of the plans to clean it up are not done at the sight of the spill, but in order to clean the mess up where the spill originated, you are going to get a little dirty. Mud on the face at the spiritual level doesn't hurt, but it sure feels messy here in the physical realm. The intensity of the problem has to be "felt" because in the creative process, feelings must flow to give the creative ability a constructive intent. Otherwise the true constructive creative ability does not flow into time and heal the world.

Impossibilities

As we look out into the world, we see many situations that make us give pause and wonder how these situations can exist. We see war, starvation, atrocities, addiction, rage, murder, molestation, insecurity, unhappiness, hate, fear, guilt, sadness, shame, loneliness, disease, retardation, death, destruction, car, plane, boat and train accidents. All of these, the above-mentioned and more, are the destructive creations of this world.

As as a society we abhor these situations and as hard as we try we make little impact, if any, on these seeming imperfections that we have to put up with while we dwell in this world. Over and over we look for solutions that never seem to be quite the answer. Since the beginning of time, the things that have plagued mankind still seem to plague him and bring him pain. Perhaps we need a different perspective. Perhaps a different way of looking at an old problem will bring a new perception into our awareness that has not been open because it appears an unlikely answer. A new perception opens a new way of seeing or understanding, and because we do not open ourselves up easily to new ways thinking, it may be a perception that is not readily accepted.

All of our "new thinking" encourages us to open up to new possibilities, and this is a good thing for us to do, but what about all of the situations in the world that are not open to new possibilities? These are the situations that have gone on for centuries and all of the new possibilities that have been introduced by humanity have not made much of a difference. What needs to be done to correct these unhappy conditions that exist? Is there an answer that will help us better understand how correction can happen?

In an attempt to see from another perspective and because the mind was not created to deal with conflicting views, we can choose another way of seeing the world that will lead it to a new awareness. The premise is this; we do not live in a world of possibilities; we live in a world full of impossibilities. When we were created it was never a possibility to experience the impossible situations that we experience and see in the world. Our mind, or the essence of our Being, was not created under such duress. Because we were not created to experience such things, we are constantly trying to make corrections. These corrections are impossible to make because from a spiritual standpoint, or from the aspect of our higher mind, they do not exist. How can we correct something that in reality does not exist? It seems to be real in our own mind, but in truth these conditions are impossible. When we deny our essence and try to correct something that does not exist, we focus our attention away from what is really there. This leads to frustration. It would be like trying to convince a thirsty man that a mirage is not really water, it is an illusion, but still he moves towards what he believes is real. We will never heal starvation or any other anomaly by focusing on the problem; only focusing on peace and Love, which are the solutions, will heal it. Love is real, the disease of starvation and problems that seem prevalent to the world are not. It is therefore impossible to heal what does not exist in the Mind of God. By looking at anything that is impossible to solve, we delay the effects of the solution. This is the same as asking; what does 3 + 3 have to do with the solution of 6? The problem and the solution must be must be brought together otherwise there will not be a correct answer. Even if no problem is evident, the solution remains the same. The solution does not lie in the physical answer, it lies in something greater, but in order to see this answer it is up to us to let go of our physical solutions to see what is already there. The answer to 3+3 is simple, but if we insist the answer is 7 then the possibility of solving a problem will elude us. The answer of 6 was the solution before the problem began. Studying the answer of 7 will not bring an answer, for this is the problem. When we try to make the solution something other then what the equation adds up to it is wrong. What is the same in every problem, for this is the solution. What is the same is that we all love, hope, care about our families, seek for happiness and security, and the list goes on. The problem is that when we believe someone has intruded on our ability to be happy, or secure, we look for ways to solve the problem elements of hate and fear are brought into the equation. This is what is different, and as long as we try to straighten out elements of hate and fear we will never see what is already there. When enough of us look away from the seeming problem, the problem will end and so will the seeming impossible situations that are occurring in the world right now. If a child is hit by a car, we do not ask what religion the child is. We do not ask the race of the child. What is the same emerges, which is the safety of the child, and just for an instant everyone has one goal. It is this transcends the physical experience and the problems of the world. Without beholding this in ourselves, we cannot see it in another.

Energy flows where we put our attention. Put it on the solution, not the problem. For every problem there is a solution that does not lie in our own personal ability of problem solving. The question of what is real and what is not real has to be answered in time because in eternity there are no such questions. Love answers all calls and when there are enough of us calling on the Source of Love in time, Love will be extended into time and heal the problems of the world, for this Love is the same in everyone. We are the ones that must look away from the seeming incurable problems of the world and return the power in our own mind to that of Love. This is true of any situation that seems hopeless in our personal lives.

When we observe something that does not seem like it will ever get solved, we must begin to acknowledge that it is an impossible situation. By this I mean that it could not possibly be real. Then call on what is the same to heal our mind and restore a condition of peace. Peace will open doorways that seemed shut, but without calling on this avenue, nothing will occur and the impossible situation will continue.

Day Fifteen

Everything has a purpose. Without a purpose all life would cease to exist. Purpose is a Law of Mind and when purpose gets tangled up with a physical experience that teaches purpose is destructive or unhealthy, the goal becomes destructive. A destructive purpose is self serving, not whole serving, because if it were whole serving everything would be destroyed. So finding a purpose that is not self serving is paramount to finding peace and changing my mind. At a spiritual level, nothing is separate, especially purpose. Goals are set to include all of creation. It is only in the realm of time that it seems possible to set goals that do not include the whole. Herein lies part of my journey, but a question also emerges: How can I join with a purpose if I am not even entirely sure what the purpose is?

It seems I have been on this journey for a long time. Constantly weeding out that which is unreal, or is ruled by the awareness of form, and striving to re-connect to the elements of spirit, thought and feeling without the intrusion of form. For I have found that it is the fear for what will happen to me physically that intrudes on my peace. Form must find its proper place among the other elements. Otherwise my purpose will be purely a physical one and true purpose is of God. I have been trying to make my purpose according to what I have learned from being physical. This has turned the Laws of God upside down and made a mockery of the Laws God created to protect His Creation, for the Laws of God are not dependent on time. Instead They are dependent on the Nature of Him, which dwells in peace. It is quite obvious that the Nature of God or His Purpose of Peace does not reign in the equation of time, for if they did the world would be peaceful.

It is the Purpose of God for all of Creation to have the same Purpose that is His. This He shares with His Creation freely and receives what He gives. The Law of Giving and Receiving at the physical level is sorely remiss at the insight of the Originator of this Law. Our physical nature tries to make it about what we give physically. The truth is that without the heart behind the physical giving of the gift, the gift carries no meaning. This is why the physical element of form must join with the rest of creation. It is out of alignment with the Laws of God and this misalignment is holding His Innocence in purgatory where it cannot see because of the darkness that surrounds it. This is why I am here, but my purpose has not always been clear for me. It has taken a long time to even connect with all of the information that could help me join with my own purpose that was not out of alignment with the Purpose of Heaven.

Sometimes I feel like I am writing a journal of a mad person. I know that once this is finished, I hope to share it. I know that this information is not for everyone. But a new era is upon the world, and in order to make it through the turbulent times ahead, a decision must be made by each individual to connect to a purpose that is greater than the form or the body that they wear. Breaking out of this mode has been challenging, to say the least for me. If I can make it easier for just one person, then the journey has been worth it. The cycle of non-believers, or beliefs that do not want this to occur, has played a dominant effect on my mind. It would have been easier to take a beating. At least the beating would have been over with by now and the healing of the body would have occurred. It has been difficult to realize that I am not in jeopardy. The only thing that has really been in jeopardy are the false beliefs that want me to remain unsettled and without the Purpose of Heaven.

ACIM says that in order to hurry along the healing, give everything one purpose. One goal that is set with Heaven as the outcome sets into motion circumstances that will ultimately place the goal under the direction of Heaven. All of Heaven leans towards the goal. Once the goal is set, it is impossible to change it., for the agreement set in the heart sets into motion the elements of change, which are spirit, thought, and emotion. This is why Jesus was able to control the elements. He had a proper perspective of His body and did not let it intrude on the true Creative Level of Mind here God dwells. In our physical experience, we have let the physical form take precedence over the other elements. In order to be Co-Creators with God and place purpose back into the Hands of God where only peace reigns, false beliefs must be corrected.

Union at a physical level is when two bodies unite. This process has the ability to make a baby. This is the greatest physical creative ability that two people possess at the level of form. At a higher level, the ability to create is much different. Because form is the end of the creative process, pure energy is the source. This is where the study of physics comes from. Watching how the creative process works at this level, it can be seen how attitude has a direct impact on the creative process.

All of nature must be placed under the control of the One Mind. This One Mind is directed by the Consciousness that evolved out of the separation which resulted in what is seen as form. Individual consciousness comes from individual purpose, or beliefs that are a result of the body experience. This consciousness does not see the whole picture of anything. All it encounters is the false perceptions of beliefs that are held in the "form" or the mind/body awareness. Once the body dies, the beliefs either move on, or will go to sleep. If the belief is sure death is real, it will believe it has died. But Jesus knew that it is impossible to kill a thought. This is why He said that Lazarus was just sleeping and was able to raise him from the dead. A body does not die because it does not know how. It has no purpose within itself and once it has served the purpose of false beliefs it rots; for dust you are and dust you will become. Thus the destruction of the false kingdom that was set up in opposition to the Will of God moves into the grave. Another kingdom dies and just like people do, beliefs that do not believe in death are misplaced for awhile until they find another kingdom or body to attach to or they seemingly haunt the place where they stay. All of this is played out on the screen of time and is recognized by the human form. Form is only the level we see or think we can understand at. If form could truly see, what would be seen would amaze and startle people. This is because what is occurring is being played out on many levels of awareness. I have been so complacent about what is happening I have not even noticed when beliefs from another "kingdom" has entered my domain. That is until I began to learn the truth. Now I can usually tell when something is amiss, but not always. I question my thoughts, and when internal war breaks out and disturbs my peace, I ask myself if this is my belief or if a belief that does not belong to me has intruded on my kingdom. I already have a full plate and do not want to accept someone else's war as my own. If I do not notice, and accept someone else's belief, this can develop into a cold or influenza. I think someone has given me a virus, but behind the virus is a false belief. If I am aware of what is occurring, this will kick in the immune system. My own belief system is literally attacking the belief that wants to take over, and my belief system will have none of it. Because my mind believes in the physiology of the body, the psychology of the mind is not even addressed. Thus our immune systems fight at a physical level, because it is impossible to fight at a psychological level where real correction occurs. Some beliefs are more subtle and just want to fit in. These are not considered a threat, but just like people, the true intention is not always known, and once they establish dominance, my body will more than likely take on the physical trait of the belief, or I will get sick because it is in opposition to what I believe at a very basic level.

Science can give a physical explanation for what is happening, but science has yet to examine the thought system that exists in each one of us. The question, have you ever seen a thought? still prevails. No matter what occurs, it must be thought about first. Thoughts do not originate in the brain, they originate in the mind. The mind thinks and the brain determines how to interpret the thought into the form level. Once adulthood is achieved, most of the form beliefs are in place and they dictate to the body, therefore to me, as to how to respond to the physical experience. The problem is that the whole creative process is placed under the direction of form, and then force and manipulation takes the place of the creative process. This projects the other elements of spirit, thought and emotion, outside of the realm of mind and into time where they become destructive because they are not developed enough to create without the direction of the mind where they originate from, so they lack focus. Displacing these elements at an individual level also leads to the dependency on time. Dependency on time leads to old age and dying. As dependency grows on time, the clock of old age that began at the onslaught of time, ticks and old age and death are the outcome.

On the other hand, a new purpose unites all of the elements and places everything in its proper order. The new purpose that I have placed on time is to learn how to bring all of these elements under the direction of the Consciousness that everyone has the ability to attain. This is the Consciousness and the Plan that God made to correct the mistake that makes form based on the false element of fear. In order to access this Consciousness, it is necessary to find innocence that has been placed in the physical realm to replace guilt. This is the woman that was seen in Revelation that gives birth. She is giving birth to the innocence that will replace the guilt ridden world that has been projected by the mind that only believes in form.

Purpose

Everything has a purpose. The purpose of reality is peace. Out of peace comes Love, beauty, harmony, joy, happiness, etc. These are the attributes that arise out of the conditions of peace. At a level of being happy, loving harmonious, joyful etc, there is no distinction of being, which is purpose, and also having, which is the extension of being. The purpose of beauty is to Be Beautiful. Nothing can have beauty without first experiencing it at the Being Level, except perhaps in form. The purpose of Love is to Be Loving. Without Being a Loving Expression, it is impossible to have Love. This is true of all the things that are really important. When we mistakenly try to obtain these ideals by getting it from another, it is because we believe that a part of our innocent nature has been lost and in order to "get" what is lost, we will have to take it from another. This now becomes the false purpose that is pursued at a physical level through force and manipulation, which in turn brings about unhappiness, depression, sadness, guilt and the like, which leads to looking for a physical solution. When the physical experience proves that innocence cannot be found by forcing or manipulating another, a physical alternative is looked for to make up for the loss, and then purpose becomes the acquisition of addictive measures that will force our attention away from what we believe is lacking. Addiction is something that is done, it is not who a person is.

In our physical experience we have learned to hold awareness captive withn the mind/body, and it is only here that we seem to be in need. At the spiritual level, there are no needs because we are limitless, but here in the awareness of the mind/body we are limited and search for meaning in the outside world where in truth the only meaning there is comes from individual perception. For instance, if the meaning of depression is given to an incident, depression becomes the purpose. Because the mind was created to seek for purpose, and depression is not a real purpose, then healing is needed to get the mind headed in the right direction so it does not perceive depression as purpose. The part of our mind that is in need of correction is held within the perception that occurred in a past experience and then stored in the mind/body. Once learned, these experiences teach that the only purpose that it is possible to have is the ones that involves problems. This changes the peaceful intention of the mind from a constructive nature to a destructive nature. The only way the mind can create destructively is by forcing or manipulating the truth, which brings into play fear. Forcing or manipulating means that something must be done in order to compensate for not being whole and because it is impossible not to be something, when we mistakenly try to "be" depressed, we look for ways to compensate for being something we were not created to be. Such as, when we believe we are not lovable, it is proven to us because it has become a purpose to the mind and depression is the reward, so we try to compensate for the feeling of depression by perhaps taking an anti depressant. On the other hand, being lovable brings the purpose of having love and there is no compensation that is needed for feeling unlovable. All of this is done at a level of mind that we are for the most part not consciously aware of. It is not the mind that is unaware, it is us. The mistaken belief that we consciously know something that the mind does not brings about many problems that we are also unaware of how to deal with.

If time is taken as a fact of reality, then time must contain some kind of being. We can be on time, but that does not prove the being level of time. It still proves the being level of the one looking at time, not time itself. The mere fact that time cannot be scientifically proven can be used to show us that we are trying to prove a false reality that ends in our own destruction. In reality or eternity it is impossible to prove destruction, but in time it is possible, and so the mind takes out its destructive tendencies on the body and also the world. This is the mind that has chosen to be ruled by beliefs that are in conflict with the true nature of Being. It is also a false presentation based on a learning experience that taught us that reality lies where it is not, which is in the unreality of time.

While residing in time, it seems as though experience is our purpose, because time is where we associate with the experiences we are having. In this state our mind believes it can become what it is doing because physical vision has distorted the facts. Physical vision is a result of looking away from our spiritual essence and becoming dependent of what the experience is teaching. When the mind does not understand that purpose comes from its being and not what it is doing, it is because it is seeing the picture of false beliefs that are writing a false reality on the walls of the mind/body awareness and then employing our consciousness to devise ways to make something happen that will prove the false purpose is correct and God is not. This is a clear violation of purpose, because purpose is of God. A distorted purpose that is held in mind must be corrected, or the error will continue to distort the function of the body and also the experience that the one in the body is having. Solutions must come from a higher state of mind that is not commonly accessed while having the physical experience. Peaceful solutions are not an attempt of trying to "get" someone to tell me I am something that I do not believe internally. Stability must be introduced so the vibration of the a false belief can to stabilize, otherwise the vibration that is out of alignment with truth will eventually lead to some kind of disease within the body.

If I was standing on a railroad track, and a train was coming straight at me, what could I do to change the outcome? The truth is if I did not make a decision to move off the tracks, then I would be hit by the train. Therefore, my decision to move is greater than the train or any circumstance that I may view myself as being in. But to make the kind of decision that will change the purpose of being hit by the train, I must first recognize that I am in peril. With this recognition, I have changed the outcome, of not only my life, but also the impact my life has on others. This is the way healing begins, which changes our purpose of self destruction to peace, for the turmoil only remains while I feel the uncomfortable feeling that I must do something. I can also choose to move off the tracks because I love myself enough to do so, for the truth is that fear will immobilize me. Fear does not provide the protection, Love does. When the emotion of fear rises, as soon as I let that go, something else steps in that says…move. Because fear is a greater sensation in the body, we may be tempted to give fear the credit for saving our lives. Truth is not fearful and the ability to move does not come from fear.

When the mind takes a body (spirit becoming flesh) it still is purpose, and its purpose is to share the qualities it was endowed with at the time of creation, which are the peaceful conditions found in Heaven. We see this in the unconditional love a baby expresses before it learns what acceptable and unacceptable behavior in a body means. The child emanates innocence because the mind is innocent. Who does not love to gaze upon the innocence of a child and have great appreciation for what they behold? This is because we recognize in the child the purpose of Heaven, which is being innocent, or that which we believe we have lost in time.

Living in time requires us to learn how to use a body and as a body matures the purpose of Heaven, which we came here to give to the world, begins to change. The eternal qualities that were recognized in the child are put aside as being "not safe" and naïve. Thoughts of being loving are overshadowed by what a child has to learn to do to receive love. As purpose becomes behavior, or how the child will obtain love, the child becomes locked into forcing or manipulating in order to "get." This is a violation of the Law of Giving and Receiving. Judging behavior violates the sanctity of being and also purpose. This happens when the child first senses something that is not part of the love idea or purpose. This first thought that introduces the idea of getting begins a fear based learning experience because getting is in denial of being. This injected fear becomes part of the child's existence by becoming part of the child's chemical make up. The chemical make up is not in harmony with the Laws of God, or the Book of Life and so purpose has changed. The chemistry of health has also taken an alternate route, and within time the new chemistry that is now entertained in the body of the child may eventually become disease, or possibly depression or something else that is psychologically damaging that may have an effect on the health that the being is relying on in error to carry it through the physical realm. Now we have a child mind whose true purpose is love, that has had its purpose changed to something else and is trying to prove that the something else is its true purpose. The child is up against odds that are impossible for him/her to win. First of all the child is trying to prove that his/her true purpose is not true by proving the Creator wrong. This will make guilt right and it will also make time real and Heaven wrong and also unreal. What are we thinking?

It is impossible to change the purpose of reality. It is just our mind that has become confused about purpose. For instance, some people like to ride a roller coaster, but one does not confuse themselves with the ride. If the mind forms a judgment about the ride, the ride loses its neutral meaning. The feelings on a roller coaster do not constitute purpose nor do they inject ideas that a person has to live with forever. It is just an experience that has nothing to do with truth. The ride through life has nothing to do with truth. It is just an experience. If there is a problem it only arises in the mind of the rider and the experience of one rider does not exist in the mind of another, so it can't be true. Truth is true for everyone. It is not selective. If a person is confused about the ride through fear it is felt within the body and mistakenly becomes purpose, then that becomes a part of the mind/body experience, and if the ride is fearful the fear changed the purpose of the experience. A person can force themselves to "ride out" their fear by forcing themselves to ride the coaster, but force is still part of physical law. Another way to approach the situation is to choose not to take the ride because, "I love myself enough not to force myself into what I really do not want to do." This is respectfully honoring the innocence within that does not desire to take the ride again. This also does not invite the dogs of fear in that are out of harmony with purpose

Once any association to anything physical has been made, the solution is to keep the integrity of our innocence. We do not want to "be" fearful, for it teaches our false beliefs that they are right and innocence is wrong. By showing Appreciation and Love by honoring innocence, we help maintain purpose, for it is always innocence that has been violated that keeps us in a state of fear. By learning how to "be" loving and lead our innocence around fear, we learn respect for the Laws of Life that keep all life in tact.

In truth, we can only fulfill our true purpose. If we take another purpose, reality has not changed. The tragedy of trying to do something that is out of alignment with reality is that while we live in time we will lead lives of desperation while trying to prove the reality of something false. The corrections that we are being asked to make is to look away from unreality to peace instead, for our reality lies in peace. Impossibility does not make reality, and living outside of the awareness of peace is impossible. Trying to live within the unreality of a mistake leads us away from truth, not towards it. The true measure of our how much we are on or off of course is by our own measure of peace. We are being asked to look directly at the false purpose we have made and recognize these as unhealthy and in direct opposition to the truth. Until we do this, we will continue to try prove that which is impossible to prove. The language of purpose awaits our decision to move in another direction. There is only one way to choose, because the other one leads to death, "for the wages of sin (or trying to live a purpose without God) is death." Our purpose, combined with the Purpose of God, is in fact God's Will being done on earth as it is in Heaven. The world will not heal without the purpose we have brought here to help heal the world.

Day Sixteen

Back in the 70's I studied with Jehovah's Witnesses. I learned about Bible Prophecy from them, but I learned about the Love of God from A Course in Miracles. Bible Prophecy explains the events that will occur in time, and this is particularly true when the Book of Revelation is read. What is not readily understood is that the symbolic language of Revelation refers to unseen forces and events that occur. Unseen forces are both good and evil, or healthy and unhealthy. Because neither good and bad, or healthy and unhealthy tendencies can be physically seen unless manifested as behavior or dis-ease, they begin as unseen forces. Another way of looking at these forces are thoughts, but the good thoughts are of a higher vibration and evil thoughts are of a lower vibration. Between the two are beliefs that are held within the self aware consciousness of individuals. There is so much going on at a level that is beyond our physical ability to comprehend, if everything that was going on could be physically seen, humanity would be amazed and a bit overwhelmed by it all.

Unseen forces bring about events that have a dramatic impact on the physical world, but because we do not physically see these things, sometimes form given the credit as having the reality. The realities of the events first occur at a mind level first and are then experienced in the physical realm. This is cause and effect. Because the physical realm is seen, and it is all but impossible to see thoughts, we tend to believe (there's that word again) that the battle is something that we will be able to physically see. Everything first occurs at the level of the unseen, and it is then carried out in the physical realm, so when someone gets angry at politicians, terror, or other physical occurrences, what is being physically seen is effect, not cause. The politician or the terrorist is the problem once removed from the source. This is why evil in this world did not end with Hitler. If getting rid of a person could end evil in this world, then it would have ended with Hitler. In this world, we fight what we can see, and because we think this is the problem we believe that if we "get rid of" the physical source then the problem will end. This is absolutely not the case; for the physical symbol is nothing more then that, just a symbol of what is unseen. This may set us into a kind of lull because we cannot actually see the real events that are occurring. These kinds of battles cannot be seen, but they can be felt or symbolically experienced, but once removed. It's kind of like trying to deal with a first cousin through a once removed cousin. It doesn't work very well and we would think this would be insane behavior if we viewed it, but this goes on all of the time when we physically try to deal with unseen problems.

Individual battles occur when it is decided to access healing instead of trying to deal with a seeming external or physical problem. When the healing process begins at an individual level, it is always the individual that makes the first move. Once the initial decision is made, then the forces of good are invited in to help with the healing. The individual begins to become informed of what they need to know and their part to help with the process. Once again, the process is still spiritual, not physical. The individual's physical part must be played in conjunction with the whole Plan for the liberation of the world. We cannot move ahead of the whole Plan by interjecting our own beliefs into what has already been decided before we were born into this physical realm. The Plan was not made at a physical level and it will not be played out there, but there can be no mistake, the battle that is being waged, whether it is being played out on a world seen or individual seen, is for the right to govern the world. To believe that the world will escape the effects of this battle is ludicrous. What are at stake are the elements that have been projected outside of the creative level of mind. Our job is to heal our own mind of the destructive nature that has forced the creative elements outside of our own awareness. We do this by learning how to be a peace giver by healing tendencies that do not align with Natural

Laws. Natural Laws govern Mother Nature and also our mind. Without understanding this, humankind is unwittingly using their creative ability for destructive purposes.

The Witness's interpretation of Revelation did have some accuracy to it, although for awhile I let their Biblical interpretation go because I lost faith in what they taught. At first though, I became enmeshed in their ideas. Eventually I broke one of their religious laws and was excommunicated or what they call being disfellowshiped. There is a difference between a religious law and a Spiritual or Natural Law; only one is interpreted by God and one by man. If it was possible to understand the Laws of Nature, then it would be possible to interpret that Laws of God. But as far as I know, man does not understand as of yet how to control the weather or make a tree grow, so his interpretation of what is acceptable to God and what is not, is a little faulty. Judgment and condemnation based on Laws that are not understood are constrictive and violate the Spiritual Law of Freedom. Studying with the Witnesses was obviously a part of my physical learning and when it was time for me to leave, I was pushed out. This has occurred many times; when it has been time for me to move on out of different situations I got a shove. Being creatures of habit, most do not like change, and I am one of those. At the time all of this occurred, I was very angry at my treatment and "believed" that I had been abandoned by God because I did not measure up to the standards of the religion, so I eventually looked for a definition of God by focusing on Spirituality. Spirituality has taught me that religion cannot place God within the boundaries of what it understands. God belongs to no religion, for He holds His Own Laws that are beyond our pitiful attempts at restricting His Love by placing Love under a physical religious interpretation. He is not physical, and the physical restrictions of religion are an attempt to explain Him physically. We do not define Him through a physical interpretation. Instead He defines us through a spiritual rendition of Love. Either Love is total or it is partial, for it cannot be both. If it is total, then it really doesn't matter what religion you call yourself, for He Loves all equally. As the Bible states over and over again, God looks at a righteous heart. To assume that a heart is not righteous because of a mistake is to judge the Home of God, for God dwells in the heart where all true emotions emanate from. How could I possibly know what dwells in the heart of an individual that He shares with God? I can't see into a heart. If I believe that behavior judges the application of the heart, then I have over stepped my boundary, for God does not judge behavior because behavior can only happen at a physical level, and it is based on past learning. If God only exists in the now, then He obviously cannot see the mistakes that we make. Not only that, if I am judging behavior, I myself have left out the ability to see or understand from the perspective of now. From the advantage point of now, everything takes on a new meaning, but this is something I had to learn. Only by looking at the past and honestly asking, what was it for? could I come up with an answer that made sense.

For a long time after my experience with Jehovah's Witnesses, because of my anger, I no longer assumed that what they taught had any value or truth, but then the dreams began. I would find myself back in the religion recognizing that I had to return because the word "truth" kept coming up. I had the dream over and over again, and tried to find if there was anything that I had not forgiven, but the dream continued. As I have worked with my dream process for quite some time, I have come to realize that once an issue has been answered, the dream stops occurring, but this dream continued. Not every night, but it would occur with enough frequency that I knew it was significant. Because I did not consider there was truth in what I learned from them any longer I assumed it must be forgiveness that was needed. I have studied the connection between the mind and body and know how the mind stores the issues that need forgiving in them. I jokingly refer to it as "issues in the tissues." I know that if the specific issue is addressed, the problem disappears, so with this significant dream, I continued try to find an answer. I asked the Interpreter what the dream meant, but because I was looking for what needed to be forgiven, I did not understand my question. If I had understood my question, I would have heard the explanation that had nothing to do with forgiveness.

Everyone has a specific Plan, and also specific beliefs that have been collected throughout their physical experience that needs a new interpretation. It is always my own interference that prevents me from hearing. I have found that if I can remove all of my associations to the question asked, I can then not only hear the answer, but can also understand what I am really asking. The question of what the dream meant referred to my individual Plan, not forgiveness. Truth lies in itself, not in the interpretation defined by religion, but because everything contains elements of truth, the elements of truth had to be exposed by the Interpreter, or Internal Guide, so I could see them and learn what the lesson was. Eventually I understood, and when I have a "Witness" dream, I understand it is not about the physical witnesses interpretation of themselves, but instead about the internal spiritual witnesses who do not interpret truth, but instead know it to be true.

Everything that I have needed to learn to carry out my individual Plan has not left me, and have not become distorted with time. The things that happen throughout our lives that leave an indelible print are there for a reason. These physical moments are like pieces of a puzzle that join us with the greater reality that is beyond time. When these moments are all put together, they evolve into the eventual purpose of the life of the individual that is beyond the physical experience. Sometimes the purpose is recognized, and sometimes it is not. Usually though, we know at some level when our mission has been completed. It is a feeling that we are done and our services are no longer needed. At that time, if a person is spiritually in tune, they more than likely leave their body and return to spirit. Sometimes though, a mind attaches to a belief, and the belief does not want to leave what they perceive as their home. Because the mind will not attempt to override the will of even a body belief, the body will eventually succumb to death.

Anyway, to get back to Jehovah's Witnesses; they have studied the Bible prophecy concerning what they call…the end of this system of things. I would admonish anyone who wants to learn what is going to happen during the "great tribulation," to study prophecy with them. Revelation, and the symbolic language of Revelation has been interpreted by many, but the Witnesses interpretation shows that the outcome of the great tribulation is not the end of mankind, but instead is a new beginning. I have since learned from the Interpreter that the new beginning means a shift in consciousness from the intellectual interpretation of the physical experience to a heart experience. The Christ Consciousness directs the awareness of Love that dwells in the heart and it will be this Consciousness that will establish a New Kingdom that is ruled by the Laws that govern the heart. Learning the Laws of the heart cannot be taught, they can only be revealed to the one wishing to learn. What can be taught are the lessons of peace which will bring individuals through the turbulent times ahead.

It is true; I am here to learn the lessons of peace, as we all are. My lessons have also involved picking up many of the pieces of the puzzle that have been left in time for the past 2000 years, examining it and then putting the pieces together so they make sense. I have been given the gift of looking past the physical interpretation that fragments everything, and looking at the pieces as a whole puzzle and seeing the truth in what is presented. This doesn't make me more special than anyone else…just doing the job for which I have been appointed.

I never in a million years would have believed this journey would lead me down this path. The passion that has burned in my heart has finally burst forth, and it was nothing like I thought it would be. The gratitude, joy and love that I have been seeking externally have finally been revealed, not in my heart, but through it. It is ready to burst forth into the world as a gift that is to be shared and then returned to me. This is the true meaning of giving and receiving, for the gifts of the heart are not gifts of time, they are gifts of Love.

My Passion and the Passion of Christ

The Journey

I have been on a journey all of my life, as well as everyone has. We all choose the road we will travel down. Some choose the road to wealth and fame. Others choose a road to poverty, although the road to poverty does not seem to be chosen. It seems as though circumstances that are beyond our control lead us down this path. What we are looking for is value. A way to bring meaning to our lives that transcends our own interpretation of life's meaning. When the road we travel leads us to unhappiness, it would be easy to point a finger at the reasons why this has happened. As I make my way down my own road, I begin to realize that the meaning I have given to the journey is all the value and meaning it ever had. The things I did like and the things I did not like were filled with my personal passion. Without this passion, I would be amiss to have these experiences in my life.

Physical passion

Passion, from a physical standpoint means that something has been learned from a physical experience that has taught me how to be passionate about being physical. A learning experience that brings passion is how we step away from our eternal associations and learn how to be physical. When we entered the physical realm we were spiritual beings having a physical experience. Up to that point, our passion was spiritual. Once our being begins to believe that the physical experience is real, we begin to believe we are the experience we are having. We now have passion about being physical, but this passion is upside down and time dependent. We now find ourselves in denial of our spirit and therefore in violation of our being. The passion must be reassigned and placed in a proper perspective so that the meaning that has been chosen for the physical experience does not conflict with the spirit or the being. Otherwise, I will continue to try to "do" something with my body so I can "be" what God created.

The Christ

Two thousand years ago, a man walked this earth. What made this man's life significant was something He introduced into time that had not been evident up until His Life and subsequent death. What He introduced was so profound, and often overlooked because it is misunderstood. We all now have the ability to tune into what He introduced into time. The time has come and we have been invited to a banquet. Because we have all been invited to this banquet, we are all invited to partake in the passion that was His. The passion of Christ was His Love. His Love was the gift He brought into time, and it was a part of The Plan of the restoration of humankind back into the fold of the rest of God's Creation that seemed to have been lost at the time of the separation of Adam and Eve from their Creator. So profound was this Love that it had the ability to transcend the death experience. Up until that point in time, this ability to Love as God had not been in this world. Up until this point, those on the physical plane only believed in the fear of God. Finally though the physical interpretation of God being a God of fear ended as God sent His Son into the world to save it out of Love. Up until that point in the history of the world, there was no hope of resurrection. It was as the Bible says; whatever you can do, do it with all your might, for there is no hope in the grave, the place where you are going. After the Christ all of that changed. A New Commandment was given. Christ said; "I am giving you a New Commandment, to Love one another. Think not that I came to add to the Law. I came to fulfill it."

In order for Him to fulfill prophecy, something had to come to an end and something new had to begin. The end of living by physical law ended. A new way opened for those who wished to understand God from the spiritual level began. A gateway between Heaven and Earth was open and the ability to understand and live by Spiritual Law began.

How powerful He must have been. How commanding was His Presence. Within Jesus was all of the Love of God contained and given to the world. One man was passionate enough to carry the Love of God from Heaven into time and give it to the world. Up until His life, this kind of Love had not been known in time. Up to this point, those who dwelled in the physical realm did not have a hope of a resurrection, but now, because of His Passion, a new way of experiencing Love was opened to those who were waiting for the promised seed. The promise was the promise of God's Love that transcended time and now that God's Love dwelled in time, hope a new kind of hope emerged in the world. Now the end of days would begin and the restoration of a spiritual paradise would begin. God would set up His Kingdom, but not the way man wanted it to happen. God has His Own Plan, but without His Love there would be no earthly passion for His Plan. It had to come to pass that the Christ would bring Heavenly Love into the physical realm to dwell in the heart of man.

So it is the passion of Christ that I look for in my own heart. This profound Love that transcends time and space is my journey. Without this passion I cannot achieve the same results that Christ did. Without this passion, I cannot express Love in the truest sense of the word. Without Love, all of my endeavors fall short of the promise of completion, because it is in His Love that I am complete.

The Puzzle

The Old Testament was given to the Children of Israel so they could understand a physical interpretation of the Spiritual Law that is known in Heaven. By using the Law in this way, they were able to come as close to a spiritual interpretation of God's Law as they could without actually having actual access to the Love of God. After the birth of Christ, all of this changed. Heaven entered the world and a shift slowly began. Slowly but surely, the Plan for the salvation of the world was put into motion. In Heaven, this took no time at all. In time it took 2000 years. Each innocent child born into time entered with a piece of Heaven buried deep within their heart. When their life was over, the puzzle piece that they came to give to the world remained. The pieces are all in place. It is time to put the puzzle together so a whole picture can emerge.

We are living in the time that the puzzle must be put together. The pieces of the puzzle must be gathered so a whole picture can emerge. It is only innocence that has the ability to attract Love but not love the way it is physically understood. Physical understanding of Love has made it partial, so it is based on a physical need to get instead of give. It is only with a physical perception that love could be mistaken for a limited ability. In order to move past this interpretation of it, everything physical must be set aside so a new understanding of Spiritual Love can emerge. This is done one step at a time.

I know that the Love that was in the Christ is also in me, but I have covered it with learned falsehoods that has hidden my innocence. I must learn how to uncover innocence so I can be recognized by God. It is my innocence that proves to the world that physical protection is unnecessary, for innocence has never been in danger. It is only in my guiltlessness that peace and harmony are restored to the world.

How many does it take to heal the world? It takes just one to have the recognition that they are totally innocent and without guilt of any kind. Our mission is to find this innocence and only this. When we entered the physical realm, the Heavens proclaimed our innocence, just like the Heavens proclaimed the innocence of Christ. The exact moment of our entry is recorded in the stars. The stars did not give us meaning, we came to give meaning to them. What we chose was written and planned and we have the ability to choose to see our own Plan if we choose to look. God did not send His Son into a world without a Plan. So specific is His Plan that each person has an Team of Advisors that is able to direct and lead individuals towards the ultimate goal of peace. God made sure that not one of His Creation would be lost. The map for each one is written in the Heavens and in the palm of a hand. The lessons are everywhere and they are lessons that when followed lead us to the piece of the puzzle that only we can supply.

The call

Do I have passion? Yes, but it does not always seem to be so. This physical experience has tried to steal my reality from me, but within my heart, Love still exists. Taking one step at a time will lead me to the ultimate goal of reaching my True Home. I am not alone. We are all in this together, and without your piece of the puzzle, I cannot fit my piece. We will only be joined through a realization that you are me and I am you. The anger and fear that I have learned in time are not real. They are stealing my joy, but I can change my mind. The greatest strength that we have is the ability to change our mind and make a new decision, but this decision is not made alone. It includes all of Heaven as it leans towards the world to save it. Would God let us make this kind of decision without His Help?

We are upon the Easter season. A time for realizing that true passion does not emanate from the body, but instead is given to us through grace. Thank You God for this realization. Thank You for Your Plan to bring about the salvation of the world.

Amen.

Day Seventeen

This morning when I awoke, my mind is whirling, for I am trying to bring peace back into my conflicted mind. The tragedy in Sri Lanka brings up feelings of hopelessness and deep sadness. I am trying to look past all of this to see something different, so I ask…what is it for? I am looking for purpose. Everything that happens must have a purpose, right? I know that there are many who believe that God is angry and is punishing those who live in the area. Some also take it as a warning from God, but I know that God is not responsible for this tragedy, so again I ask..what for?

I am reminded of a dream I had last summer. In the dream I am watching the ocean as it continually moves. I am aware of my thoughts, and as my thoughts turn to love the water turns a crystal blue. As my thoughts change to another emotion that does not support love, the water turns to a muddy brown. The dream is showing me that I am responsible for my thoughts, but I am responsible for something else. I know that I hold a certain responsibility for the movement of the ocean. My thoughts have a direct affect on the elements of water and so the physical ocean that is surrounding the globe. My own feelings of Love gives the ocean a beautiful calm to it that is represented by the color blue, but the muddy brown in the ocean represents other moods that are reflected by hopelessness and deep sadness. What is really there and is it possible that my inability to see true Love and happiness have an adverse affect on the physical ocean. If I choose peace, will it calm the ocean down or is it insane to believe that my thoughts really have this much power?

It is impossible to think without God. The impossibility of

hopelessness and sadness prove that it is indeed possible for me to use my mind without the constraints that are placed on it by Love. Why do I feel that something has been taken from me if I cannot access sadness and hopelessness? It is as if these feelings are something I really want, but that is insane. Is this what tragedy is for? To show me that the beliefs that I harbor within my physical awareness are giving a purpose to the world that is harming it? I then see the impossibility of the situation and I realize that correction is needed. Not where the symbol of the problem lies, but within my own mind, for it is here that the creative process originates. I don't want to believe that I am that powerful, for if I am then I will have to hold part of the responsibility for what I see in the world that I don't like.

It seems to be that cause and effect are outside of my mind, but if the cause is the tsunami, then I am at the mercy of outside forces that I have no possibility of controlling. My own individual consciousness that I have made that supports my belief system seems to be the only recourse I have in seeing the tragedy, but I am told no, this is not the case. There is another way of seeing this that has nothing to do with the tragedy.

This world was made to prove that it was possible to see something without God. That has been its only purpose. With this as purpose, the world is cause and the events that occur here bring meaning for the occupants. In other words, the experience is greater than God, or effect is greater than the cause, but God has given the world another purpose. This purpose is so the world cannot see apart from Him. Expression does not come from doing anything. It comes from Being a part of God. What would happen if I really knew that the seeming external elements of wind, ocean and fire were a part of the creative process that I have cast outside of myself. I have heard many times that if it was possible to harness the weather, then humankind could control the world. But if the weather is an outcome of thinking, it is an effect, not a cause. I have to go over this again and again in my mind. It is so easy to fall into the collective consciousness of humanity and just go along. The power of the mind is very strong, and up until this point in the evolutionary process, the collective consciousness has been focused on how to manipulate the external. It is very easy for me to slip back into this mode, for what the Interpreter has explained to me is beyond what is known in the world at this point, but it is going to change. The collective consciousness must shift from the ability to believe to the higher consciousness that has been put into place as a solution for the problems of the world. This transition will not be an easy one, for the law of inertia is in effect and once something has been moving in one direction for a long time, a sudden shift seems to make things worse.

Still, I am reminded that the Plan does not disrupt the forward motion. The law of inertia is not a physical law; it is a Law of Mind. Mind does not know how to go backwards, it can only move forward. My ideas of hopelessness and sadness must take on a different interpretation, or make a shift so that my thoughts are still moving in the same direction. It is just that the intention of my thoughts will have made an adjustment and I can "see" or understand this tragedy from another perception. This new perception would not be out of line with the Purpose of God, for His Purpose aligns everything and the new interpretation also has the ability to bring healing to what I see. This is the miracle, but in order to access this state, it is necessary for me to step away from what I think I know and let my own individual consciousness go.

If I speak of seeing the tragedy in another way, then I must "overlook" the tragedy, or forgive my error. If the tragedy is impossible, what is possible to see? Does God have the ability to restore what I believe has been lost, or does He see through me and then bring to me my reality? If this is so, then it is I who must see this crisis through the eyes of Love so hope can fill the land and my judgment of the sadness does not contribute to the situation.

Understanding is a Law of Mind. I don't want to understand tragedy, for if I do, my creative mind is working on the emotion that I have projected into the world, and this will re-create the past and more will suffer. The lesson is always; don't judge the experience. Forgiveness means to overlook. Overlooking tragedy seems unkind, but the fact is that looking at it inspires more tragedy. Instead, I can ask for a new interpretation that will help bring stability to the error.

So now, this brings up more conflict, for if I do not look at the experience, am I not supposed to do anything to help? The answer comes back; it doesn't matter what you do. The Laws you are learning govern your Being. If what you do conflicts with your Being, you will be led in a direction so the undoing of the situation can occur and the Being will be what is left. God doesn't care what I do. It is like the situation when Jesus was asked if taxes should be paid. He said, "give to Caesar what is Caesar's, but give to God what belongs to God." If my Being belongs to Him, then my doing nature must be brought into line so that doing does not conflict with Being, otherwise I will continue to "be" conflicted, and conflict adds to the problems that are prevalent in the world.

It seems that if I share the new way of perceiving, everyone will understand, but this is not the case. People look at me in a blank stare, and then remind me that I am deep. It seems pretty simple to me because truth is simple. Beliefs that hold relevance to fear of outside circumstances hold a powerful attraction, and I am tempted to look at the guilt I have projected onto the world again because no one wants to understand the way I do. Still, I remind myself again that this tragedy is impossible and attempt to look away towards my new perception even if no one understands what I am talking about. This is what has seemed to be the hardest; the blank stare that says, Cheril, you are crazy, but there are other times and I see the light go on and I know that a real moment has occurred and for just an instant I have become one with another in truth.

I want someone to understand my new perception, but am reminded that I am not in charge of the internal teaching process, the Interpreter is. My purpose is to help others find the Interpreter that dwells in their own mind. I know that I have been given the ability to lead the mind to the Interpreter, because I have done so on many occasions. I don't know how to perform a miracle, which leads to healing, but I am aware of how to reach out of time to the space where the Interpreter dwells. The Laws that govern Eternity are there.

It is impossible to engage the healing process if fear is present, for fear is not real and when I deal with reality, if fear is present I am never answered. I have noticed this when working with others. If they get to the place where healing can occur, if fear is present, the Interpreter will not respond to them. The first question I ask is if they are afraid. If the response is yes, then I ask them to put their fear aside so they can hear the answer they are looking for. The only thing that is needed for healing is lack of fear, and we are responsible for our own fear.

I have also found that in order to receive an answer, the question must be posed in a way that does not violate the Laws of God. In this world, we aren't too picky about what we think. There, every thought is considered a part of the whole, and thoughts that are being healed are returning to the eternal realm and are therefore under the scrutiny of Laws that are not recognized in time. I remember one dream that I had. I was amongst, what appeared to be a lot of people. I now realize they were higher spirits. I don't remember what was occurring, but all of a sudden I remembered the loss of my son. The grief overwhelmed me and I began to cry. Everyone and everything in the dream stopped. There was no motion anywhere and I realized my grief was affecting the whole. The dream was significant in that it explained the nature of wholeness and in that one instant I understood. I can imagine the impact of sadness being projected out into the world and expecting the world to cope with grief that never heals, for the mass of mankind expects time to deal with the grief and it has no idea how to accomplish this. Now that the world has been split apart by fear it must somehow cope. No wonder the ocean is rising up. It wants the form it is coming from to let go of the guilt, fear, sadness, and all of the things that mankind has been bereft at taking charge of. Because humankind, time, the ocean, the weather, or anything else in this world does not know how to handle the problem, it must come from the one who holds it, for purpose is established by the one giving purpose, not by an outside force. I do not believe that I have the ability to make my outside life such a mess, but truth is beyond belief, so I must move past my own belief into a new realm of possibility where my past beliefs hold no sway over my seeming reality. This new reality affords me the opportunity to see something else other than the mess I have made. This something else is the hope of the world that I am helping to create by not opposing the Plan that will heal the world. It is this I choose to see, not the tragedy that the world is looking at. Some call this looking through rose-colored glasses or denial, but whatever I see is what my reality will show me. It is to this I dedicate my purpose. It is to this I keep my agreements that were written on the heart before I came here. I am making a journey from the intellect to the heart, where I can remember the agreement.

What is a Spiritual Agreement?

In the physical realm, we take our written agreements very seriously. In fact, it is believed that a written agreement has more significance than one that is verbally agreed to. It hasn't always been this way, in fact it used to be that an agreement was reached verbally, and the verbal agreement was as valid as the one written on a piece of paper. By honoring a verbal agreement, we took responsibility was taken for the words spoken and even if, in the end, it was not in the best interest of one party to carry out his/her end of the agreement, once the words the words bound us to the agreement that was entered into. Words were the moral fiber of our character, and to break a verbal agreement was a violation of the character of the person making the agreement.

In this paper society, we have become less and less bound by verbal agreements and more dependent on paper agreements, it has gotten to the point that when we enter into contracts with anyone every i must be dotted and every t must be crossed. With all of this lack trust going on, it is difficult to know where truth lies. Paper contracts have become so detailed that the average person doesn't have a clue as to what it is they are signing. If the truth were known, it is impossible to cover every loop hole with signed contracts, for contracts are subject to other paper agreements and also to physical destruction. For every new thing mandated to prevent this from happening, a new way is found to cheat or deprive someone of what they have strived for all of their life. It is entirely possible that one can loose everything that has been worked for because of a paper loop hole, so the paper contracts or agreements really do not hold the security that is hoped for when they are signed. But society still dictates that these paper contracts and agreements be signed so that if there is a question, the question is hopefully answered in the terms of the contract or agreement. . The agreement then becomes a separate thing from us and we allow a piece of paper to decide what the terms of the agreement are. There is no responsibility on our part, except to follow the terms that are written on the paper. In essence, we are bound to the paper, not to the agreement. If there is a conflict regarding the paper agreement, lawyers are sought after and judgment is carried out in the legal system. This takes the responsibility off of the two parties that made the agreement and places the problem into the hands of those who have no investment in the agreement at all. This is not good or bad, except for the fact that the "heart" of the agreement was never even evaluated before, during or after the contract ended.

It seems that paper agreements are legal and binding while the agreements we speak in our heart do not have the same authority. However, in order to examine a spiritual agreement, another aspect must examined because spiritual agreements are not written on a piece of paper, they are written on the heart. Only God can read the heart. How many times have we heard this statement? If an agreement is made with the heart, and it then decided to break the agreement, can the agreement be broken without paying a penalty? While it is entirely possible to enter into an agreement without our heart involved, once we involve our heart, we have asked Heaven to enter into our agreement. The agreement is then considered more that just a contract or agreement, for now what has been entered into is something sacred. The sacred nature of the agreement or contract will continue to be in effect until the contract or agreement is brought to fruition or climax, so this kind of agreement must be carried through even though the consequences may not be understood at a physical level. God takes us at our word and when we make an agreement in our heart, and try to break this kind of agreement, we are actually attempting to break an agreement with God. God does not punish us for the mistake, but the mistake must be undone so the contract is fulfilled. Until it is, the price for not fulfilling the contract is fear. Words and deeds must resonate with each other, or a pattern of an inharmonious nature begins. This pattern is out of alignment with health and life, so the ultimate physical price is disease or death.

As an example, Adam and Eve paid the ultimate price for holding something in their heart that did not agree with what they were saying. This was the lie that violated their essence and set the world on a course of trying to live with external agreements. Once outside of Eden, their heart was no longer pure so agreements made in time without the heart involved became null and void or without life. The conflicted heart that was the outcome of not speaking the truth that was in their heart became the beginning of an era that was made without God, so they excused themselves from the Garden of Eden instead of making the correction that would have made their heart recognizable by God. This led their heart away from the truth and because God reads the heart, they could not fool Him with their words.

Our first responsibility is always to our heart, for this is the Home of God. God does not recognize the paper agreements that have been written in time, for they do not reflect His Laws. Fear of not living up to paper agreements gives the paper an authority that belongs to God. Paper agreements must make way for true commitments and communication between the word and the heart so Love can enter our agreements and our agreements become holy. Our paper agreements and contracts must reflect a new meaning if they are to continue. Everything in this physical world must be reinterpreted so it can reflect the Laws of God, not the laws that are a result of fear. Fearful agreements are not backed by the Laws of God, so they are a poor substitution for the true agreements that arise from a Loving heart.

Paper agreements without the heart involved will not hold up to the test of truth. The physical archives that hold paper agreements will be cast out of a position of authority to make way for the purpose of true agreements that emanate from the heart. Learning to let go of the paper society takes time to learn so it begins with a decision to learn how to make real agreements that do not fade with time. These kinds of agreements are written on the walls of Heaven, and what is written there has no end. The physical realm does not separate our heart from God. It seems as though this is possible because the connection seems to have been broken. It is not broken, because it is impossible to break what God has designed, but we can be looking in the wrong place for reality.

We will not find an end to the many afflictions that are occurring in the world until we learn to align our words with our hearts desire. The Home of God lies in the heart, which is our journey Home. What kind of a home have we made for Him? If it is not pure, we run from Him and put up blocks so He cannot hear us and for the same reason, we cannot hear Him. We cannot break our spiritual agreements, even though we can have a temporary lapse in memory because of the block that has been temporarily made. The restoration of the Garden, or the place that is alive in our heart is still holy because there is a spark there that belongs to Love. If it were possible to accomplish this, then the end of the world would be apparent.

Before we can live up to the agreements we make in time, we must first learn how to make agreements with the heart so our words will have meaning. This meaning is the new interpretation that leads to sanity instead of a paper chase. This decision opens doors to new understanding, which the world is in desperate need of. It is impossible to teach or learn this alone. It all begins with a decision to learn something new by learning how to honor our heart agreements.

Day Eighteen

This world is in peril. At no other time in the history of the world has there been a point when it was possible to destroy the world and all of its occupants in so many different ways. I could go on and on about the problems that are plaguing the world, and what I "believe" the solutions are, but the solutions that come from my beliefs will undoubtedly conflict with someone else's and another conflict will emerge. The alternative to this is to protect the truth, but first I have to understand what the truth is. The way to understand the truth is to let go of what I believe it to be, but because my beliefs are very strong, escape seems impossible. The realization of this came one day as anger entered my mind. I did not want to be angry, but the harder I tried to resolve the anger, the greater the anger became. I thought I was in control of my life, but here I was with this feeling of anger and also the perceived explanation for it. I began to think that the explanation was correct so I was justified in how I felt. It was difficult to turn away from the strong feelings of anger and then towards something else, because there seemed to be nothing else except my anger. Hmmm...so if I am learning that I am in control of my life, how can something that someone else does bring about inner feelings of anger and how can I restore peace to my mind? I don't want to sacrifice myself for the seeming unkindness or attack of another, and yet I see no way out except admitting my own guilt, but I don't feel guilty, I feel like I have been attacked and my anger is a defense mechanism. Swallowing my anger seems to answer the call to forgiveness that I have been taught, but that doesn't seem fair. There has to be something else that offers a different solution, but I really don't want to look because I want to be right and I want the other person to be wrong.

Somewhere in my mind I am sure that salvation is fair to all concerned. So I will return to my learning. My mind will not fight me on a decision to find the reason for my anger, so I will engage my mind for assistance rather than trying to fight it for position.

First, I know that my thoughts are fueled by my emotion, so the next logical question would be; how could a thought be tied up with an emotion of anger. The next question would be; have I ever felt this way before? The mind's memory does not separate its thoughts from the emotion of the event, so the symbol of the experience may change, but the memory of the emotion that holds the original event does not. If I have felt this way before, then the past is merely being replayed. If I do not break out of this pattern, then I will consistently be reliving the past when an experience emerges that reminds my mind of a past event learned in error. Whenever something occurs that is like the original event, I will once again feel the attraction of the strong unhealthy emotion that occurred at the onslaught of the problem.

Once I have established that I have felt this way before, I can begin to look for the original event that turned my innocent loving nature into anger, or at times a raving maniac. While I am attempting to locate the experience that defines the anger, I can ask to be placed under the Protection of a Higher Authority that has the ability to prevent my words and my anger from creating destructively, for anger and words together begin to create. In this case, because they are destructive, I will feel the effects of what I am thinking and feeling. Alone, my thoughts would not have a tremendous impact on the state of the world, but if all of the destructive thoughts of the billions of people in the world are taken into consideration, a terrible destructive force emerges. Such is the power of the mind. However, I have also been given the ability to change my mind.

My decision to change my mind opens an investigative process that invites in a team of Advisors from the eternal realm that will see to it that the best way to find the error becomes evident to my mind. I must be a "willing" participant in the process. This brings my free will back into play, for my will is only free when it is not harnessed to a physical experience that has taught me how to be an error instead of Love. Whatever I give, I will receive. If I give anger, then I will receive it. If I give judgment, then I will receive it. If I want to turn this around, then I will have to seek for new alternatives that will show me how the error has occurred in my thinking process. The investigation may bring immediate results, or it may take some time before all of the fragment of anger are brought into play that I now believe is real. Reality does not come from me, it comes from a greater Source, so when I am angry I am creating an inharmonious environment that breeds disease. When I am angry, one thought leads to another, which then leads to another, and so on. The investigation begins a process that will make sure all of the components of anger that I have collected and stored in my self awareness that relates to this particular anger are brought together under a symbolic umbrella before total healing occurs. Healing must be complete or it does not occur at all. This concept has been a tough concept to understand, because I have discovered reasons for anger without achieving a healing. I have also been aware of when the healing was complete and I even physically felt lighter. I have noticed this also with clients. They tell me that they feel like something has gone from their body. This is the illusion of; in this case, anger totally leaving the inner awareness of the body, leaving it clean so something new can enter. The first time this happened, I thought, "wow! That was amazing." Because the Advisors are very thorough, they make sure there is not one scrap of evidence left of the original anger. This insures that there are no destructive fragments left to cause destruction. This is total healing and is usually what takes time. When I first started doing this, many of the affects were immediate and sometimes startling. After awhile, the self beliefs in my mind began to "catch on" to my healing techniques, so I had to devise new ways. Eventually I found that as long as I moved beyond the form of any problem, or the physical interpretation of what was going on, and into the psychological realm, false beliefs did not understand the language of my questions. This takes time to learn because at a physical level we believe the problems we encounter are physical and do not originate within our own mind.

I was not created to lie or be deceitful, so if I am then I have learned how to do something that is not in harmony with my true nature. It is this that makes me sick and leads to eventual death. My true nature follows the Laws of Life, but when I am not in harmony with this Law, I have learned something in error. The error lies in my physical thought system that believes it is possible to have feelings, such as anger, concerning people or events. These are outer conditions and try to destroy the inner conditions of peace. Even though my beliefs that try to convince me my anger is real because they can hear my internal questioning, I learned to be privy to their tricks. Now I can move around the deceit and access the Investigative Advisors, and as long as I understood my own question, I can begin to find real answers. This has taught me that there is a difference in language of the mind/body, which points an angry finger by projecting it at someone or something else. This state of mind can only be achieved by making a decision to abandon anger, or anything else that stands in the way of truth. I really am in need of nothing but the truth. The unrelenting chatter of a belief working on an emotional problem that is held in the body that is continually giving me external reasons for the problem does not have any ground to stand on when it is not listened to at this higher state of mind. I have learned that I am a psychological being, not a physical one. The physical part of myself is having the experience, but if I experience anger I am in error and correction must occur. The ongoing process of healing seems to be unending, for every one thing I heal, something else arrives to take its place. I got a little picture once. It was a mouse shoveling manure. The caption read: I can't believe I have sown all of this shit I am reaping. That pretty well sums it up for me. My physical experience has been learned in error for it has violated my spiritual expression. The new experience that is being offered to the world is the spiritual one that is a direct contrast to the physical one. It doesn't seem so at first because it seems like such a small error, but it is like filling out a check book. An error made at the beginning, even a penny, makes all of the rest of the figures in error that follow. This is why all of the problem must be followed to the original error. This way healing is complete.

For every healing that occurs, it seems as though the need for another one shows up. The healings that seemed easy in the beginning are not so easy anymore. Some arose and it seemed to me that there could not possibly be a solution for, but I was wrong. There is a solution to everything, but the solution is never a physical one.

You always receive what you ask for. The old saying that you will never get enough of what you don't want, began to take on new meaning. I finally understood what this meant. Once the creative process is started, it recreates what is known over and over. The creative elements lie in the thinking process and once an error enters it becomes the belief system. What I learned in error showed up over and over again. I didn't have to "do" anything. There was no visualization or affirmations. There was just a decision that I did not remember making, so the solution was to find the destructive decision so that it could be corrected.

Appreciation is not a physical attribute and because appreciation is necessary to heal, I would try to fake it, but the Higher Realm is not fooled, and faking appreciation did not cut it The Higher Realm can see what the error is, even if I can't. Trying to trick myself into believing I already had achieved something that I hadn't didn't work. I tried it because I read it somewhere that it would.

If the world is evolving, the old solutions, or the old way of getting a result will not work either. I think that this is what spirituality is up against. The world is being flooded with new information that will help the world and its occupants through the turbulent time ahead. It is not difficult to change because change is immediate; it is the process of change that is difficult. It is not because we do not want to change; it is because we do not how, so we rely on what we have learned in the past. The problem is that it doesn't work anymore. Insanity is doing something over and over again in the same way and expecting different results. It's time to take the next step. The violent shifts in the weather and in the earth are signs that change is eminent. The past must be brought up to the present, otherwise the change will produce effects that will force the world to change and the consequences will be more than just a little alarming. We are not being punished for "past karma."

We are here to straighten out past karma, but we have gotten entangled in the mess and have forgotten the mission. This is why we have been given the ability to reach a state of peace and also have been given the Interpreter. Otherwise we would never be able to see past the "sin" of the beliefs that originated in time.

Emissaries that are sent to other countries are not responsible for problems that are occurring; but they are responsible for seeking ways to bring about a new understanding, which will ultimately end in peace. This is why I am here, this is why we are all here. To get involved in the politics and the beliefs of the world that conflict is not my responsibility. My responsibility is to perform the function I was sent here to perform. I cannot learn this by studying the problem. Only the solution will bring about a lasting peace that will heal humankind as well as the world. The world doesn't need another band-aid. It needs real Help that is not known in time. If humankind had the answer, wouldn't the world be at peace by now?

It seems like there should be something I can do to change the world. The desire to do something is great and I still do things that I believe will help…there is that word again…believe. All of the beliefs in the world will not succeed unless they are backed up by the Laws of God. It is the Interpreter that is needed to change the belief from impossibility to possibility. The belief would have me continually look outside of myself for a solution. Over and over again I have tried this, and it never works. The continual…try this…try this…is the endless chatter that has led me on a journey that has taken me nowhere. Now I realize that I must turn to the state of peace "ask." Ask and you shall receive. I thought I was supposed to ask for things though. Spiritual Law does not give blessings in things. Physical things are a symbolic expression of the blessing, not the blessing itself. The real blessing is the change in perception. The mistaken perception sees the material symbol and then "believes" what it is seeing is the blessing. It is still the result. Beliefs do not have access to this kind of ability to change, but I do. This has been the lesson and the only lesson. Truth is true and nothing else matters. Trying to rely on the physical aspect of the blessing has not brought me truth. In fact it has led me away from it.

Still, beliefs are very powerful, and what they look at, I look at also. The way to change this is to introduce a new way of looking, or a new perception. .

Memories of the past about the physical experience have kept me trapped in the unreality of time, but I am sure I have finally broken through to another reality that has nothing to do with time. In fact, I am beginning to learn how not to rely on time at all. Of course, I still have appointments to keep, and I keep those, but as far as my sleeping patterns go, I sleep when I am tired, get up when I wake up and eat when I am hungry. I am learning how to access my spiritual cycle that lies in peace, and is not dictated by time. Will the effects of time subside…only time will tell…ha!

The Forgotten Choice

With all of the things happening in the world, in our own lives and those that we love, we are questioning the ability of those in positions of authority to make practical decisions that will bring an end to the turmoil we now experience in the world. We are the ones that occupy this world, and because we see that what world authorities offer, as solutions to the entanglement or problems of the world, are not working it is time we seek another solution. We want a solution that works, not only for ourselves, but also for our children and grandchildren. We are not ready to give up on the world, so we find ourselves seeking for something that offers to move us beyond the solutions that have been handed down from one generation to another.

Religion has also offered solutions for many centuries, but even religion does not give an absolute solution. A solution looked at from one angle, brings another problem from another angle, so we seem to be at a crossroad with nowhere to go. It may be that we had to get to this point before we could accept something that is so radical, that it seems too difficult a road to follow, except that it is the only one that is available, and it is also the direction that we can and must take. We have heard that for every problem there is a solution, so if there is a solution, what is it?

Radical change does not necessarily have to be destructive. Einstein, Martin Luther King and Edison, to name a few, were radical thinkers. They chose a road to travel down that was not widely known, but once traveled down the direction of the world changed and life was never viewed the same. We need radical thinking to introduce something into the world that is stable enough to upset the balance of instability, for unstable thinking has become the norm.

There is a choice that we all can make that has nothing to do with what we know. It does not seem as though this choice would make much of a difference, but because the information is so radical, it will upset the balance of the world and move it into the direction of health, or healthy thinking. This healthy thinking begins at an individual level and moves outward to affect every living thing. This choice is one that is not well known or accepted at this point, but because of the ability of this forgotten choice, it can and will change everything as we know it now. This choice that we are being asked to make is to discover an essential part of our self that has nothing at all to do with being physical. It has the ability to move us beyond the boundaries of time and introduce into our lives a sense of harmony that has not been known since time began. It involves learning about miracles and how to make one happen in individual lives and how to make it happen for another. Only miracles can move beyond the boundaries that man has placed upon the physical realm, because miracles do not follow the laws of time. Instead, they follow Higher Laws that have the ability to transcend ethnic background, race, religion, creed, political differences or any problems that seem to be insurmountable. They can do this because they use whatever means are necessary to heal. Miracles do not see what humanity has made holy and so considers a violation to use for healing. Therefore, miracles do not hold false purpose and have the ability to see to a real purpose. They have the ability to look past a problem, and bring it to resolution. They do not go where they are not wanted. They have the ability to heal anything that they touch, and wait until a person or situation is open to a new solution, so they do not intrude and only come when they are welcomed. Each miracle offered to the world becomes our strength, because it is held within the peace of our own mind that learns to become unshakable. Learning miracles teaches us that when there is no conflict or unhappiness in our own mind, then there will be none in the world. We have the ability of changing the world simply by making a choice that seems too radical to work and too simple to make a difference, but the decision to use a miracle must be made at an individual level for the miracle to begin to work.

Only miracles have the ability to unite us with our spiritual nature, and bring innocence back into a world that is sorely lacking in this condition, but we are the ones that have to turn in the direction of the Help that is being offered to us. There is a book that offers us a different course of action other than the one that has been chosen. This book is A Course in Miracles. Upon first examination, the book seems to be too difficult to understand. When we choose not to understand it is because the information presented is not the way we are used to learning. It is a radical way of teaching, so it is a radical way of learning. However, when what is being taught is understood, the information in the Course is simple and offers hope to humanity. In fact, it offers *the only* hope to humanity. The Course says it is a required that everyone study the information found in therein, however when we take it is up to us. The truth is that the sooner we take it, the sooner the problems in our lives and in the world will dissipate.

Day Nineteen

So, today I will think about prayer and how to use it properly. I know this information does not come from what I know about prayer, so I will have to reach to something greater than myself in order to understand just what prayer is for. I have learned that as I write, I am drawing down more thoughts of truth and wisdom into my awareness from this Source. I know that these thoughts do not spring from my own belief system, because they are new to me and they introduce new insight into the new state I am attempting to attain. Now, if they would only stay there and my mind wouldn't flop back to what I believe I already know about prayer. I am working on re-training my mind to follow another system of thought that is unlimited in potential, but my limited beliefs continue to blab on. I know that prayer is very powerful and has the ability to awaken potential in others. True prayers are to be shared with all of the world, so the are supposed to be released into the world to add to the healing of the world.

I have had many insights and have not written them down. This is why journaling is important. Wisdom is not stored in the body; it is in constant movement in the Higher Mind and is shared with whoever is listening, open, and ready to hear. This is the true communication process and has nothing to do with physical language. Physical language however, can enhance the ability to learn the internal communication process. The desire to take the first step towards listening is all that is required. After that, everything is given. This includes the seeming coincidences that bring into focus the next step in the journey of learning to hear the internal communication process.

The desire to hear is shown by a decision to make an effort to move beyond what one believes one already knows.

Because wisdom is in constant movement, wisdom is not a physical experience meant for personal enjoyment, however it is intensely personal when it occurs. Because wisdom such as this is not a personal memory, then it is a memory that is shared with God. This being the case, then the memory brings new insight. At an individual level we may think that it is one's own personal information, but the truth is; it belongs to all of creation. New information that springs from the wisdom of the universe was never meant to have a physical patent, for once it does it is mandated by a physical interpretation, which limits it. It also has acquired restraints as the universal memory takes on a physical representation of ownership. Basically, it is impossible to "own" a universal memory, but our physical court system believes it is possible to "own" what in reality should be free. This blocks the creative potential from expanding and following the natural Law of completion. Completion is not found on a piece of paper nor in the physical courts. It is difficult to know what a person's intention is when a memory such as this is captured. One may try to use the memory for monetary gain first, while another wishes to share the memory and the money is second to the actual creative process and idea of sharing. Sharing completes the memory, while looking for completion in money prevents the creative process from expanding and being completed. It is entirely possible to make the world a place where our thoughts can be completed through the true creative process, which is inspired by God, instead of relying on beliefs that never shut up about what I can gotten by using physical law to try to harness wisdom. This is how it works at a higher level. Mind chatter just does not exist there. This is where the end of time exists, for voices that add to chatter always want an explanation. On the other hand, the end of time shows that all questions have been answered and there is only peace, so this is the peace that passes understanding.

Prayer is a way of interrupting time based beliefs by introducing peace. This is how it is possible to step out of memories of time and the endless chatter of these memories. Prayer is intercessory in that another thought is exchanged for a belief. I may not always understand what has been exchanged, because I am not sure exactly how prayer works. If I did, I probably wouldn't need it. Prayer can help find an unselected memory that is higher and not contained in the beliefs of the past. The outcome is not necessarily the miracle, because the miracle itself was made specifically to change perception. The end of miracles signals the end of time, for the miracle was made specifically to heal time. Miracles are the next evolutionary shift that will, and in fact is, occurring now and changing the world from conflict and war to peace. For every thing that we made in time, God made something better, and this is what the miracle is for. To undo what has been physically made in error. What is *made* in Heaven is not forever, but instead is used to help humankind with what it has made in error. What has been created in Heaven is forever. Eventually the world becomes a part of the eternal realm as the world learns to a place that reflects all of the Laws of Heaven. This is the last judgment of God. God does not lie, and His Statement…and He saw that what He Created was Good…must be brought into line with His understanding of Goodness, not ours. The fall, or the separation, made it necessary to introduce new means for humankind to reach God. Prayer is one of the means. The world has been given many means in order to establish the end of time and also known as the end of days, which is the Will of God. Much of this is not understood as yet in this world, and because time is still seen as having some kind of creative ability, the occupants are accustomed to using prayer as a medium of help in the physical realm to help with some time based event. Prayer is to help us understand that what has been perceived in time is incorrect and even though this is not understood, prayer has the ability to give another reality to the problem, even if we do not understand what this is or means. It is not necessary for us to understand, for prayer is beyond a time based understanding. We do have beliefs that know of the value of prayer, but because of an inability to access the Light, do not understand how it works. Because I am attached to the Light, I can access prayer and give another meaning to the beliefs that do not understand. This is in line with the statement Jesus made; 'Blessed are those that have not seen and yet believe." I thought this was referring to people, but it was actually referring to the belief system. There is still much I do not understand about the process, but I am learning.

The application of prayer is different now than it was in the days of the Old Testament. In the days of the Old Testament, only a select few could "tune into" the Language being spoken in eternity. These were the prophets, and even then, the prophet did not necessarily understand the meaning of what was being explained or saw and just recorded it. In the days of the Old Testament, consciousness was purely physical and fear was used to explain God. Therefore, consciousness was self understood and did not come from wholeness. People of the Old Testament understood that prayer worked, but they did not necessarily understand how. We now have the ability to understand the means of prayer and use it to a greater benefit, so it serves humankind to learn how to use it correctly by not offering up just what they want to offer.

After the Birth of the Christ a new way of understanding God was introduced into time. His purpose was to introduce Spiritual Love into time. Thus, the new Consciousness was born, which is commonly called the Christ Consciousness in the Western world. Prayer took on a new meaning because it was now possible to connect with the new Consciousness that had been introduced into the world. When this Consciousness is accessed it is possible to listen to the Language of Heaven that is being spoken, thus new ideas fill the world with Love. Before the Life of the Christ, this ability was only open to a select few. Now this ability is open to anyone. God is not partial, so it really doesn't matter if you're called a Christian or a Muslim or anything else. Higher Consciousness is not necessarily recognized by a religious mind. Instead it is recognized by the desire for righteousness, so the Higher Mind seeks for those who truly wish to understand righteousness, not man's righteousness, but God's. Righteousness is the desire to live by the Laws of God. These Laws are not explained by a physical interpretation or a religions idea of Spiritual Law. Instead they come through a heart felt desire to learn truth at an individual level. Prayer thus became a medium by which Spiritual Love could and can enter and heal a problem without a total physical understanding.

We call this a miracle, but as yet the world just does not understand how a miracle works. So now the question arises, what is a medium?

A medium is one who explains. Our idea of medium is different from a spiritual one. Everything is thought in the eternal realm, and everything contains spirit. Laws are also thought, so they inspire more thought and then shared with all of Creation. This is why These Laws are referred to Living Laws and are recorded in the Book of Life. What is in the Book of Life must be a part of the Light, and it is Light that gives life. So the spirit or life of the prayer is matched to the spirit of the one praying, which is found in the heart. If the spirit of the one asking is sincere, and it is out of line with the Laws of God, then it must be brought into line with His Laws so the prayer can be answered. The more an individual understands about the Laws, the greater is the responsibility to make an alignment with these Laws. This why the individual's intention in the heart is important. The Home of God is in the heart, so if the Laws of God are violated, then God cannot fulfill the purpose or the request of the heart, but there are provisions that have been made. If on the other hand, the one making the request cannot align his mind with the Laws of God, or heal the violation in the heart, the Christ Consciousness can temporarily provide the means until the Law is learned correctly by the one making the prayer request. This is not healing, but it is a way to obtain Help until the mistake is corrected. I can tell the difference because once a healing has occurred, there is no fear. If I am making a request, and the issue still brings up fear, then I need a miracle or a change of perception to restore my mind to sanity or Love. I am still responsible for my fear though. One way I have found to move around body fear is by distracting my mind by steering it away from the fearful issue. By going to the movies, singing a song, reading, or doing something I enjoy. I find when my mind does not focus on what I do not want, or a fearful outcome, a level of peace returns. This allows the Christ Consciousness to do what I cannot do for myself. This is also called the Atonement. I have had experiences that defy explanation using this. I have also experienced what I did not want by using fear as a source of a false prayer. Making a request in a fear state will not bring about the Help that is needed. This is because fear is not real, and reality can only deal with real states, so the first requirement of prayer is to restore a state of peace to the mind. It would be like trying to physically visit the state of Rocky Road. Well, the physical state of Rocky Road does not exist, so it is impossible to go there. This is the same in the Higher Realm with the state of fear. It doesn't exist, so it is impossible for Higher Help to go there. Learning to move around fear does not mean that I am the determiner of what happens next. Because there is a Whole Plan going on, what I have asked for must fit into this Plan element without disrupting it. I didn't understand this either and when my plan did not work out it was because it was in contrast to the Whole Plan that is going on to restore the world to righteousness. Even at this, I still carry beliefs that insist that know the way without this Higher Consciousness. Thus, I must make a correction or find where one has to be made. I have heard over and over again: the Plan is not of you.

Fear cannot lead anyone out of a difficult situation. Fear's purpose is terror and to hide. Hmmm…kind of reminds me of what terrorists do. So it is not possible to vanquish fear or terror through attack or defense. The only possible resolution is to replace fear in the mind with something else. Fear is pretty stupid, so it is easily distracted. If fear were real, it would be real for everyone, but because not everyone carries the same fear, it is not real.

Learning brings up many questions. Ask and you will receive is the only answer I hear. When it is appropriate for me to hear, I will and not before. I really wanted to cram it all in and get it over with, but the schedule for learning was not on a time schedule, or at the mercy of beliefs that wanted to know before it was necessary. I wanted to go from A to Z without learning the rest of the alphabet. I used to have a dream that I had lost my watch. The dream was so vivid, I would wake up and look for it and realize that it was not lost at all. These incidents were a call for me to live up to the Sacred Agreement that I agreed to. Eventually it was explained to me that I was "losing time" and I needed to get on with it. I did not understand this for many years.

There is another kind of prayer where God is directly reached. This kind of prayer is indicated by a profound sense of peace and is called revelation. Those who achieve this often comment on the peace that has accompanied the feeling that one just knows everything is all right and no further action is necessary. This happens when an individual has reached completion through God or Love. This defies any rational explanation because all physical evidence proves otherwise. It is truly the peace that passes understanding. This is customarily called a miracle when someone is suddenly cured of an incurable disease. But miracles do not cure disease, the correct application of the mind does. A miracle is not needed when God deals directly with His Creation directly, for completion is not miraculous, it just is.

So prayer is a way of allowing a Medium, or the Internal Guide, or Higher Consciousness, to take over until it is time to hear the correct solution or new perception. As long as I stay within the confines of the measures that have been provided by prayer, I am safe. Trying to dictate to the Medium or pray out of fear, will terminate the protection that prayer offers. The more I use prayer, the more I understand the potential because I am learning how to access the process that has been made to heal the world. Prayer is truly a blessing.

How to use Prayer

We live in a time when people are reaching out to their spiritual nature. People want to find their own way and receive their own answers to questions. No longer do we seem to be satisfied accepting another's interpretation of how to live our lives; but still it all seems like a big mystery, for reaching the nature of the spirit does not seem to have any clear cut answers. The question of how to find our own spiritual answers and how to be sure we are really being heard by the Powers that Be? Praying seems like a logical choice when problems arise, but how do we use prayer to its greatest benefit and how do we know if it is working?

When Jesus walked the earth, He set forth an example when He was asked how to pray by His Disciples. We recognize this example as The

Lords Prayer. In the Lords Prayer, in the first sentence we are informed that there is another realm that is not physical, for it says; "Our Father, which art in Heaven". This first sentence teaches us that it is possible to reach out of what is known, or the physical world, to another aspect of ourselves that we have grown unaccustomed to accessing. It is here that the Laws of God abide and these Laws have the ability to override any physical laws that govern our seeming problems. Physical laws seem to constrain us and keep us in turmoil when we keep searching the physical experience for answers, and there are none to be found. In the first sentence we have entered into a mode that forces us to reach beyond our physical understanding to another one that is governed by Laws that are unseen by the human eye. Obviously, if reaching beyond our own understanding of a problem does not bring results, then it would be useless to reach to that realm. We are seeking a place within where we know that we can receive another solution that will bring us peace. Heaven knows something we do not, so we are asking that we be shown a new perspective regarding a situation we are in.

Because we live in a society that demands that we always have an answer to everything, we have learned how to answer questions even if the answer is not the right one, so it may be that when we approach prayer we believe we already know what the answer should be. If this is the case, then it would be useless to ask for help if we already know. In the realm of prayer, we ask the question, and the answer is given, but not according to what we believe the answer should be. If we do not hear the answer it is because we are listening for the wrong answer. This is therefore out of line with the proper way to approach prayer, for prayer to be answered; we must be free of all of our own ideas of what the answer is, otherwise we will not hear as our attention will be focused on the answer we expect to get. The first part of the Lord's Prayer shows us that in order to move beyond our problem, we must accept a different interpretation of both the problem and the solution, for Heaven's interpretation of our problem is different than our own. If we were an expert in a chosen field, and someone asked us a question regarding our expertise, and when we gave the answer this individual argued with our answer, wouldn't we just allow them to go ahead and do it their own way? It is our own perception that is in error, so how could a perception in error have the correct solution? The problem and the solution must be brought into line so we can first understand our own question. Once we understand our question, the answer is evident. When we ask, we must cooperate with the answer before anything be achieved, so without the problem and the solution being viewed as the same, nothing will occur. In order to hear the answer to our prayer, we must let go of it and trust that there is an answer and be willing to hear whatever that answer is. This is the difficult part of prayer, for if we think we already know, we are already in error before we begin and are not likely to hear the solution.

Prayer is a form of adjustment that is made in our thinking process. When we want something in our physical life to be fixed, it is because we believe the problem exists eternally, or in time. It is impossible to ask the higher realm to solve problems in the same manner that we do physically. The higher realm is dealing with the Laws of Being, not the laws of doing, so if we are expecting to hear what we should do, we will not hear what we need to hear to make the correction. If problems could be solved from a physical level, wouldn't we have already done that? Prayer is a way of asking for a different approach to problem solving. This is the perfect way, and the more we stay out of the way the better the outcome will be. Asking correctly brings an expert to interpret our problem and solution to us. To add our own two cents is to give the solution a new meaning.

"Thy Kingdom come, Thy Will be done on earth as it is in Heaven." This part of the prayer is telling us that God has a Kingdom. Our interpretation of a kingdom is far different than the Kingdom that this prayer is speaking of. Christ said that His Kingdom was no part of this world. Being no part of this world means just that. He has no need of cleansing the world of problems, if He already has a Kingdom. We are being invited to join His Kingdom where His Will is done and can be seen from another perspective. If our questioning mind is in error, then what we see is in error also. Prayer helps correct our perception of the error so we can see what is really there. What is really there *is His Kingdom,* and our asking sets our mind on the same wave length to see what He can see or understand. While our self awareness is limited, His is not. His awareness is unlimited, and this being the case, He has the ability to bring a new Kingdom by changing our limited awareness to an unlimited one. Changing the world is useless, for the Kingdom of God is within and not a part of this world at all. Self direction is not necessary to reach unlimited potential, in fact it is where adjustment must occur, and this is what prayer is for. When we ask for His Kingdom to come, we are asking for the will of the Higher Consciousness to direct the unlimited potential of God. This unlimited potential understands only solutions, but as explained before, we must understand our own question is not a physical question, so its form must be re-interpreted. Being willing to have this happen shifts the alignment from a physical consciousness to a spiritual one. This shift is the answer, for as soon as the problem is seen from a different perspective the solution is evident.

"Give us this day our daily bread and forgive us our trespasses as we forgive those who trespass against us". We may assume that we are asking for physical sustenance when we ask for our daily bread, but The Lord's Prayer is a spiritual prayer that aligns our mind with the Christ Consciousness, which then has the ability to direct whole awareness. Because we understand eating at a physical level means nourishing the body, to ask for our spiritual daily bread means that we are asking for spiritual nourishment that can sustain us through seeming stormy weather. Spiritual nourishment shows us how we have used our own beliefs to trespass against another, and how these beliefs are keeping us locked into the error. This opens the way to forgiveness, for without forgiveness we cannot understand the transgression. Forgiveness is Heaven's Justice meted out in time. Forgiveness gives the part of the mind that believed in error back to God. With no more error, the problem that was perceived at the physical level is now gone.

Understanding the real transgression shows us that we are still innocent, and are regarded as such by God. Because we are innocent of our seeming transgressions, everyone else is also. Forgiveness wipes the slate clean and because no one is guilty, the world is free of guilt also. Removing the transgression that weighs heavily on the mind shows us the relationship of all life, and we begin to understand that there are Laws that uphold the universe that have nothing to do with the way we physically understand law.. These Spiritual Laws are our sustenance and these Laws are the Laws of life that were created for all, not for just a chosen few.

"Lead us not into temptation, but deliver us from evil," becomes, help me to see what is real. Temptation is an attempt to see outside of the Laws of God. It is a wish to make something real that God did not create as a part of reality. In truth, it is impossible to see beyond the Laws of God, but when we began to learn the laws that uphold time or guilt, we began to believe it was possible to see without God. This part of the prayer asks that our mind be aligned so we can once again see with God. Being able to see what God does restores us to an innocent state. Because God protects His Innocence, once we accept our own innocence, we are under the Law of Protection.

"Deliver us from evil" means that we have tried to build a reality without God by using false beliefs to think without God or His Laws, and so have made a fearful life. Because our memories have become distorted by a physical experience we are afraid of what we have made, and it will now somehow attack and harm us. In our true state, we are all one so it is literally impossible to move away from our own condemnation of another. "For Yours is the Kingdom and the Power and the Glory forever." Here we are acknowledging that God has given us the ability to tune into all power and glory, thus magnifying our true memories once we learn how to rely on a power and glory that is greater than our own. When we make this the end to our prayer we acknowledge that only God has the Authority to decide what is real. We also acknowledge that only His Power has the ability to give life.

When we pray and do not believe we receive an answer it is because we are blocking truth from entering. If we want truth to enter then we have to be willing to give up our idea of what the truth is. On the surface this seems to be easy, but we have made a lifetime of deceit based upon learned false experiences that have nothing to do with our reality.

The time has come for us to understand and communicate with the Language of the Kingdom. We do this by learning how to reach beyond our own understanding to the Plan that God devised to bring the world the way we think we understand it to the real interpretation of it. When we say the Lord's Prayer we are acknowledging that we do not know what reality is. It is this recognition that must occur by the one offering up the prayer. Prayer is not a mindless game; it is a request that we see beyond our own self restrictions to the wonder of the Lord. The new way of understanding prayer shows us that our prayers have already been answered. They were answered before the question was asked. Our responsibility is to learn how to tune into the solution that is already there.

Day Twenty

This morning I awoke and began thinking about the protection that has been provided for me and humanity as well, to help pass through this turbulent time. Protection was never needed before the separation. It seems that the world is confused about the difference between protect and defend. If there is anything that I have learned, it is that the meanings of words are very important at a higher level. Definitions must be specific in order for me to understand exactly what it is I am asking. In the physical realm, most of humanity has become very sloppy with their language and have lost respect for the communication process. In order to access Help from the eternal realm, I must learn what I am really saying because how I communicate is extremely important in eternity. Because nothing is unintentional or without purpose in eternity, if I want to tune into the communication of this Higher Realm, I must value what I am saying and how I am saying it. This is not to say that what I say will not be misinterpreted in the physical realm. This is because all meaning of communication and understanding is not physical, it is spiritual. Learning the spiritual communication process has left me open many times to being misinterpreted physically. Spiritual misinterpretation, which is also mis or missed communication, is experienced consistently in time. In time, many words are just tossed about without intent or purpose, but learning the creative potential of words begins a new respect for any language, for the creative potential lies in the spoken word.

I am learning my first line of protection is my ability to converse, so I really understand what it is I am saying. I do not understand my true nature, and because most of my true nature rests on the communication process, I will have to step away from my determined mode of understanding of the words I speak. At the creative level, all words create because of the intention behind them. The intention that supports words are emotion, and thought. Words are the fire in the creative process. Words that are flung around in time do not support a constructive intention and dissolve into physical elements, so they support a destructive intention, which is then played out as the seeming natural forces that humankind does not believe he has any authority over. Without understanding the potential of my own words, I will leave myself open to what I give, for what I give I will receive. Intention asks the question…what is it for, or what is the purpose? Purpose is part of the creative process and if I do not understand this, I will experience the effects of my misunderstanding. It is like speeding; if I don't know what the speed limit is…"but officer I did know what the speed limit was"…The officer doesn't care. It is my responsibility to find out what the speed limit is and also recognize that I am receiving the effects of my own action. At a higher level, it is how we think, not what we do. To believe that my words do not carry meaning is to believe that I am outside of the creative ability that God gave me at the onset of creation. Powerless is not the condition of the creative process. I came into the world to help humanity move beyond the restrictions that are believed are real. The only way I can offer assistance is to understand my own creative ability. Doing is not creative. Doing is indicative of behavior and behavior does not have the power to create. I have the ability to manipulate form, but the true creative ability is within the mind or in the thinking process. A thought is required before I can do anything, so doing is merely an outward application of the creative process, not the process itself.

So, my first line of protection is to watch my words. Not only the words I speak, but also the words that I form in my mind, for as soon as the word is formed and spoken in my mind, the mind begins to look for ways to manifest what I am thinking. I have learned that by watching my thinking process I have received results that I wanted and did not want until I finally realized that a word once formed in my mind will create. I got a lot of what I didn't want, not realizing what was happening. Now I watch what I think and if it is something I do not want, I make sure I do not form the words. But I still have to catch myself. Most of the time, formed words come from my judgment about what is going on. If I can catch myself and not form the words of judgment in my mind, I can escape the judgment that I am trying to impose on something or someone else. This is also judgment I place on myself...stupid...why are you so stupid...that was a stupid thing to say...you idiot. Sometimes it is too late and the words are put together in my mind before I realize it. Perhaps I comment on someone else's behavior in my mind or I don't particularly like the results of a project and comment on it. Once this is done and I recognize it, I ask for the creative process to stop. I can say cancel, and the words are canceled and the creative process is halted. This helps, but the mind picks up even the smallest judgment and works on it.

There is also safety net, as it were, in case I have used my mind in destructive way in the past and it is speaking through beliefs that I have made. This is the chatter that never seems to shut up. I can recognize when this happens that a belief is in control and I can ask that Higher Consciousness protect me from my own thinking so I am not using my thoughts destructively. That way I do not receive the consequences of my own thinking. Destructive thoughts only have the ability to project into the world and not into eternity, and it is the arena of time where unwanted thoughts play out their destructive intent. This is the process that is creating such havoc in the world. Asking that my thoughts be kept from harming the world, begins to process of harnessing my thoughts and thus unresolved beliefs are not projected into the world to add to its confusion. This does not excuse me from the creative potential that I have unleashed before, and I will still have to find the source of all of my destructive thinking and heal it, but at least I will not be using thoughts that I am aware of *now* to create destructively. I have to ask for this because the restricting of beliefs will not occur without my consent. This teaches me respect for myself and also brings into my awareness my responsibility for my own creation, good or otherwise. I am learning how to use my thought process the way it was intended to be used and the only way to do this is to do it right. It is kind of like learning how to use a computer. You just keep working at it until you "get it." All mistaken beliefs must be corrected. They just do not go away on their own. Thoughts that were made without God will have a choice of becoming a part of the light or be can choose eternal destruction. This sounds like beliefs have a will of their own, and I have found to a degree, this is the case. If I didn't "believe" that something could happen, it wouldn't, so beliefs are very powerful and do not want to be discarded. All of the beliefs I have made in the physical realm are not destructive. In fact, some of them are quite helpful. They are waiting for the opportunity to join with the Light and become a part of eternity. This is the separation of the sheep from the goats. I don't know how long this process will take. But there are also extremely evil thoughts that have been unleashed into the world that seem to be in control of a world gone mad. These are the dark ones that want us to believe that their force in the world is the only one and humanity will be destroyed because of their evil. The thinking of evil is purely illogical, for if they destroy the world, then they will also destroy themselves. So in control are these evil or dark ones that the world seems to be in the same predicament. It is impossible for evil to live without a mind that harbors it and until humankind takes responsibility for his own thinking process, these evil thoughts will continue to attack by using the thought process unwittingly by men whose lower consciousness is filled with an evil intent. Love does not harm through attack and it does not have to defend, because defense implies there was an attack first. It does however recognize a righteous heart and protects what it recognizes. Truth is a mighty sword that does not "see" evil. This means that truth does not recognize or understand what was created without Love. Without recognition of truth, or reality, that which has no reality or evil, dissolves…like the witch in the Wizard of Oz, it just melts because in truth it has no power. Fighting evil gives it strength, for if I fight something, I must first believe it is real. The recognition of the *unreality* of evil allows another reality to enter into my mind, and this is the truth of God. I have learned that while I believe I am in the presence of evil, if I pray, evil evaporates, for it cannot maintain reality in the Presence of what is true. It took me awhile to figure this out, as at night I was especially bothered. Now I can usually tell if something is in my awareness that is disturbing my peace. This was also a period of becoming aware of what I made that was evil and learning how to show this non-existent evil the door, where there is no existence. For it was my mind that believed in the reality of evil, so I had to learn how to reach beyond the evil that I had made with my physical mind to my higher mind that I share with God.

Evil resides in the abyss and it is this abyss that separates me from God. These are the thoughts that the mind protects until it is revealed that they are not real because they do not hold truth. The mind was created in truth, so its true function is to hold truth. Evil is not a part of truth whatsoever, and the world is easily deceived by the evil. At an individual level, each person is responsible for turning to the Interpreter to help heal the evil that is held in the abyss of his or her own mind. Without a recognition that there is evil held in the mind, evil continues to take charge of behavior and by telling people how to destroy their lives or that of another. There are many thoughts that have been made that must be recognized for their unreality, these are the demons or dark ones and once recognized by the mind they are cast out into nothingness. I have television programs that deal with evil deeds. The person that evil was using did not feel that they had a choice except to do as the evil said. We always have a choice, but if one does not know where the other choice lies, then they will rely on what evil is telling them and believe it to be true. This causes a tremendous amount of stress, because in truth no one really wants to do evil deeds. Evil is an insane condition and it is possible to say no to evil, but one must have a recourse so they can make a stand.

There are just all kinds of invisible things going on, and I didn't realize it. There are also fallen angels, or thoughts that originated in Heaven, but are now bound to the earth. Is this the Devil? Probably not in the terms religion understands and explains Satan, for Satan is blamed for everything that is going wrong in the world from a religious viewpoint, and there are a lot of beliefs and dark ones that are just below the physical level of awareness. Some beliefs are benevolent, or have my best interest, and some are just down right evil and will do anything to perpetrate a malevolent intent. The bad news is that these thoughts are really creating havoc and problems in the world right now. The good news is that the opportunity and the ability has been given to anyone desiring to do so, to tune into something else so the bothersome evil thought is no longer a factor. The ability to heal the world is in the hands of the occupants of the world, but it will not occur without Heavenly Help.

My next line of protection is to continually ask for re-interpretation. Asking for re-interpretation shows my willingness to move beyond my pattern of past thinking that is showing me what I don't want. My willingness is my agreement that I know my thoughts are in error and I am willing to place them up for scrutiny. This is how I activate the Interpreter, which then is allowed to enter my thoughts to help me find a new understanding to an old problem that is bringing about anxiety or conflict. It is still necessary to understand that the Interpreter can never tell me what to do, for the job of the Interpreter is to give another meaning to my physical reality so it does not conflict with Heaven's view of reality.

The means of healing are always given to me. If I cannot accept one mode of healing, then another one will be provided until I can actually receive the healing. The whole process of healing is to make sure that what I have agreed to is carried out. Giving up is not an option because sooner or later I will fulfill my part of the bargain to heal. Once the means are accepted the end is sure. This is means and end, so both are provided for me. My responsibility is to make the decision to heal.

There are many thoughts that my mind holds that I am unaware of. When I do become aware of a thought that is out of harmony with my eternal nature, this is when I can choose to heal. If I am unaware of the thought, I will have to wait until the problem becomes evident. The evidence always has to do with form, because form is not a part of the true creative process.

This stuff, I do not reveal too many people because the implication of what I am saying makes me a little kooky. However, I never knew how many different aspects of thoughts that there are until I began to find out how many were in my own mind. All thought begins with an intention, and this includes evil. I did not want to think that I was responsible for evil in any way, but I now know that my mind has held evil thoughts, and they must be dispelled so I can remain peaceful.

The Unseen War

We are at war. Not with anything physical but instead with what is known as "the dark ones." I hesitate to make too much out of these, but it is necessary to realize the potential hazard that these "dark ones" pose. I have come to realize the power of thought. In fact thought is much more powerful then the body. In every situation that a miracle is involved in, is releasing a fear thought from the mind and accepting the perception that the Holy Spirit gives. I have known for quite some time that thoughts do not die. This is especially true of beliefs, for when the body dies they do not move into the eternal realm. Their reality began in time, so they look to time for their reality, and because everything in time must die, it is their belief of death that keeps them here. Even at this, they still must follow certain Laws that are greater than the ones that are found in time. Thoughts that are born in time through a physically learned experience must continue in time. There are other thoughts that are of a much lower vibration, and these lower vibrations are surrounded by fear. Fear is too dense to move into the higher realm, so the destruction of all fear born error is a fact. Fear runs rampant in this world as it is now, and so we must begin to recognize when fear is present and begin to heal the thought behind the fear.

Belief is different than fear. Beliefs were made from physical experience and do not leave the mind of the thinker. This being the case, those of us who enter the physical realm are also for the beliefs that we have left behind when we leave our physical body. This is known as karma, but it is not a punishment, but rather a time of sorting out that will bring those beliefs that wish to move into the light to do so. Those that do not wish to move into the light are earth bound and will be destroyed eventually. Beliefs have the ability to "hop" from one body to another without us being consciously aware of this occurring. This is especially true when someone dies. Lower thought vibration and also beliefs have the ability to shift from one body to another. Lower vibrations attach to physical form, and literally suck the life from the individual. Lower vibrations really have nothing to do with reality. Therefore, they do not have power over us except the power that we give them. Fear is always present when lower energy is around and when we are going through a fearful time, fear feels real. But because fear does not originate in the eternal realm, it is impossible that it be real.

About 8 months ago I found within myself a dark thought that looked like a child that had black around her eyes. As I have had a lot of trouble with allergies around my eyes I was sure that this dark thought, appearing as though a child, was making its presence known to me. This can bring up fear when we internally see this kind of memory. Because it was time to let her go I began to move in the direction of healing. The child was not really a child at all, but was appearing as one. This dark one did not want to be "vanquished" as it were, and when I released her, and unbeknownst to me, she moved into the eyes of my grand daughter. My grand daughter came down with a horrible eye infection. Her eyes turned black and red down to the center of her cheeks. At first I didn't make the connection, but when I looked at how dark her eyes were, I realized her eyes looked just like the little girl in my mind. It took 2 visits to the Doctor to get her eyes cleared up. Mucus just seemed to drain from her eyes. After a few days, however, the problem seemed to clear up.

Just recently, I have been diligent on working on finding and releasing ideas that have been causing me continual torment. After one particular bad night this week, I knew I had released a horrible thought form that I had been trying to release for quite awhile. On Friday night my grand daughter spent the night with me. In the morning I got up and took a shower to go to work. I had just gotten out of the shower when she got up and walked out of my bedroom claiming that a monster was scratching at her ears. At first I chalked it up to the coffeepot making noise, but then she reiterated that the monster was trying to get her and she didn't want to go back into the bedroom. She went to lie on the living room floor and I went in to talk to her. I then asked her where the monster was and she pointed to several different areas on her body. I took my hands and pushed the "monster" away from her body where she pointed. She told me there was a "monster" on her bum. As a matter of fact she had been experiencing pimple like sores on her backside and she told me that the monster had been doing this to her. I told her that from now on when the monster came to tell him that Grandma Cheril would not let them hurt her and we would both make the monster go away.

The reason I tell this story is for everyone to be aware and not to just disregard children's stories as their imagination. Also, we want to protect our children, those that we love and those who are open to destructive thoughts. When thoughts leave one mind, if they are not healed, they go to another body and produce the symptoms that were not healed.

I realize this is not a popular subject to talk about, but if we are not aware, then who will be responsible? We are in a quiet war. We must find a way to heal the world of these lower vibrations that are attacking our children and find a way of protecting unsuspecting children and adults that these evil thoughts can and do to terrorize those we love and also the world. We have Help that can show us the way to avoid these seemingly dark ones, but we have to be the ones that are aware of what is occurring. We are greater than the dark ones, but because of the fear that is present when they appear, we believe we are helpless. This is not the case and until we choose to avail ourselves of Help that is being offered, we will continue to be plagued by an unseen war.

Day Twenty One

Everyone is looking for a way to either find creative expression or share it. Creative expression is what we share with God. Our inability to express creation is what keeps us from the eternal feelings of joy; for the creative expression is our connection to God or Love. It seems humankind, for the most part, has traded in his creative expression for a few dollars. I have done it myself believing that it was money that would solve all of my problems. The truth is that we will never be happy until the creative potential or talent that everyone carries is expressed. The problem is that we don't believe that our own creative expression has any kind of ability to "make money." This is especially true in the United States. As a nation of people, we have a special relationship with our money. There is nothing that we believe our money cannot do. Once making money becomes a goal, the alignment with Heaven creates a vibration of unhappiness. This is not to say that having money is wrong. What I am saying is that money cannot be a goal. It is a tool. For awhile we can go to work and tell ourselves that it is ok and push down the feelings of being unexpressed, but in the end, the blocking of the creative expression leads to depression, physical pain and sometimes disease.

Expression is of God. Experience is of the world. When holding back the Expression of God, what is actually occurring is an insane attempt to hold back the expansion of the universe. It is a scientific fact, the universe is still expanding and our contribution is either healthy or unhealthy, so the question arises, what has been my intention? For whatever that is will determine my contribution. I used to think that my contribution did not rest on *all of my ideas*. Instead I thought I could pick and choose at an individual level which ones would be for my own personal benefit. I now realize that all of my thoughts contribute in some way either to destruction or the health of the universe, and so I am in the process of discovering what they are and finding ways to heal them through release or surrender. The ones I release are the ones I give as a gift, and because what I give, I receive; these are the ones that are contributing to the creative expression. The ones that I surrender are the ones that I just give up. Surrender means to give up all rights to. These are the ones I don't want returned to me as a gift. On the other hand, I don't choose to give up rights to the ones that are helpful, so these are the ones I release.

Sometimes innocent thoughts just need to be healed and go Home. I heard a story once about a wall in a foreign country, and there were many people who were buried with their leader before they died. The spirits of many were trapped there. As they were unearthed, thousands of white butterflies filled the air. The butterflies were symbolic of the freed spirit. There are a lot of thoughts that are just below the level of conscious awareness or what is understood at a physical level. The way to find out what something means is to ask. I forget a lot of the time that I do not receive an answer unless I first ask. This places me in a position of constantly trying to figure things out for myself. I also think that possibly this is where self help books sometimes fail. They do not point individuals to their own internal communication system where truth is the ultimate and only real place of learning. True understanding does not come from without, it comes from within and it is the intellect that needs understanding because its understanding is faulty.

Teaching and learning through the intellect is useless when trying to understand the spirit. Reading physical material is physical communication and it is difficult to transmit spiritual understanding at a physical level. All that anyone can do is share the way they communicate at a spiritual level. How spiritual communication occurs is done individually. I don't mean to say that self help books do not have any purpose. From my own perspective, learning how to tune into the higher communication was not something I learned in a book. Before learning occurs, a decision must be made in the heart, for it is only hear that we are heard and taken at our word at a higher level, and you can't make a decision based on what is learned in a book. True decisions come from the heart, and this kind of agreement cannot be physically attained.

People learn in different ways. Some are earth signs, so their level of understanding is more logical based, or they want to see the facts. Some are air signs, so their learning comes from how they think about the experience they are having. Some are water signs, so they pay more attention to their emotions or how they feel about what is occurring, and some are fire signs, so their communication takes on still a different approach as they are usually fired up about their experiences. On top of all of this, some people communicate with themselves with internal pictures, others with what they hear, still others with what they feel. You can tell how people communicate with themselves when they go to a restaurant. One will look at a menu and look to see what looks good. Someone else will wonder what sounds good and yet another will wonder how the food will make them feel. The importance of how we communicate became apparent to me when I was doing a couples massage with a friend of mine. She is an earth sign, and I am an air sign. She spent a lot more time on her client's feet, and I spent a lot more time on my clients head. Funny how that works.

Where was I…oh yes, the creative process. Everyone was born with creative energy. It was not something we learned while having a physical experience. The creative energy of an individual can be mapped by looking at their astrology chart. Some scientists will pooh pooh astrology as being not concrete enough to determine anything…well I would say that astrology is not for the concrete. It is for the spirit, which is not concrete. Astrology requires a step towards inner self understanding. It is possible that scientists who do not advocate astrology possibly have a lot of the earth sign in them. I am pretty sure; the personality trait of doubt of the spirit would be in their chart. Because everything has elements of truth, even the doubters hold truth. They are just "living their chart," as I have found that most people do regardless of what they believe.

When someone is coaxed into training for a career that does not align with their chart and then making that their source of living, depression is sure to arise. It's kind of like telling a squirrel that he has to spend his time learning how to swim instead of climbing trees and a duck that he has to climb trees. This is ridiculous when looked at from this standpoint, and yet it goes on all of the time at a human level. Much of humankind is trying to live in constant denial of the true creative energy that he/she was designed to introduce into the world. This also places one in a position of denying purpose, and because the purpose is a Law of Mind, the individual will pay the price, for purpose is of God, it is not held in a physical experience.

Being in constant denial of my true creative ability has brought me here. It has also taught me that it is difficult to use the creative process to the full potential until the blocks I have placed in its stead have been removed from my mind. Relearning of my own creative ability has been the journey Home. The creative nature must be released in time for it holds innocence and it is innocence that will save the world. I often thought I should make a t shirt for babies that said, "If you keep me innocent, I can change the world." But our intention has been to teach innocence not to be naïve and look through rose colored glasses. My question would be, isn't this what we need? A fresh perspective is one that paints a rosy picture instead of pictures of doom and gloom. Well, the news reporters are finally getting what they have been looking for. It seems that there is not enough bad news to go around. I guess they aren't the only ones to blame because the world seems to watch in fascination when there is a tragedy. The things of the heart are sometimes just given a wisp of a mention, and then on to the next tragedy.

Awareness is where the creative process happens. Consciousness is not creative, it is directive. Why in the world do we have "breast cancer awareness"? For what we are aware of we create. Wouldn't it be better if we had breast health awareness? Then we would be aware of health instead of cancer. What are we thinking? We have fat awareness, carb awareness, war awareness, disease awareness, and the list goes on. This kind of awareness draws our attention away from the constructive creative ability that we came to share and towards destruction, for whatever is held in the awareness of the mind, the mind will produce. We now have more breast cancer, fatter people, more war and everything that we do not want, and still we are bombarded with more information that we are supposed to "digest" and keep so we can be "aware". This is the "new purpose" that we have given to the world, which has nothing to do with the Purpose of God. Still we say, we want what is good and right, but the mind set proves otherwise. No wonder the world has to evolve. If it didn't it would self destruct due to the "new awareness" that has been thrust upon it.

The way back to true awareness will lead me out of this mess. So far, there have been parts of me that have not gone without a fight. It is like that saying…everything I let go of had claw marks all over it. The mind/body wants the concrete explanation, so in consciousness I have had to learn how to lead my mind away from self aware or concrete thoughts to the Higher Consciousness where peace resides. Peace is not concrete, it is an awareness, so it is conceptual in nature. Learning this has not been an easy road, and I still find those fragments of beliefs that want me to keep my mind/body awareness as real and my spiritual one as not being real. These are the claw marks that are left by false beliefs that do not want to evolve. Learning how to change my mind with the least amount of resistance has helped. This has been when I have asked for Help from the Interpreter. Without the Plan, I would not have found the other way. The Plan has led me back to my creative nature where true peace lies.

Understanding Consciousness

What is all this about consciousness?

In the physical society that addresses the spiritual idea of consciousness, the word is used a lot, but very little is ever addressed as to what it means. Because we are entering a new era of a new consciousness, it is important to address the question; just what is consciousness and what does it mean to be conscious? We live in an information society, so there are many interpretations that explain consciousness, but even at this it is still a little confusing as to just what consciousness is. Where did consciousness come from and why is it so important? These are valid questions, and to avoid placing too much emphasis on our beliefs about consciousness, which is a physical explanation about this process, it is important to look at consciousness from a different point of view. There is the Christ Consciousness, individual consciousness, mass consciousness, war consciousness, peace consciousness and the list goes on. To get a proper understanding of what consciousness it is important to understand the Laws that the mind must abide by, for these are the Laws that it was created under. To begin with, contrary to popular belief, consciousness does not belong to the brain because thinking happens in the mind; therefore, consciousnesses refers to a part of our thinking process but is not considered the whole process or define the ability to think. Mind was created in wholeness and to be unlimited, and it is obvious that physical consciousness is not privy to either of these mind abilities. Obviously, consciousness is important, so where does its fit into our thinking process? In order to understand consciousness, we must first examine what it is for. Because the mind was created to look for purpose, the question, what it is for will help understand its purpose. Consciousness, by the mind's own definition must have a purpose, and because purpose is a Law of Mind understanding its purpose is crucial. Not because if we do not understand it will not work, but instead by not understanding we may fall victim to Laws of Mind that we do not understand. Everything in this world comes with an instruction manual, except us. It is time to dispel some of the misconceptions about consciousness and how it works. In order for it to be a rational explanation, it must make sense and be logical, so the more logically consciousness is approached, the better the understanding that will emerge.

Understanding self consciousness

The simplest way to understand consciousness is learning about self-consciousness, or your own. The first thing to recognized about consciousness is that it has the ability to pay attention. Paying attention is how an individual evaluates what is occurring, or what the individual is doing in the way of performing a task, like learning how to drive a car. When first learning how to drive, consciousness pay strict attention, and we probably "white knuckle" the wheel. With this understanding, consciousness is a teacher. The next logical question is; what or who is it teaching?

As noted before, consciousness is not an unlimited function of the mind. Because it is important to know, the unlimited part of our mind is not held within the brain, for the brain in itself is a limit. It is limited by the size of the brain, so when information passes into the brain from the unlimited part of the mind, it must be re-interpreted into a physical interpretation. This is what the brain is for. Very simply, consciousness directs, but it usually does not direct unlimited ideas, for consciousness developed in the physical realm, not in eternity.

Consciousness is an evolutionary process that was developed in order to self examine, pay attention to detail, and direct. Without consciousness, it is impossible to perform these tasks. Because whole awareness does not self examine, because it is wholly aware, consciousness is not a needed function in the Heavenly Realm. But still, because consciousness is so important to humankind, what must be examined is the implications of consciousness on the whole picture, which also involves unlimited thinking, or what is commonly known as God.

Limited consciousness, or self consciousness is only possible by acquiring self awareness, which is the opposite of whole awareness. Self awareness can only occur in the physical realm. In the Higher Realm, Laws were created to keep perfect order, and these Laws are literally written within all of Creation, so consciousness is not necessary. The Law carries all of the Authority, and because the Law is God, nothing is lacking and the conditions of peace prevail. On the other hand, self awareness is not privy to these Laws, so another method of being directed had to evolve at a physical level. This method is consciousness. What this means is that self consciousness directs self awareness.

What is self awareness?

When we are born into the physical realm we are whole aware, which means that the body we arrive in is a part of our whole awareness. So is everything else in time as we see it. As our life progresses, we begin to have self aware experiences. Because these experiences are not based in whole awareness, they must be stored in an awareness that has nothing to do with whole awareness. Therefore, they become a part of the mind/body awareness. Mind/body awareness can be viewed as the inner voices that constantly speak to us and explain our reality to us. All of these inner voices that explain reality to us began from a self aware experience. What occurs in the body, or physiologically, is that for just an instant we hold our breath and the instant of physical self aware experience becomes locked in the body and what emerges is our own personal truth. This is why there is little, or no agreement when problems arise that needs a solution. Partial or individual understanding cannot possibly solve a problem that needs a whole solution.

How consciousness works to resolve conflict

When individual problems arise, consciousness looks at all of the internal self awareness that has been stored in the mind/body, and then makes a decision based on what it believes will afford the best possible outcome. This would work, except that it only has access to self aware experiences and when a problem arises that it does not know how to deal with, a tremendous amount of anxiety is bound to occur. In addition, many times self awareness is conflicted and this places a tremendous amount of pressure on consciousness to make a right decision, but because of the internal conflict, the decision will be difficult to make. This will lead to another problem, which is looking for a way to resolve the internal conflict and is usually the reason for addiction. The mind, believing the solution is addiction, now looks to the addiction as the new purpose for the mind. Because Purpose is a Law of Mind, the mind must use purpose to create with, even if it is wrong.

The other Consciousness

Consciousness is not creative, it directs. If there are no conflicts, it directs without problem. When conflict emerges, another kind of Consciousness must be accessed. This is because the mind is the most creative force in the universe. It was created to create. If it is not creating constructively, then it is creating destructively. Conflict is destructive, so a new way must be found to direct consciousness to a new level of awareness that is not destructive. This is the unlimited awareness where the Laws of God know how awareness is supposed to work.

It is only possible to build consciousness in the physical realm. This is why we are here, to build consciousness and then lead misdirected thinking to the Higher Awareness where this world will not suffer the consequences of destructive thinking. This is called healing. The way this works is that, we learn how to lead our own individual consciousness to a Higher Consciousness, which then directs whole awareness into the physical realm to heal it. Because we choosing to allow a Higher Consciousness to decide for us, the destructive tendencies of the mind become constructive and peace is restored to the world. This is the New World that Christ spoke of during His Life.

Faith

It takes a while to build a mind/body consciousness, and by the same token it takes time to learn how to shift physical consciousness to Higher Consciousness. This is called mind training. It is difficult for self consciousness to lead mind/body awareness to the Higher Consciousness because it does not know how. This is what faith is for. Faith has the ability to see beyond the physical inability of consciousness to the higher realm where our unlimited reality lies. Trying to use individual consciousness to direct unlimited awareness will end in disaster because unlimited thinking does not recognize limited beliefs.

There is a specific plan for each individual to learn how to lead mind/body awareness to Higher Consciousness and make an exchange for what is believed for a miracle. Physical beliefs do not have access to the light, so a Plan had to be devised to help us consciously make the shift. The ground that lies between belief and reality is the miracle. The miracle is the re-interpretation of the physical experience so that it is not out of alignment with Higher Awareness.

Conclusion

The mind is the most creative force in the universe, and we do not understand it. We try to give the brain the ability of the mind because we are human and have a body and believe that only what is seen with the physical eye is real, but thinking is invisible, as is the mind. Understanding the mind begins with self understanding, but then we must reach to something greater that goes beyond what we have learned in a physical experience. It is here that we can learn the truth of Who We Are.

Day Twenty Two

Yesterday I slept most of the day. I am still trying to sort some details out that are unsettled in my mind. Taking the problems that are physical and then relating them to a spiritual level seems to be overwhelming at times. Even thought I know that this is not my responsibility, there is still something within that wants to be responsible.

I keep having this dream about living in mobile home. I used to live in a mobile home, and I wasn't very fond of it. I eventually moved out, but in my dream I am still living there. I am trying to sell it or just get rid of it, but I can't. In my dream last night, someone was looking to buy a mobile home, but it wasn't mine, it was the neighbors. I really wanted them to come and look at mine, even though I knew that the one that they were looking at was much better than mine, I was trying to manipulate circumstances and they buyers weren't buying it. I have had this dream over and over again in one way or another. This morning I decided to take another look at it and got another perspective. This is what the dream means…the mobile home represents how I feel about my physical self. There is always something better than me and I feel inferior. But it is more than that. I also feel that way about the Information I have been given to share. At one level I know that it contains the whole Plan for the salvation for the world, and yet somewhere within my lower awareness, I hear…who are you to believe that you are the one who should receive this information and share it with the world?..and this is how I feel when I share this information with others. Not everyone, but sometimes I am just looked at as if I didn't say anything, or if I did, it carried very little or no value whatsoever. I have also had the dream, these dreams occurred when I first began: I am walking down a street and there are huge homes. The bottom floor is where I live. I suddenly realize that there are rooms upstairs that I had forgotten about. These rooms are huge and they are beautiful, and the contents are beautiful, but they have not been used in quite awhile, so they need some dusting and etc. There are rooms above these rooms also. Obviously the dream was showing me that I had not explored a higher perspective, and it has been there all of the time.

    I put some blogs on my web site sharing some of the information that I have been given to relate. These insights do not come from me, but instead are from a higher awareness then what I personally know. I found a link on another site that asks what people think about what they are reading. I can log onto this site and see what others are saying about my blog. I know that I have placed too much value on what others think, but I also know what I share has value. It doesn't come from me, but instead comes from a Greater Source. It amazes me that people will say that the information sucks or that they hate it. I used to take this personally and believe it was me they were attacking, but it seems I have grown accustomed to being personally attacked, but it still hurts. This is not my information; it is a Plan that I have been fortunate enough to tune into that contains the explanation of the separation of God and His Creation, and also the Plan for the correction. I couldn't come up with this myself. I had no idea as this information was clearly not in my mind before I began the journey. Still, it has taken some time to disassociate myself from the beliefs of others. I am sure that most of the information that I share will continue to be dismissed by others until I relieve myself of the belief that others have to any ability to judge me at all. This is what the dream is about. The mobile home represents my physical belief that what I am saying must be accepted by others. This will prove that I am "good enough" and my information will be "bought" by others. But this dream has other implications. It also reveals to me my own belief about my own self image not being good enough. This dream has implications on different levels, and to leave out any of the implications is to keep the problem. Perhaps I have finally gotten the message; for once the message is understood, the dream occurs no more. Many of my dreams show that a healing has already occurred, but because I have not accepted the healing as yet at a physical level, or I still hold blocks carried by my mind/body awareness, the healing has not been accepted by me. There is still work to be done before I can share this information, for in order to share it I must first let go of any denial that is occurring in my own mind. Still I trudge on because I know that this is what I agreed to and trying to do something else will only delay the outcome.

I know everyone has received physical lessons that go so totally against the grain of truth, it is hard to learn that there is a distinction because in every truth that has been distorted, a grain of truth is still there and it is this that must be revealed. Studying what is not true is useless. By looking at the meaningless, we as a society have learned how to take the grain of truth and set it aside in favor of evaluating guilt, shame, anger, disappointment and the list goes on. As if examining why we are carrying a load of shit will somehow turn it to something else. The shit isn't real, but we are. Examining a load of shit = a load of shit. It's like examining cancer instead of the cure. Examining cancer only leads to more cancer. Likewise, examining shit only leads to more shit. It's as if we could finally understand what shit is for it would make it different. It is all in the intention, or what is it for? I am examining shit so I can find the seed of truth that is buried in it or I am examining shit to see how it works. Or still, I have found value in my shit, and if I keep it, it will somehow keep me safe. What I am looking for is what I will find or keep. If it is what shit is for, I will find more. If it is for truth, I will find that also. Finding the value will allow the rest to fall away. This is healing Looking for truth leads to truth and brings the focus of the mind back to reality where it functions properly. The lesson is; don't examine what you do not want, for you will receive more of it. But this is what my conflicts are designed to do…keep me locked into finding value where there is none, or more shit.

I have fallen into my old belief patterns very easily. I have guessed I knew what the lesson was that seemed quite evident to me in my physical experience. I decided on several occasions that God wanted me to learn that I need to stop allowing others in my life to take advantage of me. This would be all well and good, except that it still places me in a position of in one way or another being taken advantage of again. This usually occurs with someone I love and once again I will feel like I have been taken advantage of. Then I will explain it to myself that it is ok if they do it because I love them…big trick. If someone else is taking advantage of me, it doesn't matter who it is. In order to heal it, I have to find out when I learned that it was possible for this to happen. People we love do not take advantage of us, and if we feel that way it is because we learned an impossible lesson and are trying to prove the lesson is real. Once it is healed, I am not at the mercy of being taken advantage of because the emotional charge has been removed from my self awareness (where the creative ability lies) of my mind.

The mind is psychological, not physical. When a physical idea is introduced into the mind, judgment occurs. This judgment says that the physical experience is real and the psychological part of my mind must adhere to the physical application of the new physical law that I made myself. The new belief, learned in error, is in violation of my true nature, which is psychological So instead of looking for a psychological answer to a physical problem, I am forced to look for a physical answer which ultimately leads to projection and if that doesn't work then I will learn addiction as a solution. In order to get back to the psychological part of my mind where it functions properly, a shift has to occur. This shift must be introduced through a new understanding of the old, or the grain of sand that lies buried in the false perception. I don't know how to get back to my psychological state because of my belief that the physical memory is real. This is the purpose of the Plan, to lead each individual out of their own private nightmare and to the psychology of the mind so it functions properly.

The way that healing occurs, is first of all, we make a decision to heal a problem. The problem is recognized because of the intensity or anxiety that is occurring in the body. It is impossible to have an intense or anxious feeling without a body, so it is the physical belief is trying to establish itself as real. The situation will occur over and over again until I can see the real problem, which is the shift that brings the mind back into its true or psychological state. This means that the body is an effect, not a cause of an affliction that is occurring to it. When we ask for Help, the end or the final solution is promised by God, so healing is eminent. But even healing is not the final solution. The final solution is the revelation that we are one with the Creator. It is in this state that it is realized that we never left Home. Instead, we were having a dream and though that we could look somewhere else other than the Peace of God for our reality. When looked at from this perspective, it is realized that it is impossible to think without God. Here, true communication is restored with the Creator that was seemingly lost at the time of the separation. Justice has at last come into time through the healing process that was made to correct the seeming separation that occurred at the onset of time

Apple Justice

The title of this article, apple justice, is deceiving. You may wonder how there can be justice given to an apple. An apple is just an apple, and why in the world would an apple need justice? As I lay in bed this morning, it dawned on me that indeed an apple is in need of justice. Not because of what it has done wrong, but because of what the apple has been accused of.

In the beginning, the apple was given the dubious distinction of being the fruit in the Garden of Eden that became the downfall of Adam and Eve, but the eating of the apple was symbolic. It was a metaphor, or told a story of how the first couple decided to try something that was not sanctified by God. Being a metaphor, the error would prove to set a journey, which in the end, would prove that the journey was not real. The fruit was not literal, but instead stood for a new way of understanding that was introduced into the mind of Adam and Eve after they had ingested the symbolic fruit. In our physical experience, to eat something is to take it into the body and as such, it becomes a part of our being. Hence the saying; you are what you eat. The symbolic gesture of eating the apple in the Garden of Eden was quite profound. What Adam and Eve lost at the time of the eating of the apple was their innocence.

Innocence is a condition of reality or Heaven. The opposite of innocence is guilt, so the new understanding was a guilt-based understanding that had nothing to do with reality.

In the beginning, God looked on all of what He created and saw that it was good. Because Adam and Eve had used an experience to give new meaning or value to what God had created, they felt they had lost their innocence. No longer did they feel that God could look at them and declare them as being "good", so they had to go to a place where it was not so good. A place that God had not created as part of reality, and because there is nothing and nowhere that God did not create. This new place would be made, not created, so in reality it did not exist at all, and so it was, the first useless journey began. The opposite of eternity is time, so an unreal existence of time became the reality where fear, guilt, hate and conflict would emerge to prove that it was possible to live without God. Time is unreal because we believe it is possible to see things that God does not.

God knew that He could not help the couple by going into the unreal world of time with them. To go there with them would make, not only time real, but also the conditions that were afforded by time. These were and are the unhealthy emotions and attributes that are carried out behaviorally at a physical level. These conditions are known as physical law. Physical law does not understand Spiritual Law, so it tries to interpret it without a clear understanding. This makes Spiritual Law, but physical standards, faulty. When the error first occurred, a Plan had to be devised to bring the incorrect belief, or physical law, in line with correct thinking or Spiritual Law. This Plan would not make unreality a part of His creation, but instead it would make this unreal state a part of reality through a re-interpretation process. Without this occurring, their would always be a split dividing the error from the truth. The purpose of Love is to unite all things unto Itself, so a divided reality would not go on forever. This could be likened to what we do in physical society when someone breaks the law. We put them in jail to isolate them from the rest of society so that society is protected. Error in thinking had to be confined so it could not contaminate Spiritual Law, so this is the purpose of time. In truth, Adam and Eve did not leave the Garden to live in time, but instead fell into a deep sleep and began to dream that they could see something that was not there. This can be likened to having a nightmare, because that is exactly what time was made to hold. As with all things made in error, God can give them a new interpretation that can lead back to a happy dream.

Because it is fundamentally impossible to break the Laws of God, a way of distorting the Laws of God emerged in this place called time. For instance, in reality it is impossible to create without God. This means that all creative ability lies within the Mind of God, which He shares freely. In time, we do not use the Mind of God to create, we use force and manipulation, which is done without God. This leads us into deception by the belief that it is possible to "get" something through force or manipulation. Obviously, this is a huge mistake that needs correction and a part of the dream that God's Laws can be violated.

Because God does not break His Own Laws, He would have to create a Solution that would, above all else, have understanding. We do not see physical solutions as having understanding because we believe that understanding is a physical attribute, but everything that God Creates does have life, so His Solution would be able to have awareness and understand what the problem was. The Solution would have to know the truth, but also understand the deception that made time seem real. This Solution would also not be tempted to see the deception, or dream, as real. Because the mind is fundamental, the realization of the mistake would have to occur where the mistake began. The mistake the instant the mind became physical, so correction would have to occur here. So it was that God placed the Solution within the physical or lower mind where the error occurred and was held. In essence, the Solution was allowed to enter the dream state and introduce another reality. This reality was not totally Heaven, but was close enough to Heaven that the shift could be easily made, and thus the separation would end. Jesus referred to this Solution0 as the Holy Spirit, or the Great Helper. The use and understanding of the Holy Spirit is greatly misunderstood. It is only by the proper use of the Solution that we are able to make the shift that re-interprets the error in our mind. As we learn how to depend on the Solution more and more, we begin to unburden ourselves of mistakes made in the dream.

By realizing our dream mistakes, another phenomenon occurs. As the correction of the dream state unfolds a New World emerges that begins to teach us the Laws of Heaven after the re-interpretation of time has occurred. When we are in a depressed state, and look for a solution that excludes the Solution that God has provided for us, we run the risk of learning a solution that has no value. Even at that, great allowances are made for those who have decided to learn under the direction of the Holy Spirit. As long as we are continually examining our interpretation of the world and finding it lacking, we will be supported in our seeking of the new interpretation..

Now, let's get back to apple justice. At the time that God created everything, He said that it was "good". As we look around in the world today, we can see that everything is not good. The Bible tells us that the Words of God do not go out from His Mouth and return to Him without results. In other words, what was true at the time of creation is still in effect. So the world must be brought into line with the Words that God spoke at the time of creation so His Words remain truthful, and we all know that God always speaks the truth This bringing into alignment with the truth is the end of days, and not the end of the world. As with all previous calamities that befell the world, God has always offered a Plan to save those with a righteous heart. A righteous heart is evident through the faith that God is offering protection that is not quite understood, but is known is there. The physical intention of the lower mind is not enough. Imagine what faith it took for the Israelites to leave Egypt. Their faith in the Promise of God had to be great. If their intention was to stay in Egypt and have faith that God would save them, their intention would have meant that they would not have gone with Moses to the Promised Land. We too have a Promised Land, and it is the New World that echoes the Laws of God, but we have to choose it in order to gain it.

It is this Plan that uses the thoughts of the Solution that heals the world. When we believe we know how to do this, we are sadly mistaken. Many have believed that the plan rests on them and they have to "do" something to change the world. When we try to "do" something that is not sanctioned by the Solution, we are virtually on our own. This is what is meant when it is said that our good intentions are not good enough. Before we can learn the Laws of God, every false belief must be re-interpreted in our mind. It is this re-interpretation that is not in opposition to the Laws of God. The re-interpretation of the world guarantees that it will be a safe place for future generations. What reflects the Laws of God is harmless and will provide safety for those with a righteous heart.

Justice must be restored in the world. In the Garden of Eden, when Adam and Eve ate from the symbolic apple, the apple began to carry a symbol of injustice. In other words, the apple did not carry the justice of Heaven and it was not "good" because a different interpretation was given it. In order for the apple to be given apple justice, or for it to be recognized by Heaven, a new interpretation would have to emerge from Solution. This new interpretation would restore the apple as being good, not in the Mind of God, but in our own mind where we believe it is possible for error to occur. With the true meaning of the apple being restored, the world would carry a new interpretation of the apple that would not conflict with Heaven's Interpretation.

As with the apple, as we learn to ask the Solution or the Holy Spirit to re-interpret the meanings we have given to this world, the meaning of the world changes and becomes a New World of peace. This new interpretation places the world in a position of accepting the justice of Heaven. From this justice emerges a New Heavens and a New Earth because the former things have passed away.

The new interpretation of the apple is this. When Adam and Eve ate from the symbolic apple, they were concerned with the fruit. How it tasted, the color, texture, etc. In order for the apple to take on a spiritual interpretation, it would have to be understood that what seen in the apple was not necessarily the fruit as being the most important thing, but instead the creative process held within the seed or the core of the apple. As within the meat of the apple, so within the mind of man. On the other hand, the creative potential lies within the core because within the core are the seeds of creation. When we plant the seeds within the apple, we do not just get the fruit, we get the whole tree. From the tree comes the continuity of creation. The lesson lies in the ability to create, not in the eating of the fruit. The eating of the fruit is temporary and only provides nourishment to a temporary form, which is the body. It is a temporary solution for the temporary problem of hunger. What man throws away, God gives His Justice to and makes holy. The question now becomes this; what have we thrown away that God has made holy? Without this realization it is difficult at best, to understand the Justice of Heaven. Without understanding what has true significance we continue to seek for what has no value in the Mind of God.

What would happen to the world if we only gave significance to the things that God gives significance to? Would the world change? It is not up to us to decide what has value to God and what does not. If He cares enough that an apple should be re-interpreted in our mind to receive justice, how much more does He care for you and how you interpret yourself? We cannot find our own value because we do not know where to look for it. Only by valuing what the Solution values will we be able to see our own worth.

Each one of us has entered into the physical realm with a gift to give. We are here to give the gift, not get it. We do this by finding our own value. This is not achieved by anything we can do in this world; it is given to us by an act of grace. Grace is how we are to learn to live our lives through a proper re-interpretation provided to us through the Solution, or the Interpreter.

We are at the crossroads. We can choose to look for a new interpretation of the world, or we can keep trying to give justice to unreality. Giving physical value to something that has no spiritual value, does not change God's Mind. In order to heal the world, the Justice of Heaven must prevail.

The Interpreter is bound by Spiritual Law not to interfere with our physical choices, but He will help us if we realize we are in error and want to see a new way of looking at the error. For instance, when we see starving children, we believe this has significance. The Justice of God sees no significance in starving children. This is an impossible condition that holds no reality. His vision only sees conditions where everyone is provided for. This is a perception that must change. As long as we perceive that children can starve, starvation will occur. Once the value has shifted, we can stop trying to change the unreal condition of starvation. Instead, we will support the idea of an abundance of food where everyone is provided for. It is impossible to see this without it being re-interpreted for us. Without the vision of the Interpreter or the Solution, we will continue to see what is not there. His work is not complete until God can look out over all of creation, including the dream and say; "and He saw all that He created, and it was good."

We are all seeking justice, but not physical justice as it is known in time, although this seems to be so. God is kind and fair to everyone. It is time we learned of this His Justice and accept it as our own. The Solution carries a Plan that has the ability to save the world from further calamities that are befalling it. This Plan can save our physical assets and keep the monetary systems of the world from collapsing, but it is up to us to choose it, for it cannot work without our support. Re-interpretation will save our world. Only a holy interpretation learned through a new process of learning can give a new meaning to the old. We have all we need to meet the Justice of God and save the world, but we must learn how to use it.

Day Twenty Three

I have always heard that there is "body wisdom," and I always thought that if the body was so smart, why would it choose to die? I also take note that when the creative process is addressed, the body is put first; as in body, mind and spirit. Why is the body put first? Whenever healing is needed, it seems that it is the body that must be "fixed." This being the case, then why would I want to examine the physical problem first, for I know that examining a physical problem only brings about more of the problem. This is how the mind works. It can only move towards what we are looking at. The body is where the problem is stored, so if I concentrate on it, it only seems likely that I am concentrating on the problem where the solution is not. The true creative process does not involve the body at all. The true creative process is spirit, thought and feeling. These are held within the mind, not the body. Trapping the creative process in a physical experience brings about the destructive tendencies of the mind because it cannot be completed in time based reference. It must be completed within itself, for it is only here that the mind understands how to finish what it has started.

I have made many ideas that circle around the belief that I am physical instead of being spiritual. Forcing form to "be" a part of the creative process has placed form above spirit, thought and feeling. Form does not know how to direct this process. The result has been disease, depression and addiction. We are trying to complete at a physical level, that which is the responsibility of God,…oops. I finally "get it," but that doesn't stop my mind from trying to work out the past beliefs that I have made while having this time based experience.

I have been depressed my entire life. I entered this life depressed. I went to a chiropractor once who used kinesiology and he asked my why I was depressed. I really was not aware that I was. I asked him, if a man who is blind from birth know that he is blind unless he is told? I really haven't known how it feels to be without depression. But last night, I had a dream, and in the dream there was a depressed woman and she died. Perhaps that was that part of me that was depressed dying and I don't have to continue believing the depressed is a normal state.

Form is the end result of the creative process, so how can it be a part of it? Why do we make it the most important part of the process? The end result can't create; it can only be the end result. When the creative process is placed under the direction of form, destruction is the end result. This produces tremendous anxiety and stress in the body as we are asking form to produce results it does not know how to produce. We are really asking thoughts and emotion that are under the dictatorship of form to create without spirit. This doesn't even really make sense. The false beliefs that have been mistakenly placed in charge of the creative process are dictating to thought and feeling, but thought and feeling do not know how to "complete" themselves without spirit, or God. The frustrating end result is an attempt to make individual consciousness decide what should be "done". I don't know at a conscious level either, so the best I can come up with is a guess. The guess addresses physical law, which is force and manipulation. This really doesn't answer the question either, because the two choices that I have is either that I sacrifice because I have to give up something that I want, or someone else has to give me what they have so I can be complete. So, it's either him or me…some choice.

This idea occurred to me a while back…it is not if you win or lose, it's how you play the game. Playing the game is not in the completion, it is in the event. Tuning into playing the game refocuses the mind on what is happening now. Now is a funny concept, because we actually believe we know where now is. One day I was reading in ACIM, and this statement jumped out at me. It said, "the closer you get to time, it becomes space." The book was explaining the concept of time and the unreality of it. Hmm…I got to thinking how I could put this statement in physical terms. This is what I came up with. If I was going to meet someone at noon for lunch, what would separate us would be time and that time is noon. Once noon occurred, now what separates us is space, because obviously we are sitting across the table from one another and noon has passed. This is time and space. The next question that arose…what would happen if time and space were removed, what would separate us then. The answer is obvious. Nothing would, so it is here I become a part of the whole. If I am a part of the game, then which part do I play? I play the game by being my part of the whole game. I am not the outcome, nor do I play any part of it. I am the 2 + 2, I am not the 4. The four is out of my hands. But under the laws of form, I try to manipulate to get to the 4, but my idea of the 4 is faulty because it does not consider the whole game and how everyone gets to win, thus sacrifice enters. My interference does not quantify the 4, it adds another equation to the 2 + 2, so I am really messing up the end result, or the 4 so now my answer is 250 and everyone know 2 + 2 = 4, not 250. Too much input! It's how you play the game so everyone wins…it's not if you win or lose. I always thought that this statement meant that I would have to show I was brave if I lost by not showing my disappointment, and if I won, I must be a gracious winner. This has nothing to do with it. Another false belief made under the direction of form that must be corrected. Because the true creative process is peaceful all of the time, if I cannot get to the place where I understand how this works, then just being peaceful will keep me from interfering with the outcome.

    The realization that I am off balance does not necessarily bring correction immediately. I now realize that correction occurs when it will bring about the most healing into the world. When the question…what is justified and what do you want are brought together, then healing occurs. If I do not believe I am justified in my win or loss, then I have not brought the two questions together. Being smug is not to be brought into the process. Being smug is not a spiritual quality, it comes about as a result of false beliefs, and it is this false feeling that will subsequently destroy my ability to be happy because it distorts justification and also what I really want. Being happy comes as a result of everyone winning, but in this world we do not know how this can be accomplished. That is because of our distortions and concepts of time and the belief if one wins, then another must lose. Once again, winning or losing is the outcome, not the game.

Time will be collapsed eventually, but not until all of the thoughts that have been projected into it are healed. Healing brings the body into alignment with the creative process. The body, which is so cherished in this physical realm, begins to take a backseat to the beauty of the spirit. Everyone knows people who are not physically beautiful, but once they are known their inner beauty far exceeds what is seen with the eyes. The false belief that the body is the most important possession I have will eventually fade as those false beliefs are brought to the truth where they will be found wanting. With this they will disappear.

This though enters my mind: Language is the beauty of Heaven. The spoken word is carried on the currents of Love provided by God in pure ecstasy. Because in Heaven, there is no separation and everything is one, the one speaking the world is also carried on the current of bliss. As the vibrations of Love move towards the shore, the beauty of the moment is reflected back to Heaven, and for an instant, Heaven and Earth become one.

The body does not carry the beauty of this instant, but when it is endowed with abilities it does not hold, I begin to look beyond the creative process for reality. Beauty is an idea, it is not form. Without the idea of beauty, it would be impossible for form to be seen as beautiful. Now, physical means becomes the tool for holding onto a beautiful idea. Trying to fool the beautiful idea thus becomes a goal to achieve at a physical level, but because time does not hold beauty, the eventual destruction of the beautiful idea slips away. Thus, the scripture from the Bible, "man shall not live by bread alone, but by every word that comes out of the Mouth of God," or something like that. Beauty is in the word, not the form. The truth is, I have given more ability to food than I have to God. I have beliefs that claim if I eat fat, I will get fat. What this means is that instead of food becoming what I am; then I am at the mercy of what I eat. So does food have a creative ability that I do not have? Is it smarter than me? Either I am what I eat, or what I eat becomes what I am. But the world is bombarded with information that claims the creative power is not within me, it is without, so I try to make allowances. For gods sakes, we even have smart bombs. What are we thinking? Once again, projection places intelligence outside of my own awareness, or where my creative ability lies. No wonder there is fear and terror in the world. I can't fix what is "out there," no one can. There is just too much information for me to try to conform to and it changes all of the time. What I have been attempting to learn will show me another way. It is all in the peace of my Being. There is nothing outside of peace. Trying to exclude myself from peace has taught me that it is possible for a condition such as war, hate and terror to exist. It's a lie. They are all figments of my imagination and in the state of peace, they are impossible conditions that have no power over me, for peace is the state where God abides and seeks to share Himself. It is peace that will lead me Home and teach me of my reality.

It's How You Play the Game

The Old Saying

There is an old saying: "It's not if you win or loose, its how you play the game." We have all heard this expression, and we assume that we know what it means. For myself, I believed that what was valuable in this expression came from my idea of how much heart I put into the game. The problem that comes from this is that I do not understand the value of the information that is in the heart. On closer examination, I found that my interpretation of this expression was rather flawed. Not because the statement has no value, but instead because I interpreted the statement to mean what I wanted it to mean. If I am looking for a spiritual interpretation to what this statement means, then I must be willing to let go of my own flawed interpretation to find one that has value or is a real interpretation.

We are not a victim of the world; rather the world is here for our enjoyment. This statement can bring into mind the belief that I can do whatever I want, including destroying whatever I want if it brings about my enjoyment. But this is not the case. Enjoyment carries the word joy. Joy is a spiritual Law and if joy is being used for the purpose of destruction, then the Law of Joy is being violated by my physical interpretation of how I can experience joy. In other words, my sadistic idea of joy is flawed and my interpretation must be corrected so I can use the Law of Joy correctly. This is done at an individual level so our personal ideas of right and wrong are not violated and we are not subjected to fear without good reason. As an example of this, if I believe that it is ok to have an alcoholic beverage once an awhile, as long as I am not using the drink to violate my being, then it is perfectly acceptable. If I am drinking to hide a problem that has not been resolved, then the drink has become a solution to a problem I am not dealing with and therefore my physical nature, or my desire to drink, is violating my spiritual being. Using drink for violation purposes has a lot of fear involved. Also, there is a feeling of trying to hide the problem, especially from those that do not approve. Therefore correction must occur. The reason I go into all of this is to explain how I began to understand the old saying, it's how you play the game. Also, I do not want judgment to be a part of what I am explaining. Someone else's judgment will not necessarily hurt me, but it will hurt the one who is judging.

Mother's Day

On Mother's Day, my son Jamie invited me to go to a local bar and have something to eat and play Keeno. I am not much of a gambler and have really never done well with gambling. If I do anything, it is usually playing the nickel slots machine. That way I figure I can have fun and still not allow guilt to enter. While gambling, it seems like I have always been focused on the outcome. That is what we have been taught to focus on. This realization was brought into my conscious awareness as I was playing Keeno.

It takes me a while to "get" something. It usually begins with my questioning about the way I am handling a situation. As I sat playing Keeno, I decided to try to approach it from a new way. Instead of thinking of numbers that were significant, like birthdays of my grand children and children and other significant dates and waiting for them to come up on the screen, I decided to focus on receiving the right numbers. I withdrew my attachment to the outcome, or what I wanted the numbers on the screen to be, and began to listen for the numbers in my mind. When I started doing this, I began to get 3 out of 4 numbers right, and that was a winner. Then it popped into my head…it is not if you win or lose, it's how you play the game. The truth is not in the outcome of anything, it is in the journey. The outcome is merely a result of playing the game by listening with the inner ear and then following the right path instead of guessing what the path is. The inner ear is the connection to our spiritual nature that sees and knows all.

Playing the game all of the time

In the physical experience we are taught that the reward is in the outcome. In truth, the reward is in the journey. Remember when you were a child waiting for Christmas to arrive. Most of the fun came from the events that led up to Christmas. As we got older, we began to focus on the outcome. Who would get what and how they would like it. Looking at the outcome focused our attention away from what is important by forcing us to look ahead and see if we would be able to give a comparable gift that someone else was giving to us. This evaluation takes us out of the present and into a future that hasn't happened. It is also how we judge another believing we know how they will feel about our gift. When we look at the outcome, if our gift did not carry the same monetary value that someone else's did, then we feel guilty and instead of the joy of giving we experience guilt associated with gift giving, because if our gift is not good enough neither are we. We began to walk away from the Christmas experience feeling less than adequate, and even when our gifts were comparable, we began to think…all of this work for just a couple of minutes of unwrapping. The joy of the journey that is found in our being was gone and exchanged for the outcome. The outcome was then reduced to a couple of moments in time. The truth is that God is the outcome because He is our completion, but we have to let go of our own expectations. Otherwise He leaves the outcome to our decision if we have decided in advance. To interfere with our decision of an outcome is an interference of free will. Free will is a Spiritual Right and guaranteed by God.

The Outcome

Our physical experience changes the joy of the journey and teaches us that value only lies in what happens in the outcome. The outcome will happen. Our choice should not be how it will happen; instead it is how we will decide to make the journey. When we only find joy in the physical result, then the end result of our physical life is death. No wonder we live in a nation of depressed people, we are constantly moving towards the expectation of what we really don't want. In truth, the great expectation of the end result is only a great end when we learn how to let it be. When we hold the value of life to only be in the end physical result, then we miss the joy of doing and giving to others and also ourselves. We are the game, and we are the only game in town. Our being happy brings the game, the outcome belongs to God. Otherwise we would be playing the game alone, and without Him what fun would that be? Let the outcome be a surprise, for if we choose our own surprise, we eliminate God from the end result. I am sure that His outcome is much better than anything we could plan for ourselves.

Our Part

We have all been assigned a mission. When we become confused as to what our part of the mission is, we are trying to do something that we have no idea how to do. When we are confused and cannot find resolution, we become depressed and unhappy, which can lead to pain and disease. Before pain and disease set in, we have feelings of inadequacy which stems directly from guilt. This means that we have tried to step beyond what we know how to do and correction must occur so the conflict within ends. The guilt is actually occurring because at a very deep level we are trying to replace God and do His part. The truth is that we are the Being in God's Plan, He is the Doer. We find resolution by realizing that we are trying to do something we do not know how to do. Which one of us really knows how to do that which only God knows how to do? This is why physical law, or forcing and manipulation, is not a part of the Laws of God.

Play the game by becoming part of the game by learning how to be spiritually involved in it. Being is a spiritual quality, not a physical one. Ours is not to see or do, but merely to be. The end result of the game is not our direction. If we learn how to be the game and not the outcome, then we will have the end result that will be favorable for everyone concerned. A win win is the only way.

Day Twenty Four

With everything, the question…what is it for?…must be asked. This establishes purpose. Not that I can give anything purpose, for purpose is the end result, and my end result does not include all of creation, so purpose or completion is not for me to decide. My confusion comes from the belief that I am not a part of the whole, but instead alone and on my own and without responsibility except to the one that I have deemed as worthy of my consideration, which is usually myself or how I feel about my behavior.

This morning I am thinking…Spiritual Law…what is it for? My mind begins to become filled with thoughts that lead me in a direction that relies on the communication that occurs in my heart. The heart is the Home of God, so it is also where I can access the Laws of Spirit. My question now becomes, what do the Laws of Spirit protect?.. for Laws always protect something. The answer returns that the Laws of Spirit protect the creative process that is shared with God. As I think about that, my awareness shifts as I begin to think about my own creative process. I am not talking about what I "do" to make money. I am talking about the deep internal longing to pursue what I love.

This is what I love doing; sharing information that I have heard while communicating with the Interpreter. For a long time it puzzled me as to why I could not readily share this information. I knew that I had tuned into truth, but to reveal this truth to others and use it creatively was beyond my ability. The longing in my heart prevailed, and I began to be a seeker, not just of understanding, but I wanted to be happy and find purpose in my life that was not just about pursuing the dream of acquiring money. It was time for me to move on, past my chosen profession of hair dressing, and move into the desire that was activated in my heart. I knew I was reaching this point, but still the fear of not surviving my current level of living prevailed. What I began to learn was that it is unwise to mix the physical need of making money with the Spiritual Law of the creative ability. True value has to be learned but finding value in the self, and this self involves the creative process.

I know a lot of people in the healing profession that really want to help others. It seemed as though they could not use their inherent talent either, but then there were some who did. In society we hold these people up and try to mirror their success and wonder why we fall short. What I learned was that there are people who have come into the physical realm with an understanding that I did not have. This kind of understanding cannot be explained by another individual, but instead must be learned by examining the Laws of the Heart. The creative process cannot be "used" to make money. However, because the Laws of the Heart are whole and include everything, money is not excluded from the Law, but a proper perspective must be placed on value. What this means is that the value that God has given to me must be examined and understood before everything aligns. Material possessions must take their proper position in the mind, which falls *under* the value of the creative process. Without this happening, the creative process lies dormant. The more that material value is pursued; eventually the creative ability just becomes a hobby, thus preventing the Love of God, which is in the creative process, from extending His Love into the world. Being Co-creator with God *is* the creative process, and pursuing something that is not co-creator with God violates the Laws of the Heart, and this makes it impossible at best to access the creative ability that lies inherent in everyone and use it to its fullest potential. This is what all of the upheaval in the world that is happening right now is all about. It is so apparent, and yet the fear of not having money to sustain a quality of life seems to force me into frantically looking for ways to find more.

The Laws of Spirit are not founded on fear, they are founded on Love. Because the world will not find a way with physical intellect to use the Creative Expression that contains the Wisdom of God, the world will evolve. Without money or material wealth, the Laws of the Heart will have to be examined. Money, or paper, is not strong enough to hold up the economic system of the world, but the creative expression is, so it is this that must be released so the world can be saved. Without this, the world will cease to exist for there is no where in all of creation that God cannot be found. Humanity has tried to push Him out by believing that His Love does not have the ability that money does, so money is pursued. We then get mad when there is a push to get "In God We Trust" off of money. If it was realized how the mind looks at symbols, it would be realized that money has become the god of this world. God is not on a coin or dollar. His Home is in the heart. To put Him on a dollar is to try to misplace His Home.

The monetary system will not fall easily because of the fear that surrounds it. In western society we are afraid of being without it, and eastern countries claim it is evil and are hell bent on bringing it down. Neither one is correct for neither one has examined, or asked, for the interpretation that would put an end to the bickering and hatred that is occurring. Each focus looks at conditions that occur without, but the Laws of the Heart are within. Strength does not come from money, nor does it come from destroying it. Strength comes from the inner creative ability that is shared with God, and it is this that must be recognized before it can be released.

Everyone has the innate creative ability. Releasing it into the world is what will save it. Love is then released, and Love is the glue that has the ability to restore peace by establishing a Government that has Laws that echo out of Heaven, move into the heart and extend into the world as the creative process, thus Love is shared with the world and the world is saved. The creative process is not conflictive, so everyone works hand in hand. Job security is promised because everyone's part is essential, or a piece of the puzzle that is held together by Love. To leave out one piece is to leave an empty space where God is not. This is incomprehensible.

Physical law governs the intellect that tells me I must seek beyond my own creative ability to find safety. The insanity of it is, it's not there. There will never be enough money or enough things. Therefore, physical law cannot promise me security. At a Being level, I know that I have been promised everything because I am it and by pursuing what the intellect says I must get, I have left the Laws of my Heart. The Bible says…"return to Me and I will return to you". The Laws of the Heart have been put into prison by the laws of the intellect. Without releasing the innocence that is in the creative process, innocence will die. God would not allow this to happen. It is time to pay the Piper, and before all of the innocence that has been on loan to time is taken by the Piper, we must learn what we owe so we can keep the value of innocence here. It is on loan from Heaven, but we don't recognize this because we do not honor it. If we did, we would not try to change it and make it into intellectual understanding. We do not realize that when we imprison innocence by the intellect, we remove our connection to Love, for only innocence is recognized by the wisdom of the heart.

This is what I have been learning, and this is the information I have come to share. The Universe has been waiting for me to learn, so I can give this information to the world. My part is not greater than anyone else's and I am sure that I came equipped to learn this part, and it hasn't been easy. There is a collective intellect that occurs in the world and it is easy to be swept away in its current. It is not easy to break free and forge the way of the Heart. I have been told throughout my physical experience that money is what I need to survive, and I have believed it. This message has been repeated over and over again in my own mind, and has been repeated by my family and friends. But I knew that if I went back to my old ways, I would be left feeling incomplete, so I stayed to learn the lesson. Overcoming the fear of the belief that I would not survive and be left out in the cold brought new lessons into my awareness as I re-attached to the wisdom in my heart. Old patterns of self deprecation slowly but surely have turned. I found errors in my mind that traced back to another life that found me left in a place alone waiting for a promised return that never came. I did not realize that was there. Once found, I could heal it, for what I learned from that experience was that being alone was my purpose. This was never my purpose and as my awareness of my past errors occurred and I was led to healing, I learned that I would survive.

I wondered if the lessons would ever end. I begged that it would. I wondered when enough was enough, and even at this, my heart continued to open. The things that I saw and the lessons I learned went beyond anything I had ever known or experienced at a physical level, and I knew that what was occurring was to open me up to my eternal nature.

On and on the lessons went and I felt sure they were over, but yet there was still more I harbored that blocked my heart. I made an agreement, a sacred contract. I agreed to have my heart totally unblocked. In my saner moments, I told the Interpreter…let's go for it. When things got tough, I wanted to relinquish my agreement, but it is impossible to relinquish a sacred contract. Clues emerged that showed me what was going on, but I really could not make sense of these clues until later, after I had completed the lesson. My bank account got smaller, but my heart was opening. I learned that communication within the heart is very specific. In the physical realm we just throw words around without realizing the impact they have. At a higher level of communication, you have to get it right. The more I learned the Language of the Heart, the more was expected of me. The errors that occurred in the beginning that made me believe I knew it all, are no longer tolerated because at a higher level, I do know better.

I have seen what lies ahead for myself. Dreams have revealed to me what is waiting. There are blue skies…and the dream that came to me a few years ago. "I am a Messenger of Love…let me anoint you with oil." I didn't know how sacred that was. Then there is the dream with the song…"On the wings of a pure white dove He sends His Pure Sweet Love…a sign from above, on the wings of a dove." Then there is the song that they sing in the Unity Church.."Let peace begin with me, let this be the moment now." Let me not forget the one by Jiminy Cricket…"When you wish upon a star." I know what Christ meant when He said, "the Father within, He does the work." But I still carry beliefs that do not align with His Light, and so I am still struggling to "let go" of what He does not recognize as His Love.

The Purpose of Love is to unite all things unto Itself. I heard this a long time ago and remembered it. Now, as I look back at my life, I recognize that the things that I needed to remember stuck, while things that did not help me learn of my purpose did not necessarily stick. One thing I remember was the time that I had bought a birthday cake for Bruce. I had called a bakery and said I wanted, Happy Birthday Bruce, on it. When I picked it up, it said…Happy Birthday Ruth. He was only 3 or 4, but I remembered the incident. A month after his passing, it was the day before Thanksgiving. I worked next to a woman who's name is Ruth. There was a flower shop next store to the salon I worked in. Ruth went over and got me 2 yellow roses (yellow is the color of peace). On the card was…Happy Thanksgiving…I love you…Ruth. It never really struck me until later what had just occurred. Someone who did not believe in this would just say…oh that is just a coincidence. But one thing I have learned is that there are no coincidences and the Language of Heaven is not intellectual, it is intuitive. By listening, I found many messages that occurred in his physical life that would point to his continued life after his leaving the physical plane.

In time, science looks for proof of the physical. Everything we see physically has been given a physical interpretation. Much of the mysticism of the universe has been stolen through the science of form. In order to replace the mysticism in my own mind, I have asked for another interpretation that is not physical. Some of the things that I have heard are beyond belief, but my belief is not required for truth to be true.

Love is the Glue

What is the Same

We are all searching for the seeming illusive love connection. That special something that draws us together and keeps us safe and feeling secure. As we go through life, we all have had those moments when we knew we had been touched by "something", but holding onto that something and being able to refer to it beyond a temporary situation may seem to be beyond what we are capable of. To find Love, we must begin to realize that Love is not a situation or an experience. Love holds Laws that are beyond the confines that we place on It. If we want to share in this kind of Love, it is up to us to learn of the Laws that Love lives by. It is this we are seeking for, but we are looking for it in the wrong place. By learning real Love, we learn what is the same in everyone.

In each of us, Love is the same. I'm not talking about the kind of love that fantasizes and holds false expectations of others, which is physical love. This kind of love expects us to live up to capabilities that we are incapable of. Each of us come from different backgrounds and are therefore subject to our past physical learning experiences. When we enter a relationship, we bring our past learning with us. When we try to adjust love, we are in error. True Love does not make adjustments, it just is. Real Love also cannot be used as a weapon of manipulation. Manipulation is learned, Love is not, it is just known. What must happen for correction to occur is the two parties have to adjust their faulty past learning to the healing ability of Love. Once a relationship based on the Laws of Love is decided on, Love has the ability to reside and bring meaning to the relationship through a re-interpretation of the relationship. Without this the glue seems to dissolve and the relationship goes along with the glue.

It is impossible to undo Love or lose it for if this is possible, then it is possible to undo the Universe. There is a corridor that runs through the mind. Within this corridor Love resides and looks for Self Evidence. When Love finds Itself through a recognition of what is the same, it attaches to those who share the same view. It is only possible for this to happen in thought. While in the physical realm this occurs when both have decided to hold a Love thought and keep it a sacred space and as it becomes Self Evident in the lives of those that continue to hold Love it becomes a sacred agreement. This sacred agreement has the ability to heal any relationship, and bring Love to anyone that chooses to join with this higher ideal, but to choose this kind of Love takes an ability that may seem to be beyond our capability. Nothing is beyond our capability to understand, but it is different than anything our physical experience has taught us. This does not mean that there are never any problems in our relationship. It means that we are keeping safe the connection to Love by choosing not to allow conflict to become a part of the Love that has been a chosen expression between two individuals. The "space" that is held for Love remains eternal, even if the physical relationship ends, for what is accepted in Heaven is forever. Only Real Love has the ability to hold this and keep this safe. To experience this kind of Love, we must be willing to step beyond the confines of what the past has taught us and learn of our true reality that does not exist in another person, but instead is shared with all of creation in a Love relationship.

Finding Real Love

True Love is content and not form. The meaning of this statement may seem to be a little confusing until we understand the differences between being and doing. Doing requires a physical body and is ruled by force or manipulation or the intellect. Being on the other hand is governed by Laws that are greater than that of force and manipulation and emanates from the heart. These are the Laws that govern the Universe and nature. When viewed as helpful, they fall under the direction of Eternal Law. When viewed as detrimental and destructive, they fall under the direction of physical law or force and manipulation. How we behold what we see determines whether it is beneficial or destructive. For instance, a phenomenon that is seen as destructive, such as a volcano eruption, when viewed from a whole perspective is a chaotic force that in the end brings stability to the earth. New life begins in nature that takes the place of what has been taken away by the violent force of the volcano. Thus, the form that destruction has taken begins to move in the direction of stability when left alone. Force or manipulation merely adds to the destructive process. When we view nature as a destructive force, it becomes so in our own mind and we are fearful of the outcome. We try to force an outcome that we have no ability to control. The same is true of our relationships. Forcing or manipulating a relationship brings it to destruction. On the other hand, if we can look at a chaotic situation in a relationship as a chance to offer it to Love for healing, we can move beyond the problem to a solution. Thus, Love is a meeting place that is above the two individuals own agenda where a new understanding can emerge that takes the place of the old one. Thus, out of chaos comes understanding and stability. Just like the eruption of the volcano because when it happens, we cannot see how this could possibly be helpful. Out of the shadow of destruction comes new life that could not have begun if it were not for the radical change that the volcano's eruption brought.

Bringing the Memory Home

Memories are funny things in that each one brings us closer to Love or further away. When they take us far from Home, or away from where Love resides, we feel lost and out of control. This is a clue that correction is necessary. A new choice must be made to alleviate the condition of being out of sorts. This does not mean that we choose another feeling that may place ourselves or another in the position of sacrificing something that is wanted. This would hardly be fair. Sacrifice is not a win/win situation for everyone involved. We can begin to look beyond our own understanding and find a new way of understanding the conflict that appears to be happening now, which in fact has its roots in the past. The roots in the past are what need healing, not the form or the person. When we continue to look at the form, we overlook content and only the content can show us meaning. When a problem arises, it is from misinformation that has been learned that has distorted the content of our Love association. The distortion of Love is the rape of the soul. The rape on our soul is the conflict being revealed to us in the form of another human being. They are not the problem; they are only a symbol of what is really wrong.

Bringing the memory Home offers us another way of viewing the conflict that is "in our face" and showing itself to us in the form of another. Showing us the direction Home is the miracle that is extended to us when we choose to move beyond our own interpretation of the problem we perceive. Without the miracle, there would be no hope for the salvation of the world.

The Miracle

Miracles are not left to the description of humankind. Instead, they are gifts that are shared with those in the world that choose to move beyond their interpretation of what they believe they see. They have the ability to make a shift within the mind and bring it to another awareness. This other awareness is not defined by anything we think we know in our physical state. Instead, it is a Hand extended that brings us gently to the comforting Embrace of Love and we know that everything will be alright. This is the moment of "now" that we hear so much about. It is a shift out of the time and space continuum into another dimension that is not ruled by force or manipulation or physical law. Instead it is governed by the Laws of Peace. When we feel peaceful, we can be sure we have reached out of time and touched another reality that we believe is beyond our grasp.

Another Opportunity

Every day we are given another opportunity to change our mind. The problem arises from the incorrect scientific belief that we think with our brain. The truth is that the brain does not have the capacity to comprehend anything. It is merely an organ that is used by the mind to interpret the physical experience. It is a place where the mind stores information on how to exchange being into doing. As long as we make the assumption that being and doing are the same, we will continue to be in opposition to the Laws that the rest of creation lives by. As long as we look to the memories that are held in the brain, the mind will not move beyond the capability of incorrect interpretation and we will keep trying to "do" so we can "be" what we already are.

Love moves through the corridors of time calling to the child. The child has forgotten the sound of Love's call and instead hears another

voice that shows him evil. This is the voice that whispers; " God is fearful and to look upon His Face, He will strike you dead." Thus the child has forgotten about the comfort of Love and His Home and believes he is trapped in a nightmare that there is no escape from. He is an orphan that has forgotten his reality.
This child needs our protection.

We have come to time to help the child hear the calling of Love, but we have forgotten our mission because the fear of the child speaks so loudly cutting us off, it seems, from the Voice of Love we swore we would always hear.

Mistakes have been made in the past that need correction. Until the corrections are made the child does not hear the Call of Love and wanders aimlessly in time searching for what he believes he has lost and he cries believing that the master he must follow is cruel and despises him.

The corridors of Love forever remain in the mind of the one that treasures time until Love becomes the treasure. Slowly, the corridor opens and the Presence of Love moves throughout the world until peace and good will is known throughout the land. Love is established in Its Reality as the World becomes a part of the whole of Creation. This is the gift we bear. The innocence of the child is our responsibility.

We must take the hand of the child and show him that we will hear the Voice of Love despite our fear, for Love cannot enter time except through the mind of a child of innocence. It is in the moving despite our fear that the child learns to hear the Voice that speaks for Love.
Finally, when the child hears the Voice that speaks for Love, a crack occurs in the walls of time in which Love can enter and bless the world, thus bringing all of existence back to Eternity. Gone is the false witness of fear in the mind of the child. Thus, the reign of terror ends as a new era begins.

Day Twenty Five

    The elements of creation are thought, fire and emotion. The picture of a light bulb going off in the head is the firing of all three elements together. Form should be the grounding element or how it is brought into the physical level, for without the physical element the creative process would just move off without being expressed into form. This seems to have been my greatest problem; how to use the elements and then bring them into form. I seem to not want to use the form element and seem agitated at having to do this. So I can see my creative potential in my dreams, but I am having a difficult time accepting it at a physical level or ground level. I am sure this must come from deep within, and so I will have to heal the agitation at having to deal with the element that seemingly upsets me. Why am I aggravated at form? It doesn't make a lot of sense, but when I feel like I have to deal with outside circumstances that dictates to me what I must "do," I can feel myself getting upset.

    I hate outer dictates. I used to think that I would have to force myself into just "doing" what I didn't want to do, but that didn't solve the problem either. Forcing myself to do something for the good of someone else is sacrifice, and I am sick of sacrificing myself because I think I can somehow make it ok if I do. Besides, the problem of sacrificing never comes to an end. There is always something else I had to sacrifice myself for. As if I sacrifice myself enough I would finally be acceptable. I guess the question is…what is it for? If I feel it is for purposes of sacrifice, then that is what it will be for. Of course then I feel like I won't have what I want if I don't sacrifice myself. The truth is within all of this sacrifice stuff somewhere, but I will have to ask the

Interpreter for another explanation so I stop doing this. Feeling motivates the creative process, and if I am using sacrifice as a motivation, then my mind will find more ways to fulfill the role of the sacrificial victim. I don't want that anymore.

So, where did I learn that I would have to sacrifice in order to make it in this world? It seems like it is something we learn at an early age. What do I really want and what is justified? What I really want is not to feel like a sacrificial lamb. Now I can ask myself if being a sacrificial lamb is justified. I must have justified it to myself somehow at some time in order to believe it was real. I keep getting myself into the position of feeling this way. Hmmm…can't remember, but I know it is a pattern because it has happened many times before.

I can use this as a means for healing by forgiving my idea of what it means to sacrifice. I still don't want to "do" the thing that I am being told I have to do in order to fulfill my seeming obligation. I am going to choose to look beyond my seeming obligation, for the obligation is standing in the way of my peace. If I am peaceful, I can let higher awareness decide for me, and the sacrifice will end. I am going to be ok with this. My decision to be peaceful instead of making a sacrifice of myself will return to me, for giving and receiving are the same. I agreed to have all of this removed from my mind, but I still am finding things that seem to block my peace, but the block is in me. I don't have to believe anything I don't want to, and I can choose to see this another way. The outcome doesn't matter, but my peace does.

Ok…I am feeling better and do not have to control the outcome. I can let it go without aggravation being attached to how it should be done at a physical level. The physical level is supposed to ground me, not give me aggravation. Form is only a landing place for the creative process, not the aggravation. I guess I can handle this.

Still, there is also the idea that I am supposed to "do" something to create circumstances that will enhance my business. How true is that? Doing is outside of the realm of now. I used to believe that being in the now meant that I was doing something right now, but doing is not a part of the creative process, so in order to find now; I must look where the creative ability lies. This is within my thought system. God only recognizes me at the level He created me in. Obviously He is not going to move outside of His Own Awareness to reach me so I will have to move out of my time based awareness to where He is. This is where now is and it is where everything comes together as one and wholeness. This is one wholeness now. This is a part of the Plan for the salvation of the world. I got this one night as I slept. Upon awakening, I knew it was important, but did not quite understand the implications of it. As I sat down to write about it, as is normal, I just began to write. I try not to interfere with what I am hearing and have found that if I just let it be what it is supposed to be, it turns out better.

I was in a church on Sunday. I noticed the licensing from the state of Georgia on the wall that placed the church under the laws of the state. I thought to myself...this is a clear violation of the Constitution, which guarantees the separation of church and state. The Laws of God are not to be put under the mandates of physical law. This is why the Bible was written, to separate Spiritual Law from physical law. The two applications of these laws, when mixed together, are like water and oil. When I began to write about One Wholeness Now, it became clear to me that this was not to be affiliated with any physical law whatsoever. It was not to become a DBA, copyrighted, or trademarked. I wasn't even to open up a web site and protect the name by claiming rights to it. As this was made very clear to me, I put it on my web site and let it speak for itself without constricting it in any way. The Law of Freedom, which is held in the protection of Spiritual Law, prevents me from trying to confine One Wholeness Now to physical law. I realize if I am tempted to restrain the power of this statement, I will actually be a fighter against God and His Plan for the salvation of the world. I trust that there is something greater then my ability to protect this idea. Spiritual Law is greater than physical law. By constricting the Laws of God, the Laws have become ineffectual because for them to work, they must move through a mind. If the mind is in error, so is the Law because of the mind it is passing through. Freedom of Spiritual Law must reign if the world is to be saved. The intellect comes up with all kinds of scenarios as to why Spiritual Law needs to be governed by the governments of the world. This is clearly fear. How can Spiritual Law help the world if fear is surrounding it? Doesn't make much sense. At one point I would have asked...well, can't God break free of the confinement? Sure He can, but He does not violate His Own Laws, and He does not recognize what has been made real by mankind, which is fear. His Love is pure energy and does not flow when it is restricted by fear.

It is impossible to reach peace without being within the idea of One Wholeness Now. Here is freedom, security, Love and everything I want, but I still find myself pursuing a way to manipulate outside circumstances. I know it doesn't work, and yet there is a belief that constantly reminds me..."what about this. Look at this...what are you going to do about this...I have a solution." It's not a solution, for it only leads to more problems. Most of the voices do not trouble me anymore, for I have found a way to heal them using the miracle solution, but still some chatter remains. Sometimes it is just an uncomfortable feeling. I have explained it away to myself, but that is not the way to resolve the problem. I know these beliefs are attached to time and want me to believe that time and fear are real by continually giving me a time based solution that will alleviate the fear temporarily. The temptation is very strong...the temptation is the wish to make the illusion real.

I am now trying to address the situations as they arise. I look for the uncomfortable feeling that leads to the belief of separation and then ask the Interpreter for Help. Many times this occurs so fast, I don't even realize that I have moved from point a to point z and not even hesitated an instant, for if I had the interruption in the process would have been enough to introduce stability, say around e or f and I wouldn't have gotten to z. I have to recognize what is happening, for my thoughts cannot be interrupted and stabilized without my consent.

Mind does not process information by the outward symbol alone. It processes information by how it feels about the outward symbol. Some symbols are safe, like the ones that are passing in the grocery store, and some are not. These are the ones that give me an uncomfortable feeling and I want to get away so the uncomfortable feeling will go away. The uncomfortable feeling is a clue that I have processed information in the past that is now reappearing in a symbolic representation of a form or person. Mind has a lot of sensors, and it reaches out and reads the intention of the symbol. If the symbol's intentions are within the realm of my own, then I am safe. If not then I am very uncomfortable, and my mind sends out a signal that I read as…get out of here. We all have this ability. This is known as being intuitive when the degree of this process is very in tune to the messages that are dropped everywhere in time. Everything carries a vibration. The ability to pick up on the vibration that is in the symbol seems to be a gift, but the fact remains that everyone has this ability. Learning this ability about myself has forced me to ask the question as to why someone else invokes fear or uncomfortable feelings and why I am the only one feeling this way when it is apparent that no one else is. As I pondered these questions, I began to hear the Interpreter, for when I do not explain to myself what something means, I receive another answer that changes my perception. This leads to correction.

So today, I think I will just be quiet. Not trying to do anything, just be peaceful and let go of all of the burdens that seem to be howling at my door. I can be peaceful today.

One Wholeness Now

One Wholeness Now is the Spiritual Plan to restore the world to peace. Because the spiritual Plan is not commonly understood, and in fact is most often misunderstood, to explain, a new movement of thought is being introduced into the thinking of humankind to help with the drastic changes that are occurring in the world by introducing a new understanding. This understanding will correct the violations that have occurred against the Spirit that dwells within. Once humanity begins to shift their awareness towards the principles behind One Wholeness Now by choosing this alternative as a way to establish peace in the world, a New World Order will emerge. This New World Order will give the world's inhabitants a new way of perceiving life that is not out of alignment with the Laws that govern the rest of the Universe to maintain peace. It is then that the prophesy of a New World will emerge that was promised 2000 years ago.

The Worlds Justice

It was not until this century that the atrocities inflicted by men upon other men were examined and judged in a world court. These crimes and atrocities were judged to be so horrible that something had to be done to prevent this from ever occurring again. The purpose was to establish some guidelines that humankind would live by that would prevent such atrocities from occurring again. The whole world watched as the Nazi's were put on trial and it was vowed that this kind of crime against humanity would never occur again. As a society we still find such atrocities repugnant and do not understand what has occurred when men violate the basic rights of others. Still, these atrocities occur. While some men are brought to justice, there are others that do not pay for their crimes and justice does not seem to be fair or consistent. Even though we all get angry at injustice, we are still remiss in our ability to do anything to prevent such acts, except perhaps get angry. Until now, the judicial systems of the world have seemingly held all of the cards, while the vast majority of humankind had to follow the mandates of the governments and judicial systems that have not always been consistent with justice. That is until now. There is another way. We are heading into the greatest change that has occurred since the beginning of time. In order to move into this change without major upset, we are being asked to learn how to live under new Laws that have the ability to end injustice for all time. These are Spiritual Laws and have the ability to dispense justice without depending on humanity to holding a physical court. They also have the ability to transcend anything in the physical realm because these Laws do not conform to the justice of the world. Instead these Laws conform to the Laws of God, which are founded on peace.

Violations of the Spirit

We are not physical beings. In truth, we are Spiritual Beings having a physical experience. Because we have assumed the role of being physical, the experience that we are having has taken precedence over our Spirit so we believe the experience we are having has some kind of ability to dictate and demand that the universe must somehow adhere to the laws of man. This error must be corrected so the laws of man can be aligned with Laws that provide security and justice for all. Because our Spirit is governed by Spiritual Law and we try to live by laws that have been established by humanity, we are at odds with our Being or Spirit Nature and have tried to replace essence with experience. We have become so confused about our true nature, it is mistakenly believed that it is possible to mandate the Laws of God by restricting Him with the laws of man.

The Spiritual History of the World

The Spiritual history of the world began 6000 years ago. The physical history of the world was in tact long before the Spiritual History of the world began, as indicated through the tracing of physical history to millions of years ago. When the spiritual history of the world began, a new element of self evidence was introduced that began a quest for the Creator, which could only be found by seeking for the inborn spirit. Up until that point the Nature of God was fearful and was made such because fear was the nature of the world. Fear was depended upon as a source of protection and because God is a Protector of the just, He was attributed with a fearful nature. The introduction of Spiritual Law was the introduction of the true Nature of God, which is Love. The introduction of the Spiritual History into the physical world related to the time when the Love of God would be understood as the correct application of Law, which would move humankind beyond fear. Once the Spiritual History of the world began, the opportunity to unite with God's Love became a possibility through a new understanding of His Nature. Thus, the promise to end the separation that began in fear was why the Spiritual History of the world began.

The God of Love

We live in an enlightened world so it is now possible to understand God to be Love instead of the fearful God that the men of the Old Testament understood. The event that opened up the flood gates for God's Love, or Spiritual Love, to enter the world, was the Birth of the Christ. His Birth opened a connection between the physical realm and the Spiritual Realm where the truth of the Love of God came to replace the God of fear of old. We are witness to this when the Bible states that Christ poured Himself out, even unto His death. It is impossible to break a bond of Love created by God. The Christ had this connection with God so God joined with the Christ as He became a conduit for God's Love to enter time. The symbol of this connection is a bridge. Once the bridge was established, humankind was free to cross the bridge and join with true Love. This would cause the world to change forever change. It is now possible for us to cross the bridge and echo God's Love into the world and bring a new message of hope. Everything is in place, as the spiritual bridge has had the ability to give new blessings of innocence to a world sorely in need of a new perspective. The Foundation for the New World is firm and all of the pieces of a spiritual puzzle have entered this world, but the spiritual puzzle must have physically willing participants to pick up the puzzle pieces and begin the assembling process. Without physical help, the spiritual puzzle is useless, for humankind must become aware that each individual has a part to play in the establishment of peace on earth. This is why a period of adjustment is being made possible. To allow for those physical willing participants to pick up their piece of the spiritual puzzle and find where their piece fits in.

The Shift

There is something occurring in the world and everyone can feel that something is amiss. Not knowing what it is, people just go about their business in the same way that they always have. This will not continue.

Humankind will find it increasingly more difficult to conduct business as usual as the Nature of their Spirit begins to take precedent over the physical nature of man. The Laws of God work in conjunction with our Spirit Nature, which lies in our Being. For this reason, an inner shift must occur that will shift our ways of thinking from physical logic to spiritual wisdom. This shift is good news for the world, but not for those who wish to maintain using the world for unholy purposes. Our spiritual nature is not in jeopardy, but it is up to each individual to support this nature by learning how to agree and support it. Thus, the period of adjustment will occur so each person can learn and thereby contribute their piece of the spiritual puzzle and add to the joy of God. This time of adjustment was made for a shift to occur which will help each person re-establish their reality in their own mind. The shift of this occurrence is dramatic and is considered evolutionary, so there is no one in this world that will not be affected in one way or another.

The New Crusade

The new crusade is not one that will bring pain through force and manipulation by forcing others to conform to unwanted ideas. Instead, this crusade will overtake the world without a shot ever being fired. There is no right or wrong religion, so the adjustment is not involved in beliefs, instead it involves the basic nature of the spirit, which is innocence. Within every Nature of Spirit, lies innocence. This is the innocence of the world must be released to save it. The scripture refers to this when it is noted, "that a child will lead them all." Innocence is not a trait that ever came from the physical world. Innocence is spiritual in nature and dwells in the heart of everything created by God. Placing innocence under the jurisdiction of physical law has violated the heart, where God dwells. God cannot hear His Innocence because of the shadow that tries to hold innocence in contempt. Innocence knows how to deal with Natural Laws, which are creating havoc in the world. In order establish order amongst the creative elements of the world, innocence must be released before further damage occurs. The intellect does not recognize innocence as having the value that it does, so the

Plan of One Wholeness Now cannot be placed in physical hands. It is the recognition of this that will save the world. There is no other way, for this is God's Plan.

In an attempt to bring new meaning to the innocent nature, Help has been employed at higher level. This Help will provide humankind with new resources to accomplish this task. These resources are not physical, but physical results will be evident through their use. The greatest Gift to help humankind through this turbulent time is miracles. It is essential that miracles be recognized by humanity as the source that will help bring order to this world. It is also essential that humanity learn how to work with miracles so they can begin to learn how Higher Laws work. Miracles do not create, but they do have the ability to move ahead of a situation and bring the components together that will bring a new perception into the physical mind. In this way, they move ahead of time made events and make circumstances that are not out of alignment with Natural Laws. This creates tunnels in time, that when taken, improve world conditions. Humanity will literally walk into a New World as they learn how to follow miracles instead of trying to use them for the purpose of the intellect.

Make no mistake, God's Love will triumph over the lower nature. What this will mean for the inhabitants of the world will be a marked understanding of the truth and with it a peace that cannot be overturned by any physical establishment. With proper order restored to the world, the Laws that govern the heart where God or Love abides extends into the world by giving it a new meaning and a new purpose that has never been known since the beginning of time.

Our Part in the Plan

For the last 2000 years, since the Birth of Christ, the Spirit of God has been crossing the spiritual bridge through the innocent nature. Everything is in place, but the understanding of the Plan is not. The Plan of reconciliation was written within the Laws that He established in the Beginning. He has not changed His Mind and the world will know of His Peace because of His Love for the world. Because the dwelling place of God lies within the heart, it is the heart of man that must be changed so it understands that the Laws of God are His Love. We are not sinful for we still hold His Innocence. Guilt must be stripped from the human intellect through a recognition of innocence. Fear must be dismissed as the unreal state so Love can return..

Our part in the Plan is to be willing to change our mind. This does not mean that the intellect knows what to change our mind to. The first step is to acknowledge that we do not know. This acknowledgement signifies our support of what we do not understand., but are willing to learn. This is our greatest challenge, for the intellect, which was developed to live in a physical world, is in error and causing damage to the world that does not have to occur.

God's Temple

It is said the Temple of God lies in the body. This statement has been misconstrued to make us believe that body communication, which is of the intellect, can somehow give us answers it does not have. Until we understand the importance of our own Word, and how we have learned to contaminate our Word, we will not understand that the language that is held in the body is not wisdom at all. Instead the language of the body is made up of false beliefs that the intellect relies on to dictate wrong information.. This is the endless chatter that keeps us up at night telling us how to solve problems. Knowing is beyond belief because belief is not a function of the Creator. As we begin to learn or our spiritual reality, we begin to share in a knowing that moves us beyond belief. This recognition gives us a proper body identification by not inflating it or making it less than the purpose it was designed for. If this does not occur, we will continue to place body identification above Spirit Identification. Only the Spirit has the ability to understand the Law, and then share it with the lower mind, or the intellect. While we remain unaware, we will be deceived into believing a false reality over the truth.

The Universe Awaits our Decision

We have been given the means to undo our past learning that has come about as a result of a fearful physical experience, which built intellectual understanding and taught us how to avoid, force or manipulate circumstance in order to be successful in our physical experience. The Plan, on the other hand, leads us out of turmoil and conflict and into a Loving Embrace of grace.. All of Heaven awaits our decision, for we are needed to help restore sanity to the world before it is destroyed by a nature that is not designed to understand and live by the Laws of Spirit.

Each person that agrees to join with the Plan for the salvation of the world begins to get reacquainted with the language that they knew before they entered the physical realm. Instead of only listening to and hearing beliefs that were learned in the physical experience, they hear another Voice that begins to direct and Guide them to their Spiritual Reality that lies in their Spiritual Nature. As the connection is made firm it is finally realized that light has come into the dream and the path that seemed to only offer a painful end, comes to an end and a new one begins. The steps now taken are taken with purpose as it is learned that these steps are not taken alone, but in fact all of Heaven has taken a direct interest in the new direction that has been chosen.

What we are doing here

Our purpose was not decided upon our arrival in physical time. Instead our purpose was decided before we entered time, and we will not find contentment until we find our Spiritual Agreement and fulfill it. If we give ourselves a purpose that does not contain this agreement, we will go through our physical life and feel unfulfilled, or feel like there is something missing. This will seemingly force us to look externally until we move towards another decision that does not violate our Spiritual Agreement..

We were not created to "be" unhappy, depressed, alcoholic, drug addicted, or anything else that defines us in a derogatory way. We were created to "be" happy. Without knowing this, we are in violation of Spiritual Law and correction must occur so the derogatory implications are dismissed as being unreal in our own mind. It is our agreement that has brought us here to this particular point in time. We all raised our hand when it was asked who would go and help clean up the mess in the world. The world is the inheritance that God gave to His Son, and we are all Sons of God making sure that the world is a fit place for the Love of God to come and reside with us.

There is much to learn about the special provisions that have been made for us and then there is the appointed time to learn how to use these provisions. This is something I had to learn so I could give it away. If you feel like it is time to move forward in you spiritual journey, and do not know which way to go, perhaps a new road is what is needed. In order to walk down this road, you must be willing to relinquish everything that you think you know. This does not happen without an inner battle. But remember this; the more people that are willing to learn of the provisions that have been provided, the easier it is for those that have not yet made that decision. The decision to take the road less traveled is worth the effort, because you are worth the effort. Take my hand and walk with me. I will not abandon you. Together we can change the world and give it a new meaning of hope.

Day Twenty Six

God does not live in my consciousness; He lives in the awareness of wholeness. Consciousness is self made for self understanding at a physical level, so consciousness is a method of self preservation so I can make decisions based on my learned physical experiences that are held in mind/body awareness. Whole awareness does not perceive at a limited or individual level, that is why there is Higher Consciousness. The ability to use self learned consciousness and then shift it to Higher Consciousness gives the individual access to the Whole Awareness of God. Without this Consciousness, there would be no way to access unlimited understanding or Whole Awareness. This takes time and patience to learn how to shift lower consciousness to Higher Consciousness because individual consciousness is too involved in self awareness and cannot perceive that there is anything beyond its own understanding. So the first thing that must occur is a realization that individual consciousness is not the only one that exists. It is also understanding just how limited self awareness really is.

Self awareness or understanding is a result of the separation. This is explained in the Bible as Adam and Eve realized they were naked. It would be impossible to realize you were naked without some kind of self awareness. With the realization that they were naked, the beginning of self awareness began and consciousness was born. A decision to make something without God began a new state that was not recognized in Heaven. Because the Purpose of Love is to draw all things unto Itself, a Higher and better answer for the question raised in the Garden emerged. Because consciousness became a part of creation, God would have to make a Higher Consciousness that would have access to the wholeness of Living Laws where Whole Awareness reside. The Plan was to make an opportunity where it would be possible for lower consciousness to have access to whole awareness.

For all of my life I have been building mind/body, or self awareness. In order to direct my personal beliefs I had to make a consciousness that would direct these beliefs to the external world. The world began to relate to me in the same manner that I related to it, for the creative process dwells within me, not the external realm. The longer I saw how the world mirrored back to me my own beliefs, I began to become fearful of what I had made, because what I had made in error was fearful. I began to believe this fear was real, and in order to try to avoid what I had made, I try to avoid this fear by making conscious decisions that will force or manipulate circumstances so I can alleviate what is held within my own awareness. This of course does not alleviate it, and for some insane reason I believe that if I can control the problem by avoiding my fear the problem will dissipate. This is insane. If I cannot pay a bill, then I become fearful. It seems as though the fear is external, so I look for an external solution. My mind begins to churn as I seek internally for an external solution. All of my past memories of forcing or manipulating external circumstances comes into play as I look for a way to produce money that I do not have. My self awareness is trying to direct my consciousness, but it really does not know what to do. I do not know what to do consciously either, so a tremendous amount of tension and stress are the result.

Unless I realize that there is another option, I can work myself up into a frenzy. Realizing that there is another option opens up another way of solving the problem, but this takes time to learn how to make the adjustment from an external solution to an internal solution. For one thing, this world works on the premise that in order to produce results, something has to be done. The Higher Consciousness works on the premise that it can be internally accomplished with no loss or sacrifice to anyone through an understanding that the problem is a result of learning incorrectly. The revealing of the error is the solution. This sounds like it would be an impossibility, but we have all heard, that all things are possible with God. In order to access these provisions a decision of healing must be made. It is this decision that insures that the problem will be resolved once and for all. Results may or may not occur instantaneously. The decision to heal opens doors that were not there before the decision was made. Because internal Laws or Spiritual Laws are not under the same restrictions of physical or external laws, what one receives for their healing is an experience that is totally out of time as the problem just slips away.

The Plan for the salvation of the world was made so that I could have access to the Whole Awareness of God without totally understanding how it works. I can choose to have access to the Higher Consciousness, which in turn has access to the Whole Awareness of God, if I turn to this Higher Consciousness instead of relying on my own as a way to get my needs met I can depend on it to go to bat for me. Higher Consciousness can turn my need or want into language that can be understood by God, and my need is fulfilled. My understanding of this is not necessary, but I am responsible for my fear. Because I am learning how to work with my own creative process, and my own creative process has become destructive because of my own fear of what I have made, then I am responsible for it. Heaven will not acknowledge anything that is not real, but what it will do is continue to point to what is real until I can see it for myself. This doesn't mean that I will totally abandon fear before Higher Consciousness can help me. What it does mean is that I will have to find a way around the fear that is found in my awareness that I have erroneously learned to depend on as a protective measure.

If I cannot find peace and insist on looking externally for an answer my connection with the Higher Consciousness will step aside to make way for what I think I want. This does not mean I have been abandoned, but it does mean that my wish to make something in error is being honored. This is because we have the right to look wherever we want for our reality, even if it is wrong. Beliefs that have formed a bond to time will want me to seek out in the world of time for what I need, but this places me back in the position of having to force and manipulate. It has taken me quite awhile to understand how this works. My consciousness must direct and then hold with the Higher Consciousness long enough for the need to be met, and then for the problem to be solved. This means that I must be willing to hold peace in my mind, even if the problem seems to be calling for stress. What is necessary is to recognize is that the process was designed to work with me. As long as I work with it, it will help me with my perceived needs until perfect correction has occurred..

There are many ways that beliefs deceive to get us to let go of the process. They lie to us and seemingly force us to look at the physical demand of the problem or need. We are not asked to totally give up our association with the false belief, but we are asked to stand firm in our conviction of the process. The Inner Guide will vouch for us to the Higher Consciousness as long as our agreement to join with the Inner Guide or Solution remains firm. Our agreement is necessary to maintain the connection. The connection becomes broken when we stray back to the false belief and begin to associate with it. This is like flying a plane and relying on instruments that seem to go against every instinct I have. It seems like I am going to crash and burn, but the truth is the instrument is my safety. It takes a great deal of determination to use this process but it works and like I said it took me awhile to "get it." Because of my determination to understand the process and the Plan, I have received many insights. Even at this, I still have been responsible for my own beliefs that I learned in error. Without the Plan of bringing lower consciousness to Higher Consciousness, the world would be doomed to destruction, but this is not the Plan that was originated at the moment of separation, so everyone must play their part to help bring the world back to the Justice of Heaven.

Paying attention to my thinking process has taken me in seemingly many directions. But the truth is…there are only two directions to go. One is with my physical experience where beliefs are stored that make me believe that my experience is real and I am not; and the other is to use the process designed to move me beyond the experience to another level of Consciousness and Awareness that is not commonly known or used in time.

Every night I ask to be delivered from my own evil. The torment of half truths and lies seem to devour me at times. Still I trek on, feeling my way and finding morsels of truth that open the way to the whole truth. After it is all said and done, I know that I am being used as a conduit for the truth to enter the world and heal it. We all are.

Confession

Honesty

Confession is an act of honesty. Honesty is not a physical attribute, it is a spiritual one. Honesty is a result of, not necessarily being aware of immoral behavior, but instead looking within and finding why immoral behavior is occurring. The greatest act of dishonesty that we commit is against ourselves. We learn at a very young age to point our finger at others and blame someone else for our feelings and thus our behavior falls in line thereafter. To be sure, a behavioral act does not occur because of someone else. The only way we can resolve our own behavior, is to first of all stop blaming someone else. This is the only way we can begin to be responsible for our own lives and stop being at the mercy of outside circumstances. Otherwise, we will continue to be a victim and it is no fun to be in this position.

Sin

Sin is one of the most misunderstood words in the human language. Sin, from a spiritual point of view, is not in our behavior. A sin is a misaligned belief that looks externally for a solution, instead of looking within for the psychological reason. The psychological reason for sin is cause. The effect is in the behavior, so punishing behavior will not adjust sin and will not correct error.

At a Higher Level, there is only cause and effect, or sin and behavior. However, in the physical realm the effect of behavior is what society punishes. This is why forgiveness is needed, to stop the effects of the sin, or cause, that continues to perpetuate itself. Forgiveness is Heaven's Justice meted out in time, so once sin is forgiven, there is no more behavior that points to the error..

In our True State of Being, we are loving and caring and behavior does not enter into determining Who We Are. At the physical level, behavior is considered very much a part of who we are. Behavior is what we do, not who we are, and it is this confusion that keeps the world in a constant state of never permanently finding solutions that work. Let's just take a look at how a sinful nature begins.

Feelings

Laws that govern the Being Nature are beyond our intellectual understanding, these Laws state that we are what we feel. In this Being state, we wear our feelings of love, happiness, joy, goodness, etc on our sleeve for all to see. Innocent Love is not hidden and is openly encouraged and are expressed openly and shared without reservation. Our feelings are very important because they constitute our propeller that navigates us through the Heavenly Realm. Feelings also navigate us through the physical world. When we feel something, we act on the feeling, not the particular event that is occurring. Higher feelings belong to the Higher Realm. When these higher feelings get tied up in a lower experience that does not reflect Love, Who We Are becomes a physical being that has become sinful because the interpretation of Love has become distorted. For instance; if we are told as children that we get punished because we are loved, then whenever love shows up, it will show up with punishment. The punishment is not in error, not is love in error, but the two together are. The error is in our own mind, so it is sin. Forgiveness must occur so love and punishment are not seen as one, for as long as they are seen as one, they must occur together. Forgiveness is what helps us take the next step, which is the inner shift. The inner shift shows us how our understanding of love has been in error. With this, innocent love that has been defiled by punishment goes Home. This is the journey, as the intellect has learned something that was not within its awareness before. The connection between the heart and the intellect has opened. This is just an example, and the errors that have occurred that defile the heart are many. Mind/Body-Heart Connection

Lower consciousness is mistakenly using innocent love as a prisoner to keep beliefs in tact that show us that the mind/body solution is the correct one. Higher Consciousness tells us the something has been taken from Heaven's Door and must be returned, for it is in the returning of what is Heaven's Possession that sanity is restored to the world.

The physical world is the only place where consciousness can become a part of the mind. To use consciousness correctly, first it becomes associated with self aware beliefs which in turn builds the intellect. Once an intellect has been form and the belief system has been become total, individual consciousness is complete. It is then time to begin to shift this self consciousness and trade it in for a better model. This something better is Higher Consciousness. This process begins by learning forgiveness, and then understanding what the error is. This then exposes false beliefs to Higher Consciousness where the error is immediately corrected. This is because once understands what the real error is, it immediately makes the correction and returns the innocent nature back to where it belongs. This is how the mind/body awareness is united with heart awareness, and the two become as one.

The Restoration

When our innocence has been violated, it must be restored to the correct connection, which is spiritual. Innocence does not know how to operate under the physical laws of force and manipulation. It only works correctly under the Laws in which it was created under, which is Spiritual Law. Violations that have occurred that are stored in the body are the reasons for anxiety, stress and disease. In essence, the anxiety is an indicator that innocence has been lost and must be restored to righteousness, which is found in the heart. Otherwise the internal problem will remain and we will continue to experience externally what we feel internally. This is the profound effect that shows up in behavior. Because we do not know how to "do" this, we have to learn how to work within a part of our mind that we are unaccustomed to working with.

Problems cannot be solved at the same level at which they are occurring. This means that we cannot reconnect our innocence too our spiritual nature because we do not know how to intellectually perform this task. Special provisions have been made for us at this particular time to help us correct the error or the sin.

The Confession

Before correction can begin, the first thing that has to happen is a recognition that there is a problem. Instead of blaming, we take responsibility by admitting that the problem is our own. This opens up the communication process between our mind and the Solution, Who can help us make the correction. The emotion produced from lost innocence must be released from the body and returned to Love can once again express itself the way through the heart. Love is once again being moved through our innocence and then expressed instead of being imprisoned by fear.

Learning to confess, or be honest until the "sin" is expelled we learn to use this process in all situations. Because the Holy Spirit is involved, He is the Solution that God gave to us for the problem of sin, and the means to heal will be given, but it is up to us to work with Him.

All Have Sinned

"All have sinned and fallen short of the Glory of God," means that we have fallen short of our own Glory and that it can be restored. Special provisions have been made for humanity to help us rid the world of "sin". It is up to us to take the initiative and learn what these provisions are. It takes work, but God would not give us a Plan that is impossible for us to accomplish.

Day Twenty Seven

Shifting thought systems is more difficult than I thought. Not only is the language more precise in the Higher one, but everything I have learned in the physical realm has been distorted. It's not that there is no truth here; it's that the violation that has been placed on truth carries more value than the truth itself. When I speak of truth to others, many times I receive a blank stare. It is as if I am speaking in a foreign tongue. Oh, I am still speaking English, but because my value has shifted, value is not perceived in the same place.

We wonder why God doesn't hear us. It's not that He doesn't hear us, it's that we do not understand our question. The value of our question requires us to accept a new value of ourselves, but for the most part we cannot see our own value, so we approach the answer we expect from God in the same way we have posed the question. When we ask for an answer that has error attached to it, we are looking for an answer that is not related to truth. Truth cannot be found in error. The means to find truth has been taken care of for us, but most have been remiss to step up and take responsibility for hearing the Words of truth when they are spoken. It has never been truth that is in error, it has always been me and anyone else who does not take the steps necessary to learn truth and begin to separate it from the violations that have occurred. I have begun to grow accustomed to seeing information different than most people, and for the most part they agree that what I see does not necessarily agree with what they see. I am learning just to leave it alone. For instance, when I see a natural tragedy occurring, I realize that looking at the tragedy will help make more tragedy. The more tragedy is examined, the more it is understood. Understanding brings value to the mind, and what the mind values it creates more of. But the world seems to be transfixed on these kinds of occurrences. If I say, don't look at the tragedy, people think I am saying not to take into consideration that people need help and that is not what I am saying at all, so I just try to keep my mouth shut.

When tragedy is treasured, it violates our purpose and it is always the offender or the one that holds the thought that will pay the price of their own thinking. We do not physically think we treasure tragedy, but because of the violations we are mistaken.

Learning the Language of Love, or internal communication has taught me some valuable lessons. One thing for sure, if my mind is not aligned with truth, I am not available to true information. If I go into a closet and close the door, I am involved in my own thinking process. The problem is that all of my beliefs are in there with me, and so I have to contend with a bazillion other thoughts that are what I am trying to get away from. This makes for a very confused closet as every belief carries its own identity and wants to he heard. This eventually becomes unbearable, especially if there are a lot of beliefs that are angry. Eventually the vibration in the room explodes and because there is no outlet for this explosive vibration the whole house comes down with the explosion. This is the condition of the world today. There is just too much intensity for conditions to continue as they are now. There is too much input and not enough peace. It is impossible that corrupted input add to the peace of the world. Instead, it is the uncorrupted value of peace that has the ability to resolve all of the problems of the world.

If I ask the Interpreter about the wars and conflicts that are going on in the world, He tells me that they don't matter. My first judgment is to rush to the defense of my convictions that tell me there is just too much injustice in the world not to think it doesn't matter. His response is that my convictions merely add to the conflicted input that is already there. More input in the closet merely adds the volatile conditions that are already there. So what should I do? The answer is as always…stay out of it. My perceptions of what is going on are wrong. My solution to what is going on is wrong. The Plan for the salvation of the world is not of my making or anyone else's in this world for that matter. It was a

Plan devised at the beginning of time. I don't remember the assault that happened in the beginning. But still there is a part of me that wants to intrude and give my judgment of the situation. I keep telling myself that the physical solutions are not real, but I still find them. They are actually an assault on my being peaceful and keep me in a state of constant turmoil and conflict.

The language of fear has taught me how to experience fear. Fear is so far outside of who I am, that if I could even get a small grasp around this idea, I would forever ban fear from my awareness. But there are wisps of beliefs that surround themselves with fear. I don't even recognize them and actually believe that they are helpful. Seems like I would "get it" and have often wondered what was wrong with me because it seemed like I couldn't. But still I continue on the journey because I know that the language of truth is not in the language of fear that I have so treasured.

It's all or nothing. This is the agreement I have made. Still, I feel an overwhelming sense of fear at times because the Laws I am attempting to follow do not follow the laws of time at all. These Laws come straight out of Eternity and are shared with my mind via the Interpreter. Still, I wish I could have it my way just a little and have an experience that alleviates fear instead of an expression that does not recognize fear at all. I have come too far. The journey that lies behind me is in the past, and if I look for my future in the past I will return to fear. It's as if I move forward and then pull remnants of my past with me believing that somehow these remnants will protect me. But fear has no protective power. I don't know how many times I have said to someone else…I can choose not to go into the street to play because I am afraid of getting hit by a car, or I can stay out of the street because I love myself enough not to play in traffic. It is simple enough, but still I believe that there is some kind of fear that offers protection. This is known as healthy fear…what is that? Truth is not a contradiction, so either fear is healthy or it is not. Either fear can protect us, or Love has this ability, for there is nothing in between. The "gray" areas that I always tread on must be corrected, but I must make a conscious decision to make the correction for without my decision nothing happens. Still, my attempts at self correction continues. This usually occurs by trying to make something alright by addressing the situation at a physical level. Even though I know that communication and correction at this level is futile, there is a part of me that still wants to intrude. Such is the power of belief.

The power of beliefs is very strong. It's easier just to go along with them and make excuses for my behavior than correct. I know the solution lies in "tuning into' another form of communication that is not in the endless chatter that is constantly informing me of what to do to correct and explain outer circumstances.

Even in tragedy that is found in this world, there is Light. The light is not in the tragedy, but instead in the kind deeds that arise from the tragedy. The story of Lot's Wife is particularly poignant here. She was to look away from the unreality of the destruction and look at her deliverance. This took her out of the past and into the present. The longing to understand destruction is of the false belief system. The more we understand destruction, the more destruction there is. Whatever is understood is loved, then given and received. Kind of upside down when thought about that way. If I understand destruction, then I will be the recipient of more. This is a clear violation of the Law. The world just understands too much about what it should not understand and was never meant to understand. Where is the love in destruction, war, disease and hatred? The truth is, there isn't any. My abhorrence of such things does not end these problems, it adds to them. Still I look, but I can change what I am looking at by choosing to see something else. I can't do this on my own, but I can ask to see in another way. There is always hope in everything that is occurring. Within this hope is the possibility that something else will emerge that has nothing to do with the way the political and religious systems of the world have set it up, for these systems must come down to make way for the new Government that has been established. This is the hope and the prophecy that have pointed in this direction sense the beginning of time. If I am to be a part of it, then I must learn to hear the new Language that whispers to me constantly and consistently. It is only here that truth emanates from, and I can learn of my own divinity.

There is another language to tune into that has the solution to any problem that may arise. This language is the true language and the one that we all were created with. It is not the spoken language, instead it is the language that is viewed in the heart, and it is where the Love of God lives. My heart had been covered over for many years and the Language of Heaven has had a difficult time breaking through. To untangle the broken lines of communication that have attached to the intellect has taken me quite awhile and I still find remnants of the broken communication. Reattaching the lines of true communication brings about a new awareness that can only happen internally. When we are born, these lines of communication are very strong. As a child becomes more self aware, information stored in the body begins to take precedent over the lines of communication to the spirit. Eventually body communication is the focal point, and as spirit communicates, as it still does, this information is set aside as being irrelevant to the situation at hand. It makes sense, that body awareness is making the world as I see it, but I can change what I see with a new awareness. Body internal communication seems to interrupt higher internal communication, but this is so only if I let this occur. My appreciation level must shift and because appreciation is a Spiritual Law the new shift will bind me to what is real. Trying to use appreciation at a belief level is a waste of time. Truth is found in the Light of truth, not in the shadow of darkness, or belief that has never been exposed to the light.

The Language of Heaven

What is the Language of Heaven?

The Language of Heaven is the Language of Love. The Language of Love is the dialog that occurs between God and His Son. The Son who dwells in the physical realm is in need of re-learning the Language that seems to Him He has lost. He does not even remember the Language because the sleep He has fallen into is deep and seems to have taken Him far from His Home.

If we were born in another country and learned the language of that country when we were children, would we still remember the language that was spoken in our youth? Of course we would. If we visited another country, would we expect the country to conform to our interpretation of their language, or would it be that we would be the one that was expected to adjust our comprehension. Chances are that the country whose culture we were studying or visiting would not change for us. In fact it would be our responsibility to make the adjustment. Even at this, because of the special circumstances we find ourselves in, there would be patience coming from those we were learning from.

The Language of Heaven is like a language from a foreign country. We have forgotten how to speak the language, but even though this is so, it is still in our mind stored as a memory that we have forgotten how to access. The memory needs to be stimulated and reawakened. It is by our decision to reawaken that the memory of the language is stirred. Just like going to a foreign country and learning a new language, the Language of Love is step in the direction of showing an interest in learning. Without our interest, the lack of understanding of the Language remains a barrier to our communication to Heaven, where our true creative process lies.

Physical Language

Physical language is, for the most part, very primitive. Most of what is communicated by our physical language is not the whole story. In other words, body language, which is provided by internal body communication are taken into consideration along with the spoken word. Even at this, we sometimes still only get a partial story. The spoken physical language is mostly an intellectual function, which means that what we hear is heard from our experiential understanding. Experiential information is stored in the brain. This is where we make rational decisions based upon our physical learning that comes from personal experience.

I recently took a communication class, and in this class we were told that most people communicate at a level that is between 6th and 8th grade. This means that most adults have communication skills that cease to mature after the age of 12 to 14 yrs. If our intellectual ability to communicate begins to come to an end around 12 to 14 yrs., our communication is handicapped. When communication has been stunted we keep communication simple so the masses can understand what is being said. How much are we failing to understand if we are not communicating beyond a level of 14? This means that our physical communicating ability, which is in our logical and intellectual assessment of situations, is faulty and should be put up to scrutiny.

After the age of 12 to 14 is attained, communication skills are mostly inherent in the person doing the intellectual thinking. In other words, the ideas of right and wrong and how one wants their life to proceed have already been established by learning through peers and experiences. The next phase is how to accomplish a formulated goal by getting others to agree with you. This might mean forcing an issue or perhaps manipulating a situation so it can go the way of the individual's plan. In the case of world peace, there are many individuals trying to work out a compromise that is in conjunction with everyone who has their own plan and agenda on how to bring about peace. The problem is that this kind of communication only considers the plan of one who has only matured intellectually to a teenager. This is why nothing much is ever accomplished in the way of world peace. In order to find stability, a place of common ground must be established. This can only be done by finding what is the same. What is the same does not come from the intellect because intellect is established through a personal experience based on beliefs that carry their own agenda. Personal belief learned through experience cannot dictate world peace because it does not know how. Also, the reference point of personal experience lies within individual understanding and individual understanding is not global. Global thinking needs global assistance that has the ability to lead where individual experience is not a factor in the decision process. It could be that our communication standards are inept because we require and expect so little of ourselves. If we set the standards and raised the bar it is possible that the ability to communicate would supercede our own expectations. In order to do this it is up to us to reconsider our learning ability and move up to the next step. As an incentive to learn a new communication skill, we can ask ourselves if we would trust the ability of a teenager to communicate the idea of world peace to the rest of the world. Would we trust those in political office in other countries to examine world peace as an option if they too only understand the concept of world peace from the level of a teenager?

Perhaps we believe that physical communication is the only way to communicate because we do not know how to look further. Learning a new language takes time. We cannot learn how to speak the Language of Heaven by staying at a 7th grade level of intellectual understanding. It is up to each individual to expand their mind to include more than their intellect. Just as we could not learn how to speak French without stepping away from what we already know, we cannot learn how to speak the Language of Heaven without moving out of our comfort zone and learning that what we have been taught in our physical experience is not all there is.

Heaven's Language

When the intellect is perceived as being attacked, we get angry. Anger is not a part of Heaven's Language. Anger is set aside in favor of a peaceful solution, regardless of what the situation is when speaking the Language of Love. The outcome is win/win for everyone involved because the communication skills of Heaven's Language do not proceed out of the intellect, but instead proceed out of the heart. Heart expressions are ones ability to be empathetic, which is the ability to understand at an emotional level how another feels. This is beyond the intellectual understanding that is so highly prized in our physical reality. Thinking with the heart requires us to be innocent and let go of our intellectual ideas of what we need to get so an outcome is perceived as fair. Being innocent is scary and getting is not heart motivated thinking, so it seems there are two strikes against this new Language to begin with. But heart thinking observes the rights of everyone by looking for a common ground that cannot be established by the intellect but can only be seen with an innocent understanding. Do we remember how to accomplish this? If not then we are not making use of the ability that lies in the heart of all men everywhere. If we are trying to solve problems without understanding the nature, or the communication ability of the heart. What has been left out is the healing ability of Love. We have also lost, momentarily, the opportunity to allow Heaven into the problem solving process. It seems to me we all need help, and Help is here and it is now. Until we reach the point where we know that the intellect is not serving us, we will continue to serve it by allowing ourselves to believe that there is nothing beyond our belief in it.

The Language of Heaven takes time to learn. Anything that we take the time to learn serves us well and we can be sure learning how to speak from the heart will serve us. Just as a foreign language is not readily understood, so it is with the Language of Heaven. The ability to learn this new way of communicating is now open to anyone who cares to learn it. It is only too difficult to learn if it is believed it is too difficult. It is up to each individual to step up and be willing to go beyond what is intellectually understood to a new understanding that only lies in the heart. The challenge is now and the time is right. We can make a difference and heal the world by learning to speak the Language of Love.

Day Twenty Eight

Every lesson I have tried to learn on my own has been wrong, but it was not without a good intention. My good intention wasn't enough though, and so I had to set aside what I thought I knew in order to make way for what was really there. I also wanted to use what others had used, but found that this just delayed progress. I was on my own journey, and trying to use the plans that others had used actually kept me from finding what had been made for my own healing. I drilled affirmations and visualization into my mind believing that I was doing the right thing. What I did not realize was that I was working with a very creative process and in order to use these methods correctly, I had to be in the right "state of mind." To be in the right state of mind infers that there is also a wrong state of mind, so if I am trying to "program" in the wrong state, nothing happens, except perhaps disappointment because I taught myself how to do something incorrectly. I have some responsibility to learn how my different states of mind affect me. By trying to use someone else's method, I learned a lesson of how to do it wrong.

The Laws of Spirit are quite different then physical law. The Laws of Spirit are alive, where as the laws of time do not have any ability to even understand life. Time just goes forward. It really doesn't even have the ability to go forward; it is just that the universe has its own standards that we credit time for. Quite the opposite is true with the Laws of Spirit. The Laws of Spirit were written in the Book of Life in the beginning. Each word in the Book of Life is represented by the actual life of a Spirit, so the words actually speak when being read or communicated. Angels are in effect Words spoken with God and His

Son together, and They each have a purpose as is indicated when the Word of the Father and Son are spoken together. This is difficult to comprehend at the physical level as not much credence is given to the spoken word.

Written in the Book of Life are the many creations that sprang to life in the beginning. Creation is the potential of the mind when both the Father and the Son are joined. Spiritual Law, or the Words of Creation, began all means of life. The meaning of life is the creative potential that lives in individual minds. But when the thought process becomes distorted and we begin to look at a reality that does not hold the Book of Life, new forms of life spring into action that are not necessarily healthy. The purpose of the mind is to create. It either creates constructively when used under the proper conditions, or destructively when it is not.

The world, as it is now, is set up for failure. It is impossible to play by the rules set up in this world and keep from breaking a physical law. This leads to guilt, but guilt has far more reaching detrimental consequences than what is currently known. The value that is seen in the world comes from behavior, but unhealthy behavior is a physical aspect resulting from a fearful experience. This is bound to make guilt an everyday part of the physical experience. I then try to atone for my guilt by feeling guiltier. I go over and over it in my mind; as if by doing this I will somehow resolve the guilt, but guilt cannot be resolved with more guilt. That is insane. Guilt is resolved with its opposite, or with innocence. But the world wants us to be guilty and be punished for our guilt. But what would happen if everyone were viewed as innocent? Eventually wouldn't everyone become innocent? Hmmm.. the truth is, I will never feel guilty enough to finally start feeling better. Besides that, I can't be innocent and guilty at the same time. I have to choose which one I want to be. I can "be" guilty and try to make up for a past error, or sin if I believe I have to pay a penalty for erratic behavior, or I can just let it go and "be" innocent. Which ever I choose will be evident in how others respond to me, because it all comes from me. That never occurred to me before I began the journey. I believed I had to be guilty and guilt led to fear. I had so much fear in me that everything I did or attempted to do was fearful. Simple things I had to do brought about fear, and some of it was intense because I began to believe I was going to be wrong regardless of what I did. Telling myself it was stupid to feel like this didn't stop the fear, and it was surely a blessing to find out that I could choose innocence, but I had to work at it because being guilty was a way of life for me.

Just like writing in the Book of Life produces life; fear writes in the book of death. Thoughts of fear are not real, but they sure feel real when they are being experienced. They are alive in the sense that belief in them gives them a power that seems inescapable. Unreasonable fear can make the average Joe act like a crazy person, yelling and screaming at the sight of something that has no ability whatsoever, except in the mind of the one that has given it power. If fear were real, it would be real for everyone or everyone would have the same fear. There would be no deviation from the feeling and it would be impossible to escape. The mind protects fear because it was decided somewhere in the past that fear had value because it afforded some kind of protection, but fear cannot protect, it only destroys. The way out of fear is the recognition that it is not real.

I remember having a dream a few years ago. I was a spectator and watched as these two frog like creatures seemed to be hidden in a well. It was very dark, damp and dirty and these things were so disgusting that when I looked at them they made me gag. They seemed to be yelling at someone that was on the outer wall of the well as if they were taunting whatever it was on the outside to come in and get them. They were calling the outside visitor disgusting names and telling whoever was outside that they (the visitor) was the coward. All of a sudden, the visitors arm reached inside the well, and the two gross things began to scream in horror and ran away. As I awoke from this dream, I realized I had been a witness to my own fear and a Greater Presence that was showing me that my fear was even afraid of me. The feeling of wanting to gag was still with me when I awoke.

These are some of the nasty things that are made to replace what was written in the Book of Life. Some of the other things are demonic and live in the part of our mind that is known as the abyss. They come up from the depths of hell at night when we are asleep. I have experienced them as a paralyzing force when I have tried to wake from a dream and just can't. They are the feeling that there is a presence in the room that is evil. This is the evil that attaches to drug addicts, alcoholics, and people who are obsessed with murder and killings. A good example of this is that prison in Iraq that Americans used after Iraqi soldiers used it for murder and torture. The evil never left the prison, and when the Americans came, the evil invaded their awareness as they slept. This was not the "normal" behavior of these soldiers, as friends and family members will attest. The power of thought is very strong, but because we give behavior more ability then thinking, we do not correct where the problem originated. The jail should have been torn down and the evil thoughts of demoralizing others would have had a difficult time invading the minds of the soldiers stationed there. Some would argue that they had the inclination to do this kind of behavior or it wouldn't have happened. Perhaps this is true, but why would you put a man of honor with a serial killer and expect that honor would not be defiled in some way? Why would we test such a theory, when in fact a serial killer holds thoughts in his mind that are evil, while a man of honor has to go to sleep, and evil attacks when we let go of what we believe to be acceptable behavior in waking hours. Once evil attaches to form, or the body, the body carries forth the evil of the thought believing that the thought is real. Evil can tell a person anything and it can even sound logical, but when questioned and looked at from a distance, an evil thought makes no sense at all. Afterwards the question remains…why?…but there is no answer, and so the price is guilt and dishonor for unworthy behavior.

    Nothing appears in this world the way it really is. Everything that is form has another purpose other than the one that has been given it by humanity, but we don't believe it because humankind has forgotten how to access the Laws of Heaven, so we go on trying to make rules and laws that work outside of the creative ability that lies within. I wonder when I will learn this lesson. I wonder how long it will take me to arrive. I see it just around the corner, and yet still have not "touched it" because I am not able to use the Law the way it is supposed to be used. To know it and yet not believe it is an oxy moron, and the part of me that wants to keep on believing what is not real is the moron.

The End of Time

The end of time is the end of all questioning. Questions only occur if one does not know, so when one ceases to question, one knows the truth. To be aware of truth, or know the truth, one is aware of their own innocence. The stains on truth are the questions brought on by the presence of the shadow. The shadow is merely a learned experience that was not expressed with Love. Therefore, the shadow is a result of fear. The seemingly unanswered questions are the stains that seem impossible to remove from our mind. They are represented to us in form and come in the way of unhappiness and pain. To try to keep the shadow from harming us, we try to force or manipulate circumstances that seem to be coming at us instead of from us. We blame, get angry, or feel sad at our own expressions gone awry. We actually believe we can force or manipulate circumstances to keep our own shadow at bay. But the shadow is ours and is emanating from our own presence.

If I stand outside alone, and see a shadow, the shadow is mine. I cannot force or manipulate the shadow so it isn't there anymore. I would call this ridiculous if someone believed I could. Yet each person, in their own way resorts to this when situations occur and it is seen and believed that the situation shadow is not really theirs, but instead coming from another to them, so they resort to reaction. The only thing wrong with this is that we were not created to react, we were created to act. Reaction to the shadow creates intense feelings of anxiety and we try to escape, but it is impossible to escape from oneself. Wherever you go, there you are. So a lose/lose situation is made and we keep going around in this insanity until we at last realize that we are caught in our own deception. Time was born to make this deception possible. The end of time is the realization of this insanity. The journey through time is an empty journey that needs our belief in the shadow, for without the shadow, time would not be evident.

Housing a shadow gives a false impression that it is possible to force and manipulate other people, and they won't know about it. The true purpose of forcing and manipulating is to mold physical matter into a new shape. Forcing or manipulating others or circumstances is out of character with the Creative ability and will bring about intense feelings of something being wrong within and needing correction. Trying to correct by forcing or manipulating is trying to "do" something with our mental prowess that it was not designed to perform. The mental level is psychological, not physiological. When our psychological being is mixed with our physiological doing, the only thing that can emerge is the shadow.

Sooner or later the shadow is revealed as not having any reality and is lifted from the psyche and ultimately the world. The lifting of the shadow reveals the end of time, for time cannot exist without the shadow of guilt of trying to give a psychological meaning to life through the physical body. It is true, only a body can produce a shadow because this is where the shadow lives. The guilt of living outside of the psychological nature of Being and Natural Laws is where the shadow must remain until its unreality is recognized as an intruder upon the peace of the world. As the shadow begins to fade, future generations are relieved of the dark guilt and the world is restored to peace. Thus, time ends as does the need for guilt of trying to make true what never was.

Each person, when they are ready, begins to deal with the shadow of error that they have learned from a physical experience of guilt. The shadow reveals the symptom of guilt and the unbecoming behavior that is a result of mixing that which was never supposed to be mixed. Trying to deal with the symptom of guilt makes the symptom real and the solution unreachable. The real problem is not the symptom, but instead is the shadow of guilt. While we look to cure the symptom, the shadow continues on and we are deceived into believing that we are cured. The symptom may be cured, but a healing did not occur because the shadow remains. The symptom reoccurs as the shadow once again reveals itself in another guilt ridden event. We say the disease has returned, but it is really the shadow of guilt. As long as we try to fix the symptom, the shadow will elude us. The shadow is not tangible, but because we are so accustomed to dealing with the tangible, we try to make the shadow into something we can touch. The fact remains that the shadow has no life, outside of the one that is cast with the body and because we believe in the life of the shadow it becomes real. Therefore, it is the effect and not the cause of our woes. We must stop looking at the shadow as having a life of its own, because the words of the shadow are death. The shadow is not written in the Book of Life, so it is the cause of death. We make up what we believe in, and now we are afraid of our own shadow.

The end of time reveals that there is no shadow to believe in and the end of time is possible to reach. The place where the end of time is revealed is not found in the body where the home of the shadow is. Instead it is found in a place of unlimited thinking, so this place can only be found in the freedom of the mind. The mind, being created without a time limit, is not limited by time. I know, I have been to the end of time, but sometimes I forget. Sometimes I try to deal with the effect of the shadow, not realizing it is me that the shadow is claiming life from. The shadow is tricky and plays deceitful games in my mind. It seems to have breath and a reality apart from me. When this happens the fear of the shadow becomes apparent. The burden of trying to deal with the shadow has been intense. Not because it is real, but because I have believed it was. Therefore, it is always the belief that casts the shadow, not truth. It is my true reality that I share with the Creator and I find the end of time.

It is getting better. I am not so easily tricked anymore. I know where the end of time is. It is here that the shadow can make no claim on me. I can carry the end of time back with me into my time associated physical experience and be aware that I have the ability to choose the shadow or the end of time where my innocence has returned. It is this realization that is the healing of the world.

It is time to move beyond the barrier of the shadows of guilt and let the sunshine in. The shadow of guilt and shame is an impossible idea. But it seems we want our guilt and believe it is somehow healthy. Guilt is a condition of the shadow. Do we want to keep the walls of time open with such an unhealthy idea, or would it be better to find a way to close the walls of time and perhaps find out that time wasn't real at all.

This physical experience and the lessons of time is a bitter one. But the healing is sweet. The job of revealing the shadow as unreality must become the focus for the world. We are in the midst of an evolutionary change. The likes of which has the ability to literally destroy the world. It is not reality that is making the change destructive, it is the shadow that has tried to cast the light outside and make the shadow real. We have another alternative to choose from that can lead us away from the shadow and back to the Light so it can be seen throughout the world without interference from the shadow. This other choice does not come out of what is known in time; instead it comes from our reality where our innocence is real and there is no shadow to hide our innocence from us.

The world is our inheritance, but we are ill equipped to take charge of our inheritance because of a belief in something that isn't there. A major shift must occur that will force humanity to look away from his intellect, where the shadow resides. Instead, we will all learn how to look to the wisdom in the heart, where Love is revealed. This is the end of time and the end of the shadow.

Day Twenty Nine

When listening to music, what is more important; the notes of the music or the space in between the notes. It seems that each is equally important, but when music is listened to, the focus is on the music and the spaces between the notes are as nothing. But if the truth be known, without the spaces, the music would hold no meaning.

Most of life is looked at like a song. The what is physically seen and heard are everything and the empty space is nothing. But within the empty space lies the potential of all of creation. Once something has been made, it is difficult at best to change the meaning of it. The old cannot be improved by trying to adjust the old. A new way of looking at the old must be added, or the same old thing remains. The empty space is the only place something new can be introduced while keeping the old in tact. The empty space holds all of eternity, which holds all of the worlds solutions, but when the focus is on what already is being played and how to change it, it creates an impossible situation. The old way of doing does not want to give up its position to make way for what is a new way This is why many times affirmations do not work. Old beliefs do not make considerations for new music and because we are used to the old music, new music is an intrusion. The old rhythm of music that has been rehearsed over and over again makes this rhythm real to the mind, and the mind does not like to give up the music it knows, so another approach must be introduced so the old music remains, but the melody takes on a new rhythm that does not conflict with what is old. In this way, what is old becomes new. This is the inner shift that occurs that does not introduce more fear but instead brings about a whole new perspective to an old situation or conflict that is seldom recognized as belonging to the past. Music learned in the past is not threatened by a new note when it is introduced with the same melody. I have the ability to keep what is old and learn what is new without upsetting the delicate balance I have strived to attain. This slowly but surely brings about a new flavor to my life as I learn what I have been listening to is there, but it no longer is fearful. This is the Plan that has been made for those who wish to learn that there is another way. I really did not understand that this was the direction I was heading in when I decided to learn a different way.

Windows and doors open up constantly, but if I do not see them as a new opportunity I stay in the same arena if I do not recognize the opportunity as being a part of what I want. It doesn't matter where I go…there I am. I can't out run my problems because I take them with me and they keep pace with me as I go. The seeming terror that problems represent is merely brought about as a symbol of my own past. The problem occurs over and over again until I recognize the room as being my own past learned in error. When I finally recognize it as being the same room I can ask for a new thought to be introduced that will bring resolution to my terror learned in the past. It is here that a new opportunity opens and the music can shift from terror to a melody of peace.

The room that I always seem to enter is time; for only in time can I see form. Eternity does not hold form, so it must be that the only place in all of creation where it is possible to see something that is not a part of reality is in time. That is why it is an illusion. It is in time my perception shifts from my innocent or being level of existence to my doing or guilt level of experience. Doing is behavioral and I can only be guilty if I have done something wrong. On the other hand, being innocent is internal.

It is entirely possible to see thoughts as they are occurring internally. This happens all of the time when I am sleeping. I remember one dream that I had and I was being shot at by a dream figure. I suddenly realized I was having a dream or what is commonly known as a lucid dream. I asked the dream figure who was shooting at me a specific question. He said he didn't know the answer to my question, but asked me if I remembered entering the door downstairs. When I said I did, he told me that the guy who was standing at the door downstairs could give me the answer I was looking for. The implications of this gave me pause to try to sort out exactly what this meant. It seemed as though a person in my dream had feelings and knew things that I did not. Eventually I understood that this dream figure was a part of my own psyche, but not just a figment of my imagination. Instead I began to realize that my thoughts were more than just something I had. I began to respect my thought process to help me learn about myself. Eventually I began to wake up with the idea in my mind that I too was just a thought. But this took quite a bit of time, as the fear of recognizing my own reality of being just a thought would be sure to invite all kinds of terror into my mind.

I still find that many of my thoughts have attached to the physical world, although I am learning how to detach from what I have believed to be true in the past. Completion and endings cannot be found in an insane world. The only thing that can be found in insanity is more insanity, and the definition of insanity is doing the same thing over and over again and expecting different results. Isn't that what is happening in the world right now? There is nothing new under the sun because we won't allow a new perspective in. We are so afraid of losing what is known, we keep insanity as a form of reference so we can make sure the future remains insane like the past. No one wants to give up their belief of what is right, even if it is wrong. Well, it is reasoned that it is the best that is known at this time, or our best thinking got us into this mess. What's that? It is the same garbage that has occurred over and over again with just a different label.

A New World is opening up that has nothing to do with what I see from a physical aspect. What I am attaching to mentally is a new reality that is much brighter than the one that I have known here, in time. I don't tell many people this. I usually don't even approach the subject because I am already considered weird. I just don't see life the way I used to, and thank God I don't. I still find pockets of fear, but I have learned how to move around it so it does not seemingly steal my power as easily as it used to. I have learned how to work with the Laws of the mind, under which it was created, but there are still things I find that need correction, but at least I recognize when a correction is needed most of the time.

Well, I only have one more day. Deciding to choose to find 30 days of peace has brought in new insights. I know now that there are levels of existence that I have only just had a tiny glimpse of and there is no end to what I can witness to if I so choose. I will ask what it is I should see on the last day I have dedicated to peace.

First we Learn to See Another Way

At the moment of our birth, we still have the ability to "see" eternity. As we go through physical life, we begin to look at something different that distracts us from the eternal or inner vision that we were created with. As innocence begins to look away from eternity, innocence begins to learn something else besides innocence. The innocent nature is very unique in that it learns very quickly what it is being taught. It always trusts that what it is being taught is the truth, even if what it is learning is not a total truth, and will try to conform to what it is being shown. It seeks for mirrors, or what is the same, to mirror back its reality. When what is not mirrored back as the same, innocence assumes that it is in error. This is why children do not like to be told no. No means that their mirror is incorrect, and so they generally cry at the word no. Mirroring is a form of communication in eternity. Mirroring is a way of seeing or understanding the Self, for what is mirrored back is the evidence of the One. This mirror is known as the mirror on the mind. In eternity, when one occupant of Eternity looks at another, what they gaze at is the reflection of themselves. Because spirit only looks at spirit and reveals itself, all true feelings of love, joy, and peace remain in tact. All healthy feeling is contained within the thought of another, for what is given is exactly received and then returned to the giver. This is why in reality that giving and receiving are the same.

Think of your own reflection as you gaze in a mirror. What do you see? It mirrors back to you your body, but does it reflect how you feel? In our physical experience, we learn how to use a mask that can cover the mirror. We learn how to use the mask, because we learn at a very early age that it is not safe to reveal our innocence to another. When innocence is violated, a shadow forms begins to form over it, and this is the mask. The shadow seems to carry value, and we begin to turn to it as a source that is reliable. We learn at a very early age that the mask is safer than revealing our innocence, so we grow a shadow that belongs to guilt. Honest emotion is eventually hidden behind a veil that seemingly protects our innocence. In the physical experience, we exchange what is deemed as honesty in the spiritual realm, as an external condition, and when it takes physical form it is called lying. However, the external condition of physical lying to conceal behavior does not touch the heart of the matter. Being true to the self and others is about being honest about how one feels. True feeling lies in innocence, not in the shadow that teaches how to be dishonest with ourselves.

The physical world has been established to condone dishonesty. I say this because before lying can occur, we must teach innocence that it is incorrect in its assumption that being naïve' is ignorance, and it is not safe to follow the feelings in the heart. Conditions in this world has placed humanity in a position of defiling the gift of innocence, and then punishing it for not complying to honest conditions the way the physical world has set it up it. Thus, the mirror grows cloudy with each new dishonest trick that is learned, and the shadow becomes the seeming source that supplies reality to the light of innocence. This is an impossible condition, for it is only innocence that lies in the heart that God sees. How can He see it though if it is covered with a shadow? God does not see partially, He sees wholly, so a partially blocked awareness prevents Love from giving comfort to His Innocence.

Light and darkness constantly flows across the mirror in the mind throughout the individual's life. Sometimes the child emerges in laughter, but as the child becomes an adult, the lighthearted laugher isn't so spontaneous anymore. Laughter may occur at the expense of another because the shadow cannot see the real reason for laughter. The lessons of the shadow that have been learned in time cannot reflect Heaven's Light, so light is prevented from entering the world. The innocence of the child still lives behind the unreality of the shadow, hoping that the fear that made the shadow will somehow protect it. The light in the mirror has not gone out, but the shadow distorts the perception, and once the shadow begins to be the main source of dependence of the child, the shadow only sees the external world, and so it is the child must see what the shadow looks upon. All the while, the child cries, because it is in a seeming reality that it does not know how to cope in. We touch this child on occasion when the mask has been stripped away and we have been called on our inappropriate behavior. We try to explain it away, for buried behind the behavior is our lost innocence.

Who would the world blame and call a monster if all that could be seen behind an inappropriate deed was the innocence that lies buried in ourselves? How quickly would we be willing to judge and condemn innocence, if all we could see was what God created? If we saw our own wounded child in the eyes of another, would we want revenge, or is that what the shadow wants? Who we listen to and what we see reveals what we choose reveals our loyalty to innocence or the shadow. What we are loyal to is our treasure, and because innocence is seemingly buried behind darkness, in order to reveal it, we must learn how to look behind what is not being revealed. The shadow wants the child to die, because it wants to be proclaimed as real. The insanity of this is that if the child died, the shadow would no longer exist, for in truth it is the child that provides life for the shadow. The mockery that the shadow has made out of our lives can be seen in the quiet desperation behind the mask that the shadow holds up for the world to see. The shadow is not who we are, it is what we have become by learning something we were never supposed to learn.

We live in a world of shadows trying to make sense out of insanity. If we are to bring sanity back into this world, we must release our innocence out of the cage that the shadow has placed it in. Our innocence has been pointed and laughed at long enough. Shadows cannot reveal what lies in the heart, but innocence can, so this is what we must learn to reveal. We do this with a healing process that has been specifically designed to help release our innocence back into the Arms of Love and thus heal the world of the insanity of the shadow. When we step close to the truth, the fear of being revealed to more pain forces the child to move deeper within the shadow. The anxiety of this fear becomes intense in the body, and because we do not recognize our own child as calling out, we recede also. The only purpose of the shadow is insanity and there is no end to depths of this insanity, as it is continually played out destructively in the physical world. We believe these destructive circumstances are beyond our control, and point to them as the source of our unhappiness, depression, disease and addictions. We have become a victim in our own nightmare because we have forgotten the innocence that we carried into the world to heal it.

There is a story that relates to a man that saved a town from the rats that infested it. This story is called The Pied Piper. The Pied Piper had a plan to rid the town of rats by playing a flute that would mesmerize the rats to follow him. The Piper demanded that price to be paid for his service. The towns people were eager to be rid of the rats and agreed to pay the Piper the price he was asking. So, it came to pass and he proceeded to perform the task of ridding the town of rats by leading them over a cliff into the ocean. Thus, the rats all drowned and the town was free of the infestation. Quickly, the heart of the town changed and when the Piper demanded payment, he was denied his just reward. Not realizing the ability of the Piper, the town settled in for the night secure in the knowledge that they were now rid of the rats and they felt smug in their ability to cheat the Piper. Big mistake, for the Piper's ability was grossly underestimated by the town. When the town awoke in the morning, all of the children were gone. The Piper played a melody only the children could hear. Because of their innocent nature, they followed a melody out of the town, never to return. The town was unaware of what was occurring as they slept, and so when they awoke, the mistake was realized and great sorrow arose. It was too late. The towns people had a chance to be honorable and teach the children how to live by honor, but instead they chose dishonor. The false belief that they could win by cheating the Piper was a mistake that had irreparable consequences.

Imagine a world without innocence, for this world is upon the threshold of losing what it claims it treasures the most. The payment of the Piper must be met, otherwise our innocence will leave as the Piper plays his flute while we sleep. We do not believe it is possible for innocence to leave the world, for we also believe that innocence belongs to it. We are wrong. Innocence belongs to Heaven, and Heaven is perfectly capable of playing a melody that only innocence can hear, thus leaving the world without the influence of Heaven. Our physical children are merely a symbol of the innocence of Heaven. Innocence lives in them because they are not full of the shadow.

The lessons that innocence brings on the wings of children can lead us to our reality, but it is not without a price. The price is the undoing of the lessons of the shadow, which will allow humankind to free the innocence that has been imprisoned by a false experience that claims the experience is real and our innocence is not. It is impossible to keep the lesson of the shadow, for that is the price that the Piper is asking to rid the world of the infestation of evil that dwells here. We have all agreed we want something better, but are unwilling to pay the price. The treasures of the shadow involve external pleasures and physical objects that are not recognized by the Higher Mind. The price is the willingness to relinquish, not the physical symbols, but the attachment to these symbols. The attachment to these symbols are recognized by fear and greed and a desire for more. It is the attachment to the symbols that keeps innocence in prison. The false assumption that we can get something without being willing to make an acceptable exchange is an error on our part that we cannot afford to make. Heaven knows its children, and knows the melody that its children hears. The pittance that we throw Heaven, in the way of what we do not want, has been justly noted. We will not be "saved" from disaster by not taking action. Faith without works is dead. Imagine how much faith it took for the Israel to leave Egypt without understanding the plan that Moses revealed, as it was revealed to him as they journeyed into the Promised Land. The steps that are taken in faith towards healing and releasing the innocence within ourselves must be taken, lest we wake up one morning and our innocence all be gone. How will we know when it is gone? There will be no more joy. There will be no more Love or an honest ability to be happy. There will be no more intense anxiety, for the shadow feels none of this. The anxiety rests on the child because of its inability to move beyond what the shadow has taught it.

There is a Plan to save the world by using the innocence that is already here. This Plan lies within the innocence that has been covered over by the lessons of the shadow. In order to release this Plan into the world, we must be willing to relinquish these false lessons that we have mistakenly learned as our reality so innocence and the Plan can be revealed. For two thousand years, spiritual innocence has been entering time so that when the time is right, it can be released into the world to heal it. All aspects of this Plan is here and it is now. It began with the Birth of the Christ. He opened the gateway between Heaven and Earth with a Love that was not evident in the world until then. With each birth, innocence brought into the world what was needed to completely heal it of the effects of the shadow. When the time was right, mass healing would begin as innocence was released into the world and the Plan would emerge, whole and complete. That time is now and we must hear the call lest innocence be called Home without completing its mission. If this occurs, the world will no longer have a purpose and it will self destruct.

Make no mistake, Heavenly Bodies are intensely interested in world affairs. Not because of interest in the shadow, but because It's Innocence is on loan to the world and we have been entrusted with the Treasure of Heaven. Think carefully before you offer something that is unholy to God, for the shadow would have us believe it knows what is acceptable to God. The faith of the shadow is not what is wanted by Heaven. Heaven is calling to It's Innocence, and it best be the individual that works in conjunction with Heaven's Plan to free what is Heavenly owned.

There are Teams of Heavenly Advisors, Guides, and Angels. When we purposely call on Them, They have the ability to help us release the innocence that has been entrusted to us. We are much more than the shadow, and until we learn how to reach beyond the physical interpretation of what we believe God is by learning from His Innocence, we will listen to the shadow in quiet desperation not realizing that there is another way.

Morality is not a physical attribute, and it cannot be monitored through behavior. The Laws of Heaven do not hear the laws of time and so do not adhere to the laws of the shadow. What is considered righteous in this physical world is not even taken into consideration in the Spiritual World. The only sound that innocence hears is the sound of Heaven. We have all made sacred agreements that are bound by Heaven. This agreement lies within, and will not be revealed until we choose another way that will lead us out of the insane conditions that prevail in time. We are responsible for what we choose to see, and the ability to see beyond the shadow is our birth right. Let us place this birthright into the Hands that will lead us Home.

Day Thirty

Salvation is dependent upon my being able to see something that has always been there, but I have not acknowledged because I have been looking at something else. There is another way of seeing everything, but as long as I only acknowledge what I see with physical eyes, then I miss the wholeness that is presented Now. The circle of life presents itself in another way when I am open to moving beyond my own perception. The basic idea that I have needs is presented as a circle of life. If I look at the circle of life like a Ferris wheel and if I put what I think I need on the Ferris wheel, what gets off after the ride is still a perceived need. But if I can see my need presented in another way, as not being a need at all, but instead a call for love, then when the Ferris wheel goes around again perhaps I can see my need presented in another way. Perhaps I can see that my need was really a call for love presented as a physical need. The next time, instead of a physical need, I can change my mind and put a call for love on the Ferris wheel. Now when the Ferris wheel goes around, I can see the perceived need being transformed into a new way of seeing the problem. Now I can see that my call was not for the "thing" that I thought would save me. Now I can see that what I really, which was love, wanted never got off the Ferris wheel. It was me that got off and began a journey looking for things that represented the Love that stayed on the wheel. As I go around the wheel with a physical need, all of what I think I know about a problem and how to solve it will remain the same.

I have placed myself in a precarious situation, for all of the problems that have presented themselves are seemingly in my life to help me find more fear. This fear is merely an indication that I believe it is possible to lose my Love Source. The purpose of the problem has to shift as I go around the wheel, otherwise I will continue to believe that the result of anything I face is fear. The end result of anything should be Love just like the beginning should be. This is the circle of life. The journey is the intention. The destination is Love, but if I have chosen fear as my destination, I have chosen impossibility, and the impossibility of the situation will continue to be impossible. It is impossible that an impossible situation will suddenly become possible without an interruption in my thought process. If impossibility gets on the Ferris wheel, impossibility gets off. Still, I seem to want to try to figure it out so I can salvage my wounded self esteem at a physical level. I want to show someone that I am better than the impossible situation. It is impossible to figure this out when I am locked into form. Love is not form; it is content and only getting on the Ferris wheel with this understanding will help me change my mind when I get off. When I finally "get" this my mind has been changed.

It wasn't always like this. I remember when things used to work out. As I have gotten older, I have learned to believe that I am in charge of the outcome, but I'm not. Still the question emerges…what should I do? The answer returns…do nothing. Let go of the whole situation and see what happens. But yet I am afraid. At some level I know that this situation is reminiscent of the past, but it sure doesn't feel like it. I seem to know what the problem and the solution are, but they are fragmented. Neither has taken the same seat on the wheel of life, and so I have learned to settle for what I don't want. The problem and the solution must sit in the same seat and go around the wheel together…like $1+1=2$ or the solution. The problem and the solution brought together will bring an outcome that solves the problem. Whoever heard of a mathematical problem without a solution? The right answer is always completion. I can feel the completion within when the answer has finally arrived. When the answer is my own it is conflicted, so I do not feel complete. Completion or the solution is Love's answer, not mine. This can be my only solution to all questions. Not love the way I understand it, but instead Love that is extended from the Realm of Peace. I do not know how to give this kind of Love, for I believe I have lost it and have to get it outside of myself. I also know that it will extend from me into the world when I remain an open channel. The frequency of Love is a vibration and extends to the furthest galaxy when I am willing to receive it. This will change the world, and also the Universe. Everything must reflect God's Love in the end. When the Universe stops expanding, the purpose of Love has been completed or made manifest in time and space and it will end. Perhaps I shouldn't say end, but instead will become a part of eternity, with no boundaries. The perfect Plan, when fully perceived and executed, is the inclusion of everything everywhere.

Everyone who comes here is still looking for what they believe they have lost. But most of the time what is settled for is less than Love. Over and over again, it is believed that some scrap of the illusion or unreality will provide completion. But completion lies in Heaven and the only solution is Love. Still, it is hard to get it through my head that this is an illusion. Maybe that is it..the answer is not in my head at all. The brain what has stored the memories of my physical experience. Physical consciousness lives there and believes in form as my reality. But form is not my reality, Love is. Making the switch is necessary now. I can't go back, but I still have this lingering guilt. I have made many strides in the past month, and I know I am going in the right direction. I have decided that I will continue to move past the guilt and fear that I have been associated with, and learn of my True Reality. Fear is an illusion that I have made and I can choose again. I remind myself over and over again, saying the affirmation that doesn't work. I know it doesn't work because it is the shadow that is repeating it. If I could just say it once myself and mean it, the affirmation would have meaning. The answer is not in the affirmation or the visualization. The answer is in the healing. The affirmation and visualization has always been targeted at the physical solution, but the physical condition is the illusion, so how could it be the answer? It is the anxiety that the physical problem reveals that must be addressed. The anxiety does not reside is what my physical eyes see, it is in me!! The anxiety is the sin because it carries fear. Fear is the destructive enemy that in the end destroys the host, or the body, that carries the fear.

I haven't been able to "feel the fear and do it anyway," either. Tried that and just succeeded in scaring myself more. The conclusion is that there is only one solution, and that solution lies in finding, and then attaching the plan made for individual salvation. Using someone else's plan just doesn't work., well, it hasn't' worked for me However, the value in another's experience is not to be tossed away, but by the same token only the Interpreter has the ability to lead a person to their own plan. If I use what has worked well for others, what was made for me will never be revealed. What I look for I find. It has always been that when I needed to hear what I needed to hear, and a book held the information, then the book presented itself to me. I didn't have to go in search of it, but I believed I did. When I did, I set myself back by trying to reach the goal of another. By the same token, I have taken classes with the specific goal in mind of finding a clue to my own healing. With this attitude, I did find what I was looking for. My journey is about me. It is not what someone else plans for me that doesn't even know me.

We all want someone else to be the solution or have the solution for us. That way we don't have to do the work and won't be wrong. This alleviates me of my own responsibility. Perhaps that is my anger. I wanted someone else to tell me what to do, and when their plan didn't work, I got angry. To see the source of my anger about this matter helps me heal it. I am never upset for the reason I think. It thought I was angry because I felt taken advantage of, but I was really upset because I wanted someone else to give me the answer. With this revelation, I can now let this go. I am responsible for finding my own path and the road to healing. I am not responsible for healing myself. I don't know how. That is the purpose of the miracle.

I am trying to tie up some loose ends, seeing this is the last day. Last night, I could hear two critters in my house. They were probably mice. I have heard them on and off for the last couple of weeks. I used to be able to vanquish them by focusing on peace. That would mean I would totally obliterate their sound in my mind and focus only on a peaceful state. That hasn't seemed to work with these two. Perhaps there are two beliefs that I have not brought to truth to be healed. Everything on the physical plane has another interpretation. Only by giving up my interpretation am I able to see what the truth is. Learning from what I see physically has brought me into the world of symbols. I can see how the mind uses everything in the physical realm as a symbol. Either it is a symbol that represents Love and life, or it is a symbol that represents fear and death. There is nothing in between. If death is fear and is representing itself in a symbol, then I have to make a correction. I can't correct the symbol, for the symbol is fear is my own. Otherwise I wouldn't be afraid of it. The false belief that God is fear must be erased from my own mind before I am completely at peace. Recognizing that a correction has to be made is not difficult; it is finding where the error occurred so correction can be made. That is what the new purpose of my physical symbols represent. Car problems can symbolize that my physical energy is in question. If steering is the problem, this may indicate that the direction I am going in is not necessarily in the right direction. When someone tells me they are having trouble with their furnace, or water heater, or they hit a curb, or their house has a problem, I look for the psychological equivalent of what the symbol is trying to explain. Most do not believe they are that powerful to affect their physical circumstance, but we either create constructively or destructively. Nothing happens by chance, and usually the symbol of the event is looked at as being a coincidence and not coming from ones own mind. What is true cannot be partially true, or only when I want an interpretation that does not indicate my own psychological problems. We are remiss in understanding the full potential of our mind. The brain interprets the physical experience, and usually incorrectly. On the other hand, the mind interprets in ways we do not recognize. All problems can be addressed when a symbol is applied to the problem. But understanding the symbols at a conscious level takes an ability to "see" beyond the physical interpretation of the symbol.

Just one more thing I would like to add before I end this 30 day venture. This was the equation I was given for creation. Thought is 1…emotion is 1…intention or passion is 1. $1+1+1=3$. Three is the outcome of thought, intention and emotion. It is the creative process and new spirit energy is the result. Spirit is alive and when the creative process is engaged, new life springs forth to bring about our desire. We supply the thought and the passion, but God supplies the emotional equivalent. The emotion is the completed process of the creative process. The complete process is an expression, which then returns to us as we learn how to use the creative process. The error occurs as we learn to believe that God, or Love is fear. When we learn in error, instead of being completed in Love, we find incompletion in fear and continually seek for ways to remedy this. The problem is that the physical experience, where we first found fear, cannot produce the kind of Love we are seeking.

This is the equation for incompletion: Thought is 1…passion-1…and emotion-1…when an equivalent is given to physical form another 1 is applied. This equation formed at the beginning of time. Before that there was no need to allow for form. The new 1 was individual consciousness, so new allowances had to be made for consciousness. This was and is the Plan to bring physical consciousness and what it directs, or the world, under the Laws of Heaven. The equation of $1+1+1+1=4$ must include the Laws of Heaven, for without these Laws, death is real and life must be surrendered unto death. It has taken millions of years of physical history and 6000 years of spiritual history to reach the perfect conditions so consciousness could be included as a part of the constructive creative process. The world is on the verge of an experience that is so new, and when the evolutionary shift is completed, nothing will remotely resemble the world as it was set up at the beginning of time.

The Plan to allow for the physical experience, or consciousness is under way, but the physical world must become aware of what is occurring. Without this realization, the Plan to bring form into the spiritual expression will fail. Spiritual expression must move through all of creation unhindered, so that Love, and not fear will be addressed as the creative potential that dwells in all. Without this realization, fear will continue to be used mistakenly as a healthy element that God provides. God cannot be both, fear and Love, for they oppose one another, and God is not a contradiction.

Individual consciousness cannot define expression, for that is the function of spirit. Up to this point, form has been the error in the creative process. In order to alleviate the error, or the sin, form must be included, and properly perceived.

The Plan makes allowances for form. The new purpose of firm brings into focus a grounding element that helps mankind attach to Mother Earth, and thus become a part of all of the physical realm. Reaching out of the physical realm into Heaven begins the establishment of Peace on Earth as it is in Heaven. The Plan does not destroy form; it merely gives it a new interpretation. Eventually, forcing or manipulating form merely becomes a way of expression, just like a child plays with toys. There is no external agenda in playing, just expressing and being joyful. The truth is that nothing needs to be created in time. Everything that is already perfect already exists, but at this point remains unexpressed in the physical world. Perfection cannot be perfected through a physical interpretation, but it can be perfected by a Heavenly one. This is what the world is being offered. We would be foolish indeed not to wish to learn how to become a part of this earth changing event.

The lessons I have learned and are still attempting to learn have seemed extreme. Because I have read so much, I remember having experiences that I have read that others have had and believed that I had reached a plateau and I could finally rest, but that was not the case. I am still letting go and releasing so I can bless the world with what I have been blessed with. My goal still remains the same, even though I am weary of the journey. I know I have the ability to have the same understanding that Christ had when He walked the earth. Because we do receive what we ask for I will trudge along, continuing to look for answers that lead me to my ultimate goal of a new Consciousness that transcends the physical experience of time.

The Walls of Time

The walls of time are fragile and the seeming protection that is afforded its occupants can come crashing down at any moment.

Love waits for any opportunity to slip quietly past the protection that time seemingly provides. A momentary lapse of the awareness of time is all that is needed and a quiet remembrance slips through the barrier, and ever so gently shifts the awareness of hate that seemingly holds the gate shut to the beckoning call of Love. An instant is all that is needed to shift the world from that of hate to a world of Love.

Be still and listen. The instant of Love returning Home is occurring all over the world. The dwelling place of Love is being opened, one instant at a time and revealing something new, as the world becomes a spiritual playground.. Love waits on a welcome call. The instant before we answer the Call of Love is perceived as being fearful, so many times we do not answer. The erroneous perception views events that are happening that seemingly foreshadows the total annihilation of the world; and therefore our own, but the war is not with the world or time. Instead it is with the violated *purpose* that time has brought to the world. The purpose of time has been guilt and fear and it is fear that has overtaken the heart. It is the heart that is the Home of Love, and Love will not co-exist in a fearful state. The war that is occurring is for rights to the heart, where the new Kingdom of the world will rule.

The offerings of fear lie scattered about in the heart and are polluting what Love would claim as It's Own. What is seen in the world of time is the out picturing of the manifestation of fear and guilt. The stench that is caused by fear violates the once secure heart, or the Home of Love. Love could not and would not remain homeless forever in this time based world. It is time for Love to return Home, but fear will not retreat without a seeming fight. The fight occurs, not on the battlefield of the world, but instead within the heart where fear tries to hold its ground by enhancing what it stands for.

The Army of Heaven has been assembled and the war trumpet has sounded. The King is coming. Fear strikes the heart of man because all of the external things in time he sees occurring. These are in fact an external reflection of the fear that is held in his heart being played out in the arena of time. Amazingly, he finds comfort in this fear, and tries to keep himself from the instant when Love could enter and return his heart to holiness. The Home of God has been corrupted long enough. God has set a time when this would end. This time is upon us.

It is impossible to fight this war in the physical realm of time, for time is not real. To fight a Holy War in time would make the home of evil real. There is no battleground in the world as we know it. This world merely reflects the events that are occurring in the war for the heart. The real war is indiscernible from a physical level. Because the eventual outcome is the abolishment of time, man is fearful that he will find himself homeless. It is in fact the fear and guilt harbored in the heart that has been learned in time that tries to hold onto the territory and hide it from the healing Presence of Love. We would have God join the seeming nightmare and fight a war with the physical conditions we supply and on a physical battlefield we supply. God's Army protects and preserves by holding what is holy, but not on a physical battlefield. This holy army has no need to destroy the world, for Love does not destroy. The Heavenly Army looks for instances to shift the heart and expand the Kingdom through Love. It is our willingness to join with the Cause that is needed. We are not being asked to fight a war. A little willingness is all that is needed to shift the world from one of hate to one of Love.

The Army is creating opportunities for the occupants of time to learn of the New Kingdom. Each shift reveals, at first the hatred found on the heart, and once realized the heart returns to Love. An ancient hatred has become a present Love and the world that thought only time could be called home, finds a resting place so pure that Heaven Itself abides within and finds comfort with us there.

There is no hate and there is no fear. We made it up. We are not in danger, except from a perceived nightmare that has the ability to house war. Take the war out of the heart and Love will return to It's Home. What happens then? Time cannot tell because it doesn't know. The only ability that time ever had was to move forward. But once Love has returned Home, this world and all of its occupants give way to a New World, which has the power to build a foundation of peace that will never be threatened by war or the evil ideas that the evil heart worships. How long does it take? Just an instant. In every instant we choose to go with empty hands to our God and return with something new and so clean, it has the ability to wipe away every tear and put an end to death. Time is not in danger because it was never real; the instants we choose to be with Love are. One instant is the same as many instants, for they are all the same for they lead us Home.

The very fabric of time is being shifted away from the evil thoughts that live in the heart of everyone who occupies and believes time is real. We can choose to join with the Crusade of Heaven, or we can choose to remain with the foul stench of fear and guilt of a corrupted heart. The choice is ours, but the outcome of this war is not. Once the outcome is evident, the war is over. What has been placed before us is life or death, and we must choose life, not only for ourselves, but also for future generations. Who will volunteer their services? Who will open their heart and allow the New King to enter and bring a holy instant to the world? This is how the Holy War is won and how righteousness is returned to the world. You need do nothing except be a willing host for Love. It is through a willing heart that peace is finally restored to a world that has lost its will to fight. Nothing else will work because the Plan for the salvation of the world must come through the Purpose of a Greater Awareness than our own. The time is now and it belongs to the world; but the holy instant is our joint inheritance, which cleanses our heart and gives it back to Love.

Join with me. There are specific provisions that are being given to humankind to help survive this evolutionary process. One of these provisions is learning how to use the creative process or talent that we hold with Heaven. We are at the cross road of life and cannot turn back the clock. Placed before us we have been given a choice of life or death, and we must choose life for the world to survive.

The world will be restored to righteousness through a conscious willingness to become a Co-Creator with God. It is up to humankind to open him/herself up to a new understanding that is born in the heart where the creative process lies. It does not lie in time. There is nothing there to create with, except perhaps death. Specific guidelines have been revealed to help us during this time of evolutionary change. There is a Plan that we can access that will provide all protection for anyone choosing to join with it. Time doesn't have to be the enemy; it can be viewed as keeping pace with our learning, when learning is done under the proper conditions. The choice is ours, but the outcome is not. Join with me and make a mighty noise of peace that will be heard even unto the Heavens. What we give is received and returned to the giver. How the world is changed from hate and war, is as simple as choosing peace to come into the heart. This is the greatest calling you could ever answer, and within this call is everything you want. It is promised by God.

God Bless.
miracleresponse.com

Printed in the United States
42730LVS00003B/232-246